NEW POWER OF FACE READING

ROSE ROSETREE

JAICO PUBLISHING HOUSE
Ahmedabad Bangalore Chennai
Delhi Hyderabad Kolkata Mumbai

Published by Jaico Publishing House
A-2 Jash Chambers, 7-A Sir Phirozshah Mehta Road
Fort, Mumbai - 400 001
jaicopub@jaicobooks.com
www.jaicobooks.com

Published in arrangement with
Rose Rosetree
116 Hillsdale Drive
Sterling, VA 20164, USA

To be sold only in India, Bangladesh, Bhutan,
Pakistan, Nepal, Sri Lanka and the Maldives.

NEW POWER OF FACE READING
ISBN 978-81-8495-722-8

First Jaico Impression: 2015
Second Jaico Impression: 2016

Printed by
Trinity Academy For Corporate Training Limited, Mumbai

Cast of Characters

You,
Power-Packed Reader

Ava

Shirley

Cliff

Matt

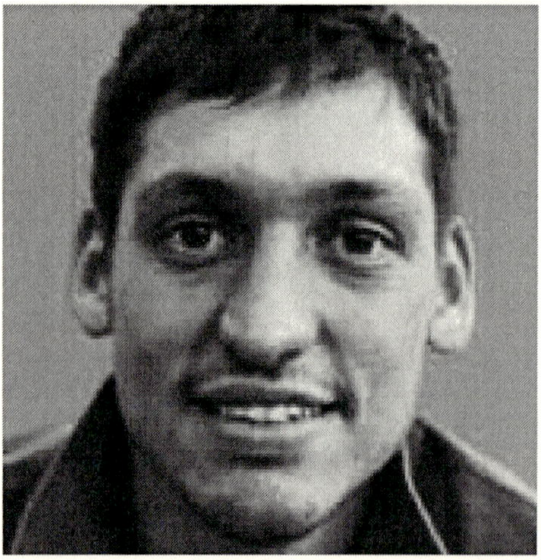

Fred

Praise for Rose Rosetree's Face Reading Secrets®

"It's like she's known you forever... but that's crazy, because you just met. Still, she has described you perfectly, and not just your surface traits."

— *The Washington Post*

"She doesn't immediately seek feedback on her accuracy. She sits back, confident that she's at least partly on target. When she does ask, it's with a flat sense of curiosity, like someone peering out of a rain-splattered window to check on a storm's progress."

— *The Washington Times*

"[Governor John Engler and Mayor Terry McKane] were highly skeptical... [but] both men said they found Rosetree's readings uncannily true."

— *Lansing State Journal*

"I decided to send her a picture of myself... with the caveat that my wife would 'check' her report for accuracy. 'She's got your number,' was my wife's simple response."

— *The Catholic Standard*

"As Rose Rosetree says, 'The truth of what we are shows in our faces and each face, in its distinctive way, is perfectly beautiful.'

— *Style* (Hong Kong)

"At The Heart Institute, Dr. Keon preferred not to comment himself [on Rosetree's profile of him], though his secretary was happy to offer her view of the analysis. She found it surprisingly accurate.

"Said Sue Slater: 'I've worked for him for 16 years, and I'd have to say this lady either knows someone in Ottawa, or she's awfully good.'"

— *The Ottawa Citizen* (Canada)

"Rosetree's goal is to demolish societal standards which separate so-called good looks from bad. All facial features have meaning and value, she declares, regardless of their popularity or apparent lack of appeal."

— *Aloha Magazine*

"[County Supervisor] Moore said [Rosetree's] assessment — especially the part about saving money — was accurate.... 'I shop at Frugal Fannie's. Does that tell you anything?'"

— *The Fairfax Journal*

For *The Orange County Register,* Rosetree profiled local newsmakers. Profiles included both gifts and potential challenges. Their feedback was published as part of the newspaper story:

- Frank Phillips, District Attorney: "This profile is so accurate, it's almost scary."
- Amy Christ, Philanthropist: "Amazingly accurate."
- Benjamin Gilman, Representative: "Very interesting. It sounds very plausible."
- Gilman's long-time friend: "If I had been asked to describe Ben Gilman, those are the words I would use. The woman is something — how on earth does she see all this?"
- Dennis Greenwald, Middletown Pharmacist: "Only two people could have written this assessment, my wife and my mother… I tell you, I don't know who this lady is, but she must be living in my house."
- Mary McPhillips, Orange County Executive: "Come on. This woman had to know who I am."
- Maurice Hinchey, Jr., Assemblyman: "I'm quite amazed by this. In fact, it's remarkable. I didn't think anyone knew me that well."

"Rosetree's motto is 'God don't make no junk.' For her, every facial feature tells a story. So, if you want an edge in knowing if he's Mr. Right or Mr. Way-Wrong, if he's fling material or worth a long-term investment, don't just read between the lines — read his face."

— *Flare Magazine* (Canada)

"Face reading performs a real deep service to people in terms of self-acceptance. When you learn how to look at your face and you understand what it means, you end up with a real appreciation of how you look."

—*The Indianapolis Star*

"So far, response from co-workers at the paper has been incredible — even our publisher, who's not one for handing out compliments, sent me a message saying he found it fascinating."

— Letter from Tim Lucas, reporter for *The Indianapolis Star,* sending clippings from this article

"Forget Cupid's arrow. Reading faces is a more reliable way of finding love."

— *USA Today*

"Well, I have to tell you, most of the stories I write don't generate this much interest. Clearly the nation is hungry to find out more about face reading."

— Email from Cathy Hainer, reporter for *USA Today,* after publication of her interview with Rosetree

Rowan

Valerie

Annette

Oliver

Lloyd

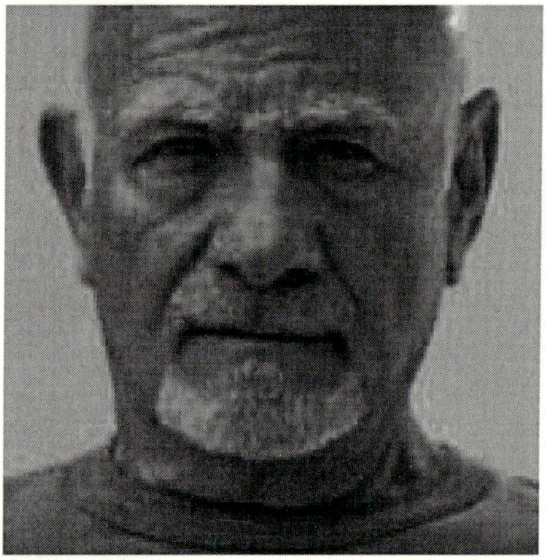

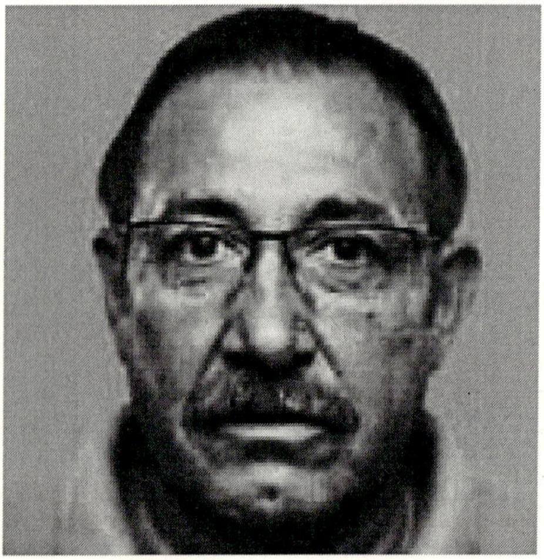

George

Jesse

Kathryn

Alexander

Wayne

Joyce

Madison

Anthony

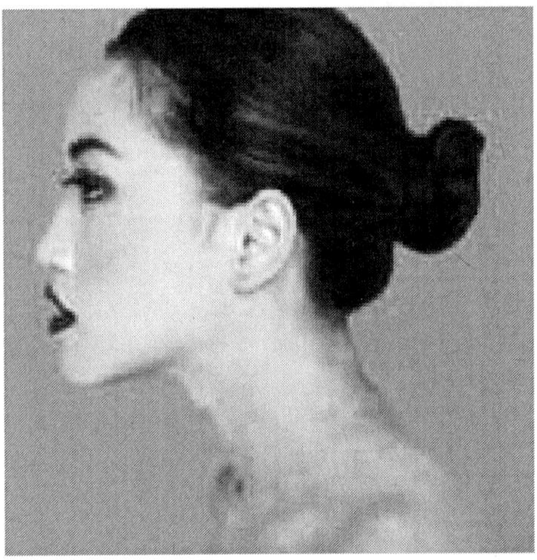

Helene

Gary

Foreword

From the earliest times, human beings have had to read each other's faces to survive. Our brains evolved via face reading. As a result, we are all natural-born face readers.

Systematic study of faces started with the shamans. Generally it has remained an esoteric understanding for the rare specialist. For instance, the Chinese system involves an apprenticeship training process sometimes lasting 40 years. Therefore, systematic forms of face reading have not been readily available.

In the West, during the Middle Ages, this began to change. A man by the name of Lavater began seriously studying and drawing faces, starting an unusual tradition of seeking to make face reading public domain.

Historically, however, we humans have been effectively paranoid (that is, intensely judgmental). Due to this pattern, face reading literature has been harsh in the extreme. Once I read this:

"A concave nose is one step away from animality and bestiality."

Now who has concave noses? Most children, for starters.

No wonder only the most dedicated students of physiognomy attempt to survey the full range of literature in this field, 60 titles since Lavater that I, personally, have encountered.

As I was reviewing this literature for my first book on the meaning of facial features, I ran across a little gem of a book called, "I Can Read Your Face." It was Rose Rosetree's first work in this field, unlike anything I had seen before. It was the first face reading book that came from the heart — and the real truth of the matter.

Now, years later, Rose has written what I consider to be another breakthrough book, applying face reading to everyday situations with lots of examples to concretize what she is talking about. She makes face reading understandable, easy to learn, and memorable.

Her communication style is refreshingly upbeat, zestful, enthusiastic, and passionately involved (like her lifestyle, to judge from her anecdotes and my personal experience of her). Beneath the surface, you will find a depth of understanding about people and the meaning of faces that doesn't exist elsewhere in the literature.

Rose works from the realization that every human characteristic involves both a set of talents and a set of challenges. Then she proceeds to show us how to more deeply appreciate every person we encounter.

Her general approach is that we are all in this together, and that we need to love ourselves and each other to make the whole thing work.

In effect, she is picking up and transmitting a collective soul change that is happening now.

What it all comes down to is that if we don't move to coming from the heart, we human beings won't enjoy being human much longer.

I believe a massive transformation is taking place and Rose is part of it, teaching us how to put it into action in our relationships with ourselves, with each other, with the community, and with the human race.

Her loving wisdom-sharing will stick to your soul. This new book is a delight to read, a revelation that leads to transformation. I heartily encourage you to join Rose Rosetree in this great evolutionary adventure.

— Narayan Singh Khalsa, Ph.D., Boulder, Colorado

Contents

Photos of Our Cast of Characters

Foreword by Narayan Singh Khalsa, Ph.D.

PART ONE: Start Smart

Chapter 1. Power 1
Not Same Old, Same Old Face Reading ✦ You May Be Wondering ✦ Ethics ✦ Discretion ✦ Scary?

Chapter 2. Where Does Face Reading Come From? 11
How I Developed Face Reading Secrets® ✦ Distinguishing Features ✦ How, Exactly, Do You Do That? ✦ Reframing ✦ Life Lessons ✦ Controversy Prejudice ✦ Read Faces in Today's World ✦ People with the Nose Bonus

Chapter 3. How NOT to See Like a Face Reader 23
Census Taking ✦ The Perpetual Beauty Contest ✦ Status Reading ✦ Seeking Health Updates ✦ Color Gazing ✦ Worrying

Chapter 4. Expression Reading 29
Expressing... The Intent To Deceive ✦ Mood Reading ✦ Most Annoying ✦ Quiz Yourself on Face Watching Habits

Chapter 5. Practical Advantages 35
Develop a Face Reader's Curiosity ✦ Six Distinctive Steps. ✦ Become YOUR Kind of Power- Packed Face Reader ✦ Use Intention to Empower Yourself

Chapter 6. Cast of Characters 41
Introducing our Cast of Characters

Chapter 7. Mirror Skills 43
Which Kind Of Mirror ✦ Prepare Your Face Physically ✦ On The Level * Sideways Views ✦ Beware Multi-Tasking ✦ Time, Not Measured By Counting "Big Honkers"

Chapter 8. Where Will You Read Those Secrets? 49
Ava Demonstrates.

PART TWO: Read The Secrets

Chapter 9. Starting With Starter Eyebrows 51
Distribution Of Hair • Overcome Shyness • Perspective, And Not Just About Eyebrows • Level with Yourself • View Photos On The Level, Too • Tell Left From Right On A Face • Meet Fred Again. And Again.

Chapter 10. Eyebrows, Continued 63
Eyebrow Hairiness • The Limits of Eyebrow Plucking • Eyebrow Shape • Keep that Expression Pleasant * Startup Hairs • Eyebrow Height • Conversational Pauses • Eyebrow Range • When to Prepare for Emotional Drama • Unibrow • Tricky Facial Characteristics • Calm Down (Even More) • Wondering about Cosmetic Surgery? • A Second Opinion

Chapter 11. Eyes 79
Lower Eyelid Curve • Interpreting The Wariness Index • One More Way to Keep Friends • Horizontal Eye Set • Calling All Golfers • Deep-Set Eyes • Eyelid Fold • Question This Offensive Term • Eyelid Fullness • Anchors • Advice to the Lovelorn • Double Whammy Eyelids • Eye Angles • Lying

Chapter 12. Ears 107
Ear Length • STUFF • Ear Position • Wavelength Alert • Ear Angles • Earlobe Size • Earlobe Fixation, Attached Vs. Unattached Earlobes • Ear Circles • Ear Circle Proportions • Don't Translate Backwards from Behavior to Face Data • Protruding Ear Borders • Vote Smarter as a Face Reader

Chapter 13. Smiles 127
Smile Quiz • The Problem with Reading Smiles • How to Interpret a Smile • Learn to Detect Fake Smiles

Chapter 14. Cheeks 133
Dimples • Cheek Prominence • Develop More Inner Power • Cheek Padding • Cheek Emphasis • High Cheekbones • Setting Deadlines • Cheek Proportions • Do This Favor

PART THREE: Superb Physiognomy Skills

Chapter 15. VERY Interesting 151
Easy Does It Best • How to Handle a Somewhat • Eye Angle Quiz • Develop Your Eye For The VERYs • More Sophisticated Visuals • But Very WHAT?

Chapter 16. Noses 159
The Limits of Work • Nose Length • Noses In Profile • Bumpy Noses • Better Bossing • Nose Padding • Why Race Matters Less Than You Were Raised To Believe • Combination Nose Padding • Nose Tip Angle • Nose Tip Size • Nostril Size • Conflicted over Your Nose Data? • Nostril Shape • Major Compassion Awakeners • Dating a Nostril • Your Best Sales Prospects

Chapter 17. Mouths 185
Lipfulness • Dare to Go Counter-Culture • Lip Proportions • Mouth Length • Outsmart Celebrities • Mustaches • Outsmart Celebrities • Commitment • Overlips And Philtrums • Special Gifts from the Lip Fairy • Mouth Puckers

Chapter 18. Jaws 205
Jaw Width • Jaw Definition • Pointy, Angular Jaws • Angry Jaws • A New Sense Of Proportion • Largest Priority Areas • Smallest Priority Areas • Why Priority Areas Can Change

Chapter 19. Chins 223
Chin Bottom Shape • Scary Little Chins • Beard Bottoms • More About Facial Hair • Chin Thrust • Fake Profile Pix • Chin Length • Chin Width • Macho Knobs • Extraverts or Introverts

Chapter 20. Sex 241
Good Reason to Review All You Have Learned • Conclusion

Acknowledgments 245
Face Reader's Guide 247
Index 251

Online Supplement at www.rose-rosetree.com

Dedication

Like warriors, the faces of strangers
went off to do battle. Somewhere. As usual.
I stayed home, admiring the safe faces
    I knew and trusted.

Home, where my own face in the glass
went unquestioned, familiar, comforting.
Except I hungered for more of a world,
    with new faces in it.

After their battles were over, the strangers returned
with ineffable sweetness inscribed upon every feature.
I could look at them easily now, and find the same self.

We had one.

PART ONE: START SMART

1. Power

Like you, Power-Packed Reader, my fascination with faces didn't start off as a lust for power. That came later.

Oh, I'm kidding about myself. And I'm hoping about you.

But it is true that face reading makes a person more powerful. Knowledge is power. And since most people don't have a clue about the kind of in-depth knowledge available from faces, you will have a competitive advantage when you can look and learn, rather than overlook.

What will you be seeing? Face reading does *not* mean looking at expression, which most folks assume is the ultimate insider's view. At this point, let's simply make a distinction between **expression reading** and face reading; in our next chapter we will explore the difference more fully.

Does it shock you to think of reading the physical face? **Face reading** has been practiced for thousands of years. Its formal name is **physiognomy** (fizzy-OG-nuh-me), which means interpreting people's faces to learn about who they are inside.

Such an advantage for you, reading the Secrets available through this kind of attention! One side benefit is discovering new things about your own face *physically*. Sure, it's likely that you will discover meaningful characteristics never noticed before, like your Ear Position and Nostril Shape.

When interpreting that face data, you may discover wonderful new things about yourself *inwardly*, too.

Since 1986, I have done thousands of face readings for people like you. And most have made surprising discoveries about themselves, starting with the physical level.

How could this be? Before, these face wearers didn't pay close attention. Why should they? Most of their face parts didn't seem meaningful.

Not yet.

But all your face parts can become meaningful, effective immediately. So you might want to keep a couple of mirrors by nearby while exploring the power of face reading. Mostly, you will need just one hand mirror. For profile viewing, use two mirrors for that thrilling Sideways See-Self Mirror Trick you learned long ago.

Discoveries about your face physically will be part of the fun ahead. You are going to learn more than that, though. This how-to will instruct you in *how* to do face reading, *why* to do it, everything except *when* to do it.

That part you will have to figure out for yourself.

One chapter at a time, I will emphasize practical ways that face reading can increase your effectiveness in life. Which is why I'll refer to you as a "**Power-Packed Reader**."

Investigating faces can help you to achieve your goals in life. Indirectly you will awaken something that is often missing in people like you, people who care about understanding others: Personal power.

Which would mean what exactly?

Power means effectively pursuing your goals in life and achieving them.

Using personal power, or being power-packed, means sticking up for yourself, rather than serving others so hard that you forget to do that sticking-up part. As a Power-Packed Reader, you already have skills for sticking up for yourself; now that can be improved by activating your face reader's superpowers.

Only one person on earth has the job of advocating for you, and I sure hope you know who that is.

As a Power-Packed Reader, you will be developing the unique **power of face reading**. Why could that be so useful?

For starters, the power of face reading can help you to improve communication skills. This excites many of my face reading students, and not only the sales professionals who want to earn more money. All of us find ourselves in situations where we need to sell ourselves and negotiate with others.

- On a job interview — for any kind of job — wouldn't it help if you could get inside information about your prospective boss?
- Once hired, couldn't you serve your clients better if you knew more about them?
- What if your company should downsize? Might your ability to read people help you to survive as one of the fittest?

A great *Peanuts* comic strip delivered this punch line: "I love humanity. It's just people I can't stand." Face reading helps you to deal with those silly people. You learn about one silly at a time, one cheek at a time, one sale at a time, one friend at a time.

The power of face reading can also upgrade your standing in personal relationships, especially situations where you are likely to feel the opposite of powerful — like singles events. Or meeting your prospective mother-in-law. Or enduring your grumpy new next-door neighbor, the one with the drooling Rottweiler.

What do all these situations have in common? Lacking an abracadabra wand, you are stuck with people. They are stuck with you. How can you both make the best of it?

Without power, you are left wishing those strangers would be nice. You hope they'll see the real you (which is, of course, magnificent). You wish. You smile. Mentally, you cross your fingers.

Except your mind doesn't have fingers! That's merely the most obvious reason why this sort of wish won't ever make a person feel, or be, powerful.

Wishing deepens faith but knowledge brings power. If you are wise, you will wish to see *the best* in all the strangers who enter your life. And I don't mean reminding yourself of a cheery slogan, like "God is in this person; so as long as I can ignore the revolting remainder, I suppose we will get along fine."

Nor does seeing the best in a person mean slapping on a quick label. Some folks assume physiognomy means you decide in 30 seconds whether a person is "good" or "bad."

Aw, come on. We're mixtures. If you want to learn about problems as well as the pretty stuff, don't worry. That can be arranged.

Face reading informs you of practical things, like:

- How your new date makes decisions, spends money, works most productively, handles details.
- Why that seemingly laid-back co-worker is anything but.
- Whose sex appeal makes everybody go crazy, not just you.
- Who is a deep-down nonconformist.
- Which important person at work uses body language to convey exactly the opposite of what she feels.

To read these Secrets, start with curiosity. Then add a willingness to look at human face parts when they are right in front of you. In person, on a newspaper or magazine, your favorite photo, online at a dating website — any of those will work just fine.

(If you think you know friends on Facebook, wait until you *really* see their photos.)

The face parts you will investigate are richly varied. Add nuanced interpretations from this humanistic system of physiognomy and you will gain practical insight into character.

I call it "**Reading the Secrets**" because of the range and accuracy of these insights.

Power-Packed Reader, reading the Secrets can remove any stereotypes that keep you from seeing people as individuals.

You might even avoid having those people bore you ever again. Right now, can you name someone really annoying, someone you deal with often, someone who bores you until even your socks turn droopy? Let face reading help you to appreciate that person in an entirely new way.

And why not also claim your power by using face reading to prevent burnout at work? Do you come into contact with so many people that their faces are starting to blur together?

Sure, a vacation might help. But the cheapest and best vacation could be a few hours with this book. Give yourself a deluxe vacation... from limiting ways of looking at faces. Your own face included.

Not Same Old, Same Old Face Reading

When was the last time you looked in the mirror and thought, "Wow, I love every single thing about this face of mine"?

This contemporary face reading system can help make that happen. More traditional systems? Not so much.

Ancient face reading must have some value, or you wouldn't find it today at places like Ginza, Japan's deluxe shopping district. But mixed in with the good parts are some very outdated notions.

With all respect to sages from the East who began reading faces around the time that other sages started jabbing each other with acupuncture needles, consider the historical context. Again, with all due respect, haven't human beings evolved a bit over the last five thousand years?

Back then, what was the individual's place in society? If you came from a poor family, how much social mobility did you have?

And what if, as a woman, you wanted to work outside the home? Here's a hint: In Japanese, even today, one word for wife means "Woman who stays in the house."

Family status determined your life, if you happened to live as a woman in Asia. Same deal in plenty of other places as well. No wonder folks were anxious to learn about fate. How far would they be able to go, using free will under such heavy restrictions?

Back then, society was rigid compared to today. Your place had more to do with your family's position than any effort you might make on your own behalf. At best, you wouldn't dishonor anyone.

Well, living today, don't you aim higher? I believe so strongly in freedom, my whole face reading system is based upon that: Freedom plus respect for each individual.

Yes, respect. Most of us don't respect our own faces nearly enough. No client has ever come to me pleading: "Help, I have fallen out of love with my face. When I see my face in the mirror, I am no longer thrilled by the magnificence of my visage. Bring back the delight!"

My clients, you see, are grownups. By contrast, my son at age three loved his looks so much that he would dot the mirror with little kiss marks. When was the last time you or I did that?

Enthusiasm over your looks need not be confused with vanity, either. Excessive pride in one's appearance differs dramatically from self-esteem. As healthy non-narcissists, we do have the right to pick up a mirror and thoroughly like what we see.

Now that you are older than three, much of what you observe in life, in the mirror or elsewhere, is covered with layer upon layer of social conditioning. Symbols, memories, fears, and habits of criticism all can distort that image you see in the mirror.

Not the least important of these associations is how your view of your face links up to your self-esteem. Bad face equals bad self.

Unfortunately, few of us like our faces nearly as much as deserved. May a spontaneous enthusiasm increase within you as a result of this skill set!

Power-Packed Reader, long before studying physiognomy, you have been schooled in some weirdly distorted ways of looking at faces.

For example, you have been influenced by advertising. Advertising? Talk about weirdly distorted!

All those images of celebrities and models — each one has been cosmetically enhanced, cleverly lit, probably Photoshopped. That glamour object has likely been surgically altered as well. Scariest of all (to me, anyway) each face is framed with a professionally perfected hairstyle.

In short, even models don't look as good as their photos. No wonder the rest of us do not generally look that good either.

All this is mighty discouraging. We advertising viewers can take this discouragement so deep, we take it for granted.

Enter face reading, a free kind of help for self-esteem. You deserve that help, even if you don't come right out and admit consciously that you could like your face more.

How can you receive major self-esteem help through a mirror plus some easy-to-learn new skills?

As you will discover, just about every detail about your face means something wonderful — the proportions of your lips, the chunkiness of your cheeks. My system of Face Reading Secrets® is based on this premise: *God don't make no junk.* Still....

You May Be Wondering

Just how **accurate** is face reading? Since turning pro as a physiognomist in 1986, I have read faces like crazy. At the end of those readings, I ask for feedback about my accuracy.

About 99 percent of the time the response is positive. This system is so easy to learn, students like you can have a high level of accuracy, too.

For instance, I once got a call from Gladys* a faraway client from 10 years before. Evidently she appreciated the accuracy. Because she said:

"I'm starting a new job. If I send you a picture of my new boss, can you read him? It's really, really important."

Of course, I did. When you have skills, it's easy to read faces with reliable accuracy.

Joe also telephoned me after a conversational gap of 10 years. "You ought to see my copy of your face reading book. It's a mess, I've used it so much. By the way, I'm a millionaire now, and so are the other salespeople I've trained. Your face reading has a lot to do with it. So thank you."

Of course, accuracy matters. You won't be reading people in some hypothetical, theoretical world.

Well, I suppose you possibly might. However, most of us have to make a living, or get good grades in school, or otherwise deal with non-robotic individuals where we want more than vague theories. When we profile people, we want the truth.

With the system of Face Reading Secrets, you will get that.

Ethics

Power-Packed Reader, you might also wonder, is it **ethical** to snoop into people's lives by reading faces?

My short answer is "Yes."

For the long answer, let's use an example. Say that you are looking for a job. Don't you find out all you can about a new boss? Job interviews don't tell all you need to know, either. (Just ask Gladys.)

What a charade, some of those interviews! On the surface, those who play the game discuss formal business matters with unnatural politeness. They move their arms and adjust their expressions as though playing the famous parlor game.

---

*In pursuit of discretion, all first names used alone in this book, like "Gladys" and "Joe," are fictional. Stories about them are true, however. The big exception will be our thoroughly fictional "Cast of Characters," who will be introduced later with all due pomp. Full names in this book, like "Timothy Mar," are real names for real people.

Below the surface, a frantic search ensues, though less obvious than when playing the official game of "Charades." During the game of "Job Interview," everyone becomes a profiler:

- Checking out clues to personality
- Listening for signs about character
- Trying so hard to get at the truth

If that job works out, you will probably spend more time with this work partner than with your love partner. When you are cooped up together, what will that be like?

Considering your perfectly understandable need to know, how would you react if your friend Joe offered you first-hand information about this mystery person? Would you hesitate to listen?

Then why hesitate to grab the first-hand information for yourself... by reading faces?

An inside scoop on that work associate might reveal the difference between a great choice versus a potential disaster. We can make an analogy to graphoanalysis, the study of character based on handwriting samples. Did you know an estimated 80% of businesses in France and Switzerland rely on graphoanalysis? Handwriting analysis has been taught in universities in Germany, Italy, Israel, France, and Holland.

Wherever you live, it pays to learn about the inner person. Face Reading Secrets can provide similar information. It's easier to learn and, of course, easier to access.

Managers have studied with me to help them make better hiring decisions or to bring out the best in staff already hired. H.R. professionals find the results comparable to more complicated personality tests but much easier to administer. All they need do is look at the job applicant.

One manager put it best: "The face is a walking résumé."

Perhaps you have heard a story about President Lincoln, who was asked to appoint a certain man to his cabinet. When Lincoln declined, the reason he gave was, "I don't like the man's face."

"But the poor man is not responsible for his face," protested his trusted adviser.

Lincoln disagreed. He said, "Every man over 40 is responsible for his face." Lincoln was right.

Discretion

Could face reading ever be wrong? Sure, if you try reading the face of anyone under the age of 18.

So don't. Kids haven't had enough time to form a face of their own. If you are a parent, you have seen how fast they change. On Tuesday, Baby Gladys looks more like Mom; Wednesday she looks more like Dad. One year Gladys' adorable nose threatens to take over the rest of the face; next year, her other face parts catch up.

So it's better to let those unpredictable faces develop at their own pace before slapping labels onto them.

Sure, you will probably read kids' faces anyway. (My husband and I started reading our son the day he was born.) Just don't confuse impressionable young people by reading their faces *out loud.*

What if you are under 18 yourself? Can't you learn to read faces?

Smart! You can never start reading faces too early. Power-Packed Readers can be found in every age group.

By the time you are ready to vote, you could become a master physiognomist. Actually that could come in handy with voting, among other things.

Take lightly whatever shows in *your* face until it turns 18. And please don't give your friends face readings until they turn that age. Growing up is confusing enough without worrying over your physical face while it's still developing.

Instead focus on adults, especially teachers and other authority figures. Considering how much power they have over you, you deserve the advantage of reading their Secrets.

Scary?

Newbies can have fears about face reading, even perceptive and talented and very, very sane people. For instance, I often hear this question:

What if, after you learn face reading, you can't stop yourself?

As if. Face reading does not turn you into some kind of weirdo, where you drive yourself and others crazy. (At least, crazier than otherwise.)

After you learn to read faces you won't obsessively go for the deep stuff every time you see a couple of ears or a chin. This is a skill. Turn it off or on at will.

Think of face reading knowledge like a supercool TV set. When you choose to learn more about people, zap!, turn it on. Otherwise, why click your remote? Pay attention elsewhere.

If face reading doesn't drive people crazy, what effect does it have? Will anyone in your life find it scary?

This particular system of physiognomy combines insight with affection for people in all their quirkiness. Once I was hired to read faces at a party where people enjoyed my comments so much, they extended my booking until it lasted 11 hours.

In general, face reading can help people to like you more than otherwise. No guarantees, but this really could happen.

When you have the intent to connect with people more deeply, this changes the level of the relationship... even if you never announce that you are reading faces.

Automatically your intent to connect deeply will invite that other person to reciprocate. After all, can't you feel when people actively reach out to you versus going through the motions of a conversation?

As a face reader, you will still need manners, a skill set learned separately. Face reader or not, would you normally approach a woman who is a total stranger, supply gratuitous comments about her nose, and expect her to thank you?

Face reading ethics, as well as good manners, dictate that you read faces aloud only after asking permission. The notable exception is reading faces of public figures, such as politicians, reality show stars, website owners who proudly show their faces online, etc. Anyone with press coverage, publicity photos and all, is fair game for energetic literacy.

Back at reading faces of people in private life, beware. When Gladys gives you *permission* to read her face, that is one thing. Don't confuse this with something very different, her giving you *respect.*

Just because Gladys agrees to some face reading, does that automatically mean she plans to take your words seriously? Unfortunately not. Could be just the opposite. Some people will test you mercilessly.

Well, are you going to be a Power-Packed Face Reader or not?

Years ago, I was hired years ago by a personnel company to add zest to their convention booth. When Joe stopped by for his free reading, I cringed at his loud, obnoxious voice. And such manners to match! Still, I did my job, describing talents and challenges that showed in Joe's face.

Five hours later, he returned. Quietly Joe said, "I just have to tell you, until today I have always hated my nose. What you said made a bigger difference to me than you can ever know."

Likewise, only you will know what a difference face reading can make for your own self-esteem, communication, success, and overall power in life.

2. Where Does Face Reading Come From?

Timothy Mar, the world's greatest living face reader, stood before me. I felt scared. He had been asked to read my face — not by me, but by a man who was trying to impress me, Joe.

What led to this pivotal point in my life? It was 1975. I had attended my first meeting of Mensa, an international club for people with high IQs that I had joined in the hope of making some friends. Unfortunately I had just been treated to what, with all respect to the astute Mr. Mar, was the most boring lecture I ever heard in my life.

The great man stood in a room crammed with people like me, certified smart but totally ignorant about physiognomy. The former diplomat held up his latest face reading book and announced, "I want all of you to buy this book. So I won't tell you anything that's in it."

Salespeople, take note: This is not a highly effective way to sell books.

Of course, Timothy Mar had to talk about something for the next hour. He was our featured speaker. So he told us how nice it was for him that he could read faces.

The audience fidgeted and would have texted friends if mobile phones had been invented yet. Unaware that I was attending the birth of my future career, I yawned.

Joe, seated next to me, was likewise hoping to make some friends that night. Evidently he found my yawning attractive. So Joe followed me to the front of the room, along with about .04 percent of the listeners in the auditorium. We, the curious, the survivors, plied Timothy Mar with questions about face reading.

Finally the renowned Chinese face reader spilled some real info, commenting on noses and foreheads and cheeks. Eavesdropping from the sidelines, I was having great fun.

Then Joe decided to impress me. "Please read her face," he asked Timothy Mar.

I flinched in advance, certain that I was about to be humiliated.

After a brief professional assessment, Mar said, "Beautiful."

My head swiveled around to see this person. Couldn't be me!

Then he said, "Teacher."

I gulped. In the past four years I had done little else but teach classes in personal development. Teaching was my life.

Shy or not, I finally dared to make contact with Timothy's eyes. Unfortunately, he was now looking worried, extremely worried.

After a polite pause, the august physiognomist glared at me with an expression of great horror. "But you shouldn't pluck your eyebrows."

I looked back with an equally intense expression. It wasn't horror. It was shame. "But I don't pluck my eyebrows," I mumbled.

Although I waited to find out more, Mar slammed his mouth shut.

How I Developed Face Reading Secrets®

As months and years followed, I read all the books on face reading in the English language. At least I started them all, then finished the ones that appealed to me. For a while, I practically lived at the Library of Congress, which offers free access to most books ever published in America.

Definitely, I was hooked on face reading. It made such intuitive sense that a physical face could be meaningful.

If your expression could count, if your body language could reveal yet another layer of truth, what was your long-term face supposed to be, glopped together like potato salad?

Yet my research took a great deal of intestinal fortitude, perhaps not unlike what it might have taken to study all the potato salad recipes in America's cookbooks.

For instance, I discovered what was allegedly so horrible about my eyebrows.

The system of *siang mien,* old as acupuncture, has come down through the ages as fascinating but pretty judgmental. Classical physiognomy is organized around concepts like "The best mouth" and "The best eyebrows."

What if you lack these particular items? Then *siang mien* will tell you cheerfully, and sometimes in great detail, how you are a loser.

My notorious eyebrow characteristic , for instance, involves Distribution of Hair in Eyebrows. Technically, mine are extreme "Starters." (You will read more about Starter Eyebrows in the "Eyebrow" chapter, coming up soon.)

According to *siang mien,* the interpretation is simple: "A person with eyebrows like this will never accomplish much in life."

After I worked my way over to ears, the *siang mien* text instructed me about Ear Position. Such a fascinating discovery!

There was even good news. I had something relatively unusual, ears in a high position. Then came the bad news:

"He will have his greatest success early in life."

What was so terrible about that, aside from the obvious gender problem? When I read this pronouncement, I was well into my thirties. Apparently (unbeknownst to myself) I had already peaked.

At the gorgeous Library of Congress, I studied other face reading systems, too. My favorite classical physiognomist became, and continues to be, Lailan Young, author of "*Secrets of the Face*."

Other face reading authors didn't impress me so much. Really, was I going to be inspired by the bestselling "*You Are All Sanpaku*"? The author used an eye characteristic to predict early death. This didn't appeal to me, hunting for death not being one of my hobbies.

Macrobiotic face reading was another popular system I investigated. Briefly. I dismissed interpretations of face traits along the lines of, "Your mouth shows that your mother ate too many dairy products."

What could I do about that, grab a time travel machine and then vanish my pregnant Mom's grilled cheese sandwich before it entered her mouth?

Gradually the desire built within me to keep what I liked about physiognomy and develop a different system to interpret the rest. I wanted to create a system without dire predictions. It could be a loving system that would be helpful to people. It could be based on the premise that "God don't make no junk."

Using my intuition, which had been developed by years of meditation, I asked inwardly about the meaning of face data. If Starter Eyebrows didn't mean failure at life, what could they mean? How about Ear Position?

When answers came, I tested them on myself, then on friends, and eventually paying clients.

"Yes! It's so true," they said, and not only to the cheerful parts.

Eventually I would go on to trademark this system as Face Reading Secrets®. (At the time of publishing "*The NEW Power of Face Reading*," it is still the only system of physiognomy registered with the U.S. Patent and Trademark Office.)

Other books on physiognomy may be based on *siang mien* or Personology (a well-researched but, to my taste, depressingly deterministic system based on genetics, physiology, anatomy, and neurology), or health-related forms of face reading from the East.

Many physiognomists do a mix-and-match. Also note that physiognomists trained personally by me may have received additional training in energetic literacy, so they can supplement face reading with other skills: Aura Reading Through All Your Senses®, Empath Empowerment®, etc.

By contrast, it's quite possible that you have encountered writers or teachers who use large portions of Face Reading Secrets® without acknowledging it. One rather wacky example is that I googled "The Power of Face Reading" while preparing this new book. On October 23, 2011, there were 141 million hits. By March 28, 2012, the number rose to 222 million hits.

As of August 16, 2012, make that 453 million hits.

I'm pretty sure that most of those hits aren't from me or face readers whom I have personally trained. Very flattering, though!

This author's work in energetic literacy is constantly growing and developing, plus I delight in mentoring students up to a professional level of skill. Power-Packed Reader, this book is your introduction. I have shaped it to emphasize ease of learning and practical uses.

Distinguishing Features

The single biggest influence on this modern system of face reading is... the concept of personal style.

Power-Packed Reader, you are probably more familiar with a related term, **lifestyle**. That means a way of life, as in choosing a healthy lifestyle to prevent heart disease. Or dressing up for dates to attract the crowd you would like to join.

During the 1960's, when I first learned this concept, lifestyle emerged as an exciting way to use free will. Lifestyle includes a set of behaviors, some social roles, maybe even wardrobe choices.

That's right, lifestyle is a choice. If Gladys' couch potato lifestyle brings health risks, such as a heart attack, she can change that lifestyle. Which would be wise, unless Gladys is keen on racking up extra reincarnations.

Over 50 years later, lifestyle is no longer a leading-edge concept. Most folks are familiar with the it. However, they don't necessarily know about a related concept that is newer, **personal style**.

This means a person's comfort zone with behaving in a particular way, or being sensitive to a particular aspect of life.

Gladys, for instance, might have her own adorable and distinctive way of being a couch potato. Perhaps that personal style is related to her special excellence with love, all her hobbies, and everything else she does.

Personal style is not something to change. Rather, a wise person goes with the flow. Ideally you learn to accept how you are in life, then make it magnificent.

Get the contrast between personal style and lifestyle?

- Lifestyle is surface, and relatively easy to change.
- Personal style runs deep. It takes a whole lot of effort to change. And why bother?

For instance, let's consider personal style about conformity. Some people care deeply about belonging. Their manners are great. And when they break the rules, they know it.

By contrast, other people are geared more toward independence. They automatically do things "my way." Afterwards (if ever) they notice what other folks expected.

For me, it was a breakthrough to realize that face reading could be used for interpreting personal style in life areas like social conformity.

How, exactly, do you do that?

First you see the face data. For instance, to what degree do Joe's ears stick out from his head. Then you interpret your findings in the context of Joe's need to belong to the crowd. (Read more details about the Ear Angle category in the "Ears" chapter.)

Why would conformity be related to Ear Angles, rather than some other face reading category?

Don't blame me.

That's the symbolism of the face, a spiritual alphabet. It is what it is. When anatomists analyze the structure of the human heart, they study how it works, not invent it.

Similarly, physiognomists study. We don't invent. Our job is to do our honest best to explore what is there. Since face reading explores a spiritual level of truth, the research is carried out in consciousness rather than a physical laboratory.

Some folks believe this is possible, while others scoff. In the words of Henry Ford, "If you think you can do something, or you can't, in either case you are right."

Folks who believe in the power of face reading will get to benefit from clearer self-knowledge, improved communication, etc.

Scoffers just benefit from their sense of superiority.

Everybody gets something. Evidently you are in the non-scoffer group, willing to consider the possibility that studying face reading data (like In-Angled Ears) can reveal helpful information. Pursuing this system of physiognomy, keep in mind two things — quite apart from the actual ears:

1. Reading personal style is different from assigning a fixed destiny. Your personal style can change over time, just like your lifestyle. It's up to you.
2. Unlike lifestyle, however, personal style isn't necessarily something to change or improve. Instead, personal style is something to value about yourself and others.

Whether ears wing out like flying buttresses, or stick close to the head (more like window shutters fastened with extra-strength Velcro) either characteristic gives its owner at least one advantage in life, a definite talent.

Reframing

Beyond pegging personal style, another way to enjoy the power of face reading is **reframing**. This means taking something that has bothered you in the past and putting it in a different context.

By way of analogy, say that you have inherited a family portrait. It's great. Except the frame for the picture looks hideous, a blotchy old wood with weird curlicues at the edges, and many a ding and dent.

Somehow that picture frame emphasizes the "warts and all" aspect of your relatives.

Imagine that you keep the painting but change the frame to something better. That new frame is tasteful, shiny. Maybe even gold plated.

Automatically you stop seeing warts. Instead, you notice the sparkle in each person's eyes.

That's reframing, Power-Packed Reader. And it can be done figuratively, not just literally. Face Reading Secrets will help you to reframe things you can't stand about people (self included).

Persistent problems are often related to soul-level talents, wonderful talents. Whatever gift you have, there's a related life lesson, like the flip side of a coin.

Yet most of us don't associate the head of a coin with the tail, the upside with the downside. To do this requires reframing. Power-Packed Reader, it can be a huge reframe, discovering how foibles and frailties are connected to a person's most distinctive strengths.

Let's take the example of Joe, with his very In-Angled Ears. Although he's highly sensitive to good manners, he may be easily annoyed by people whose manners are, frankly, lousy.

For years it has bothered Joe that, try though he might to be a nice person, in this respect he still acts like a snob. At elegant dinner parties, he'll catch herself muttering, "Where did she grow up, in a barn?"

Enter the perspective of Face Reading Secrets. Joe learns that his snobbishness about manners reflects his high standards. It's the flip side of having such social finesse.

In this system of face reading, I refer to "**potential challenges**" that go with your talents. Every item of face data goes with a talent plus a potential challenge. They are presented together to help with reframing.

Joe, for instance, might stop beating himself up about that old barn idea. Next time he might catch himself mid-grumble and think, "Why expect everyone to have manners as good as mine? Hey, I have a special talent with manners. Maybe I can afford to be more patient with people who don't."

With enough reframing, Joe might spontaneously stop having that snobbish reaction in the first place. Then he will have mastered one of his life lessons, overcoming a challenge, making the most out of his sacred personal style.

Life Lessons

Have you noticed? The place where you live is **The Learning Planet**. It's a one-room schoolhouse. Kindergartners sit next to graduate students. None of the grades are labeled properly. And, like it or not, each of us is receiving a spiritual education.

It's an extremely public school.

Funnily enough, externals like social status, wealth, and fame don't necessarily reveal how well your classmates are doing at their spiritual lessons. People in high places can be highly evolved, or barely human, or anything in-between. The meek (who inherit the earth spiritually) may have any corporate job title... or none.

How can face reading help you succeed here at The Learning Planet? You learn which life lessons another person is studying.

Half of a life lesson is to recognize your gifts, develop your talents.

The other half demands that you learn to handle the flip side of your gift, the corresponding potential challenge.

In chapters to come, you will read about both in juicy detail.

Does face reading also inform you whether or not someone has learned a life lesson?

Interestingly, no.

Aura reading can tell you, however. And you don't have to pursue psychic development to read auras on anyone you like, in person or from regular photographs. Just seek out instruction in more advanced techniques of energetic literacy.

For practical purposes, though, it's enough to read faces. Spot those life lessons, one item of face data at a time. Gift + potential challenge can add up to inside information that will help you to handle people way better.

Also, those insights will help you to handle your own challenges better. Reframing, like other forms of charity, is best begun at home.

Controversy

To summarize, Face Reading Secrets offers insight into life lessons, both gifts and the challenges that potentially go with them. Such a perspective enables you to reframe your own shortcomings and those of others.

This is a loving system, based on the premise that "God don't make no junk."

Rather than assuming that physical face data is simply a meaningless collection of genes, everything about facial features becomes informative. You can appreciate people more by reading their Secrets.

Nonetheless, face reading is controversial. It contradicts some common assumptions that folks make about reality. For instance, have you ever heard the idea that faces are entirely shaped by heredity?

Agreed, heredity is part of the truth about physical faces. But it's not the entire truth, and it may not even be a particularly useful kind of truth in the context of face parts.

Truth has many levels, you know. After all, a cell from your hand, when seen under a microscope, seems entirely different from the hand you wave to greet a friend.

Yet both these perspectives about your hand are true, due to life's many interlocking levels. One of our privileges as human beings is the freedom to place our attention, at any given time, on whichever level of life we prefer. We can make a mountain out of a molehill or a molehill out of a mountain.

When you are being a scientist, sure, consider facial characteristics as pure genetics. But even the greatest scientist may exit the lab sometimes and just be a person.

As a person, your life will be enriched by the more holistic level of face reading. It combines something physical with something metaphysical.

What is the relationship between your soul and your physical face? Your mind-body-spirit system out-pictures your gifts, based on what's available in the gene pool.

Sometimes it's a pretty long reach in that pool to locate the face data under consideration.

For instance, one face reader told me that, in his family, there are four brothers. All of them look alike except for "The rebel." And his face looks completely different from all the others.

Coincidence? Not to a face reader.

Here's another example. Think of any couple you know who have been happily married for at least 10 years. Haven't their faces started to look alike? Well, whom did they inherit that from, their kids?

Another possible explanation is that, as face readers have said for thousands of years (long before modern-day genetics), there is a reciprocal relationship between the inner person and the outer face.

Beliefs have consequences. If you believe that your life is determined by heredity, you limit your free will. Face Reading Secrets offers you the chance to take responsibility for your looks, just like other aspects of your life.

As you look deeply into faces, you will be amazed how much they change over time... and in ways that validate each person's spiritual journey.

Not all systems of face reading are as free willish as this one. For me, the most fascinating aspect of reading faces for character is celebrating the impact of free will. Faces change in meaningful ways over time.

Before you start researching those changes, Power-Packed Reader, it's smart to start with the program offered here. Learn to read people one at a time, here and now. Later you can get good at reading faces from photos. After that, sure, use comparison photos to track meaningful ways that someone's face changes over time.

Prejudice

How about the racial aspects of a face? Some newbies fear that "physiognomy" is just a fancy word for "prejudice."

Look, I can't defend all that has ever been done in the name of reading faces. About the system of Face Reading Secrets(R), I know for sure:

- This face reading system is *not* a pretext for judging people as good or bad. It is an opportunity to learn, not judge.
- This face reading system is *not* deterministic. Instead, it celebrates free will. Your face changes over time in ways that reflect the evolution of your soul.
- Also this face reading system is *never* about putting people into racial categories.

Which face data will you examine in our program? Power-Packed Reader, I'll show you plenty of fascinating categories about shapes and angles and proportions within a face.

What won't we include? Skin color, the texture of hair, or the color of eyes — which is where folks generally go to shove strangers into a racial category.

Because society has schooled us extensively in stereotyping, many beginners at face reading do expect certain features to go with particular groups. That doesn't last long.

When you look, really look, you will see individuals. That's the fascinating part.

Once, when I was interviewed on national television, my host asked this question: "How can you read faces of black people when they all look alike?"

Shock waves ran through the studio audience.

Interestingly, this talk show host had coffee-colored skin and blue eyes. Probably she, herself, was a mixture of black and white. So she definitely knew better than to ask such an insulting question. Only she wanted to stir things up.

Publicly few people today would come out and say "All black people look alike" or "All Chinese people look alike." We don't say it but sometimes maybe we think it.

However, stereotypes are true in only the most superficial sense.

Gladys, a friend of mine born in Taiwan but raised in America, told me this before she made a trip to China:

"It's going to be such fun to walk down the street and have everyone look just like me!"

Oddly enough, guess what happened on that trip? No matter how large the crowd, Gladys never had trouble recognizing her husband or son. This "look-alike" aspect she referred to was mainly a matter of coloring.

Usually it is.

What Gladys prized, I suspect, was her cultural heritage. Ethnic categories are wonderful as a means to value your heritage. Definitely one can feel an ethnic pride that celebrates history, ancestors, culture.

Unfortunately, another type of ethnic pride that has brought places like Bosnia the horrors of "ethnic cleansing." Face reading is a different subject altogether.

What if you have been conditioned to see the ethnic part first and foremost whenever you see people?

Then see it and move on. As a face reader, you have freedom to choose which aspects of people you will observe. Only you can decide, "This particular time, is it to be molehills or mountains?"

For instance, say that you are taking your first look at Joe, someone who just asked to friend you on Facebook.

- Will you match Joe's features to a racial stereotype?
- Or will you seek (and find) an individual?
- Will you scan Joe's skin for blemishes, like a dermatologist trolling for patients?

Of course, given all your social training, here is what you are most likely to do: Visually weigh Joe's physique (and character?) in terms of fat.

With practice, you might be able to estimate perfectly to the quarter ounce. This could be useful for something, though I'm not sure what.

Aha! So you are interested in something more meaningful? Smart! Because weight and skin and racial assessment reveal zilch about how Joe ticks. Face reading uses the surface of a person to explore the depths.

Still, maybe you are still wondering:

Are face readers supposed to voluntarily blind ourselves to racial characteristics?

Reading people deeper is not about blinding yourself. Instead, face reading gives you something more interesting to view than color of eyes or skin, or hair.

There is so much more to see about faces, for instance, than whether a person has so-called "slanted" eyes (more on that in our Eye Chapter). (And if you are like most beginning face readers, what you read there will really surprise you.)

As a physiognomist, your job is simple. Look at one person at a time. Locate one item of face reading data. Then interpret it.

That's all, folks. Identify the information and interpret it.

Each face has dozens of characteristics to choose from — way more interesting than playing matchy-matchy with stereotypes.

Read Faces in Today's World

Radical search for ethnic purity mostly went out with Hitler. In today's world, millions are doing the ultimate opposite: Mixed marriage, interracial marriage.

Back in the day, this was even considered illegal, labeled with that ugly word "miscegenation."

Well, hello! Intermarriage has arrived, leading many to wonder:

What about faces of biracial or multiethnic people? Can face reading work on "those people"?

Perhaps you have been raised to believe that certain facial parts, like noses, always go with one ethnic group. Well, let's take a look at real faces, in real human reality.

Some people have an extra chunk of nose that hangs down below the nose tip, between the nostrils. Cosmetic surgeons call it a "Hanging Columella." I prefer to call it a "Nose Bonus."

Here's what that item of face data means, whatever your country of origin. If you have a Nose Bonus, you have a talent that shapes your career: Service motivates you.

Service. Not money, not status, not how fast you can reach the current Facebook limit for maximum number of "friends."

Instead, you have an instinct, a calling, to serve others through work. And this motivates you, shaping your personal style when doing a job.

What is required for you to stay interested in that particular job? That particular kind of work must help people, really help them, in a way that matters.

What's the related potential challenge? When you don't believe, deep down, that you are helping people through your work, uh-oh. You can't stick with that job, whatever you are offered in terms of money or status.

Darn, there goes your fine executive job, with the huge expense account. To earn this, all you had to do was find sneaky ways to get teenagers hooked on smoking cigarettes.

Incidentally, what does the meaning of the Nose Bonus have to do with race? Exactly nothing.

Turn the page to see some examples.

People with the Nose Bonus

Dr. Martin Luther King, Jr., *African-American civil rights leader*

Dr. Albert Schweitzer, *German medical missionary*

Anwar Sadat, *Egyptian political leader*

Leo Esaki, *Japanese physicist*

Henri Bergson, *French psychologist and philosopher*

Jacinto Benavente Martinez, *Spanish playwright*

Odysseus Elytis, *Greek poet*

Aung San Suu Kyi, *Chinese-American chemist*

Maireadé Corrigan, *Irish pacifist*

Har Gobind Khorana, *Indian-American biochemist*

Camillo Golgi, *Burmese human rights activist*

Dag Hammarskjold, *Swedish leader, U.N. Secretary General*

Ivan Pavolv, *Russian psychologist*

Rose Rosetree, *American physiognomist*

Lloyd, *from our Cast of Characters*

Alexander, *from our Cast of Characters*

See photos for Alexander and Lloyd near the front of this book; official introductions are coming soon, in Chapter 6.

Power-Packed Reader, by the time you have looked at a person long enough to spot three or more items of face reading data (such as the Nose Bonus), what will happen?

You're likely to see that face as belonging to a real person, not a stereotype.

3. How NOT to See Like a Face Reader

Gone are the days when you ate like a kid, though I hope that cookies still taste at least as good. Just remember your old ways for a moment. It relates to how to see like a face reader.

Kids are purposeful in how they eat. They discriminate with the zeal (if not the sophistication) of a Zen master.

During a childhood phase when all you wanted to eat was potato, you could extract that from any casserole with unerring aim. Flinging squishy peas to the left and icky carrot cubes to the right, you would spoon your way to exactly the morsels you wanted.

However otherwise limited your coordination, once you put your mind to it, you could remove every flake of parsley, no matter how minuscule. Potato, only potato, is what you would toss into your mouth.

Kids are great at paying attention. In fact, a friend of mine who works as a magician has told me how tough it is to do sleight-of-hand for an audience of five-year-olds.

"You can't fool them," Ken Norris complained. "The way tricks work is that you distract the audience while doing the business end of the illusion.

"But young children won't be distracted. They see everything that you are doing, including whatever you are trying to hide.

"Typically at the end of a trick, I say, 'Ta da!' Then the kids say, 'Now what?'

"Those smart little kids are still waiting for the magical part."

The magic of childhood doesn't lie in someone else's illusions. Likewise, the magic in faces doesn't lie where we grownups have been schooled to look. As face readers, we can bypass layers of training and simply see what is.

This comes easier than you might think.

But first let's draw attention to how much you have been doing with faces all along — not physiognomy exactly, but plenty of ways that you were trained to register info about people's faces, whether you consciously meant to or not.

Old Habit #1. Census Taking

Seriously, Power-Packed Reader? You are telling me that you have never been paid to work as an official census taker?

Could have fooled me. Chances are that you have been collecting demographic statistics ever since the age of five. Within seconds of seeing a stranger's face, you fill in your unofficial census form:

- Male or female.
- Old or young.
- Skin color (Which is then used to cram that person into a category about race.)
- Alive or dead (You may not see many of the latter walking down the street. But if you did, trust me, you would notice.)

How fast these demographics whiz by! When not reading faces, sure. Feel free to tag people that way.

Of course, anybody can do quick census taking. You, by contrast, are about to start reading the Secrets.

Old Habit #2. The Perpetual Beauty Contest

Say that you are checking out faces at an online dating website. Attractiveness can count so much, sometimes that is all the date-seeker cares to see.

Strikes me as sad and creepy. Maybe even dangerously limited. For safety's sake alone, anyone considering an Internet romance might choose to learn how to read the Secrets.

Psychological research documents that most people select mates with a similar beauty quotient. Thus, if you are a 10, you probably won't date a 3.

No wonder so much of what passes for face reading — or profound psychological inquiry — or soul mate recognition — really comes down to cuteness screening.

Often our attention is drawn to a stranger's image, rather than the actual face. Physical features pass our test when framed by the right hairstyle and makeup.

"Yes" or "No," we decide. Face audition over!

Quick sorting of candidates for your affections, in person or online, can be fun. Being on the receiving end, however, isn't nearly so delightful.

In either case, I implore you. Stop the face judging. Substitute face reading, something else entirely.

As a face reader, you can take a break from society's gigantic obsession with gorgeousness.

- Who is good looking?
- Who is better looking?

- How will you be judged, given the vast ongoing beauty pageant that is life in the 21st Century?

Well, here's some good news. As a face reader, starting now, you can answer questions like these with another big question: Who cares?

If you really want to check out faces for beauty, you need no help from me. But I'm going to teach you a fine alternative.

How refreshing to have something meaningful to look at, some reason to check out the physical face besides scoring a person's looks on a scale from 1 to 10!

Old Habit #3. Status Reading

Of course, you have been taught how to read social status, scanning faces for clues to class, wealth, and lifestyle.

No, you didn't necessarily take an official class about class. Like it or not, you have been schooled by one snobby group of people after another.

Ever since you met your first "in crowd," snobs taught you to research faces for clues about who (supposedly) belongs in one social group or another. Who looks successful? Who looks pathetic?

By now this is most likely a habit. When meeting somebody new, you will do a super-quick facial check for broken teeth and number of piercings, large visible tattoos, how makeup has been applied, etc.

If you are a woman over 50, you will probably notice how well other women have cared for their skin. Richer people take way better care. They have time. They buy product. So this kind of facial assessment also becomes a way to learn about class.

Male or female, if you are upper middle class or richer, you probably do an extensive survey of facial clues to status, from how eyebrows are groomed to the quality of the facelift.

None of that status reading habit makes you a snob, necessarily. You have simply adapted to seek what you needed to learn, much as certain cavemen needed to tell which type of rock made a good weapon.

Today, status reading is the kind of hunting most humans do best. Certain facial expressions inform us of status, as well.

For instance, try this status reading experiment. Open a magazine like "Vogue" and behold the deadpans of professional models in the fashion photos. Personally, I have never understood why this jaded look sells off-the-rack clothing. Too many of these women look as though they have been starved, then stretched on-the-rack.

Power-Packed Reader, you have probably learned how to distinguish such faces from newspaper photos of war victims, close to death from starvation. All this counts as lifestyle and status reading, not face reading.

Old Habit #4. Seeking Health Updates

Sometimes it's tempting to try reading health from faces. Physical or psychological wounding can show in the way a face is held.

Depending on your experience, you may be familiar with subtle cues revealing a certain kind of alcoholic, or brave adjustment to chronic arthritis, or other clues to physical problems.

Depression, sexual impotence, cruelty, shame: Based on what you have been through, Power-Packed Reader, you may have learned to recognize a full collection of sad nuances.

These problems show to you as obviously as the presence of a chin, even when other onlookers don't see a thing.

Consider it admirable knowledge, hard won and useful. Still, let's not confuse this with face reading. Thank God, face reading can help a person to lighten up!

Even if your lifestyle requires that you routinely deal with the suffering on faces, you owe it to yourself to look at faces in ways that reveal the Secrets. Shadows of tragedy instruct us, but so can the gentle light of talent.

Personally, I am not interested in studying the health implications of faces. I'll leave that to acupuncturists, osteopaths, chiropractors, and other practitioners who specialize in physical health.

You know, the people who have skill sets to actually *do* something about the problems they find. Beware practitioners in any aspect of life who merely diagnose problems without being able to fix them.

Face Reading Secrets is included in my overall method of Energy Spirituality, which contains other skill sets to remove emotional and spiritual blockages. Whichever skill sets *you* have learned to help people, you may actively use your growing perceptiveness about faces as a supplement.

Old Habit #5. Color Gazing

Sometimes new face readers are surprised that I don't include coloring in my system. Why not?

For every pure heart that's bedazzled by the sheer beauty of your skin tones or hair color, dozens of people use coloring as an excuse to categorize you, then not really see you at all. And not only the aspect of race, as supposedly shown in skin color.

- For instance, what if Gladys makes a poor choice of lipstick color? (According to your taste.) Can you ever respect her, ever again?
- What about wanting to gaze into Joe's sumptuous eyes, toying with the right name for their chocolate hue? How would that differ from staring overtly at the rest of his sumptuous body?

Color gazing is fine but it ain't face reading.

By asking you to eliminate color as something to notice in face reading, I'm not saying, "Never again enjoy looking at colors on faces."

If it helps, think of physiognomy as going on a short-term Color Fast.

By disrupting your normal view of faces as mostly color, you can jump start seeing new face data — equally beautiful and way more informative.

Literally thousands of times I have shown people facial details they never noticed before. What on earth do you think they were looking at all those years? Color, color, color.

Old Habit #6. Worrying

What if you feel worried about being not terribly observant? Fear not.

Power-Packed Reader, I doubt this one book will stop all your worrying in life. But at least I can reassure you about worry related to being observant as a face reader.

If you are observant enough to read these words on a page, you are observant enough to become a face reader.

So stop any worrying. Instead, consider this: Until you knew that facial characteristics were clues to character, why on earth would you have bothered to notice?

Reading faces is like reading words. Before you became literate, letters like b, d, p, and q were just lollipops. By now you can tell the difference. It's easy to become observant once you have a reason.

Similarly, face data adds up to a kind of alphabet. When you know what to look for, you will see it just fine. And once you master this form of literacy, I think you will find it amazing how much you do see. Effortlessly.

Sometimes I'm hired to read faces at parties. Pitted against a live band or a square dance, still the face reading goes on. I have lost my voice, trying to squeak above the music.

Even then, I have had no trouble at all, seeing the p's and q's of a face, then interpreting what it means in physiognomy.

Face reading is like other skills in life. We're observant about what interests us. Your new habits for reading the Secrets can become perfectly portable, life skills that only improve over time.

4. Expression Reading

Are you fascinated by expression? Television has trained us all to become expert expression watchers.

Power-Packed Reader, do you remember that once upon a time you had to learn how to watch TV? And it was hard. For instance, you were supposed to park your butt and stop running around the room.

As for the opposite end of your torso, the face part, shocking discovery! TV watching taught you that facial expression was the key to important scenes:

The drama intensified.

Main characters were shown in close-up.

Background music grew louder, like little arrows pointing to faces of the main characters.

Soon you caught on. You were supposed to look at eyes and mouths. Expression showed there.

Changes to expression were the main point of the story, whether a cartoon or a movie for kids or whatever else the grownups let you watch.

But is that really true?

Once again, Power-Packed Reader, it's helpful to realize that truth comes in many layers. Expression does have advantages as a way to learn about people. Nonetheless, it has plenty of drawbacks.

Expressing… the Intent to Deceive

In real life, unlike TV viewing, expression watching can be dangerous. In real life, creepy people aren't identified as such. Focusing on their expressions can distract you from using your common sense.

What does the person say and do, apart from acting so darned sincere?

Apparently nice, and never publicly nominated for an Oscar, real-life villains can be really good at deceiving others through expression.

However, occasional lying is done by perfectly nice people as well. Sometimes maybe even you. Even if you shade the truth with the loveliest intentions to spare people's feelings. For instance....

Leaving the boring party, it's so tempting to paste a sweet smile on one's face. Makes it so much more convincing when you mouth an excuse for leaving early, then say, "I'm so glad I came. I had a grrrreat time."

Deception starts early in life. It doesn't feel like lying necessarily, so much as slipping into an emotional space, then conveniently deciding that *this* is the part of the truth to tell.

Say that Gladys glares at her five-year-old, Joey:

"Were you just eating that cookie?"

Conveniently, Joey remembers the microsecond between finishing the last chocolate chip and when Mom entered the room. "No, Mom." he says. "I was just bouncing on the sofa."

A face full of innocence stares right back at her. Oh well.

Expression can be unreliable for reading even a five-year-old.

Power-Packed Reader, never confuse reading expression with reading the Secrets.

Mood Reading

Apart from deception, expression has other disadvantages as a way to learn from a person's face. Expression shows mood, and mood is a passing thing.

As months go by, reality pushes away fantasy. How many times have you heard a friend's sad story begin with words like these?

"I trusted Joe because he looked so nice."

"Nice," on a date or job interview, reveals exactly how much about Joe's long-term behavior?

Exactly nothing.

What has expression revealed about Joe's personal style with power or intimacy or work?

Nothing, not really, except whether he likes what is happening at one particular moment.

While doing volunteer work at that animal shelter, perhaps he's thinking about smoking a really choice cigar after he leaves "the stinking hell hole."

Maybe Joe volunteers only because he likes picking up tenderhearted critters of the human variety, and he smiles as a civilized alternative to licking his chops in anticipation of the delights to come.

For more dependable insights, Power-Packed Reader, might I recommend face reading? Unlike expression, face reading data can't be faked, which makes for a far more accurate reading.

Most Annoying

I find it pretty annoying when folks tell me, "I know all about face reading" and they really mean "I pride myself on reading expressions."

So far, Power-Packed Reader, I have mentioned the transience of mood and the prevalence of deception. I have even hinted at the passivity of watching faces as if simply watching TV.

But my most searing indictment of expression watching is that it is so ridiculously limiting.

All too often folks who could become perceptive face readers… settle for breadcrumbs at life's banquet of insight.

"Eyes are the mirror of the soul," they say. Gladys believes this, for instance.

This attractive young woman loves staring into the eyes of potential dates. Gladys is convinced this reveals deep truths. Right now she's speed-dating, sitting kissing distance away from Joe. Gazing into his seductive eyes, Gladys has convinced herself that she is x-raying his soul.

Is she ever fooling herself!

No insult intended: Gladys has great innate smarts for soul-reading. Could she become a fabulous face reader? Definitely.

Her curiosity and innate smarts could help Gladys to develop the full power of face reading. But no amount of innate smarts can substitute for owning skills.

Same thing if she had the desire to become a racecar driver, a lumberjack, a brain surgeon. Technical skills are needed to support any enterprise that is potentially tricky.

Soul-seeking Gladys could benefit from learning a thing or three about how to read the soul in a face. Her regular reading skills — Gutenberg-type literacy — developed after learning some skills, right?

That's why Gladys is able to read the words on this page. She uses her full smarts as a regular reader because, back in the day, Gladys spent plenty of time acquiring skills.

Back in elementary school, Gladys learned phonics. She practiced for years with the help of skilled teachers. All this woke up Gladys's inborn smarts for regular reading.

Face reading is a form of energetic literacy, requiring comparable skills and practice. If you want to consider face reading as tough as rocket science, I'm flattered. But regular Gutenberg literacy makes as good a comparison.

And, fortunately, learning to read the Secrets can develop way faster than regular reading skills, let alone the preparation required for rocket science.

Back to Gladys at her singles event, soul-level truths about her prospect, Joe, could be available through his eyes. Ditto through reading the rest of his face. Except Gladys stares at his eyes alone, since this is where she thinks all secrets will be revealed. TV has trained her well.

Gladys grows so excited during her two-second research. She can tell that Joe is:

- Happy and positive. (In this particular moment.)
- A good person. (In this particular moment.)
- Interested in her. (Definitely.)
- Lusting after her with barely concealed drool.

Sorry. None of this counts as really reading the man's soul. Joe's soul is a deeper level of truth than his passing emotions, passable manners, and a promising degree of sexual interest.

Want examples? They're coming up, chapter by chapter. Reading the Secrets is *all* about investigating the soul.

What can thrill you most, if you do want to read someone's soul? To a skilled face reader, the entire face mirrors the soul. Not merely the eyes.

You are going to learn how to read any adult's soul in detail, feature by feature, with accuracy. Meanwhile....

Quiz Yourself on Face Watching Habits

Here's a quiz to help you assess some old habits. What does it mean to you now to see a face?

AnswerTRUE or FALSE.

1. Observing a sales client's expression helps to put you in control.
2. Never trust someone with beady eyes.
3. Never trust someone with shifty eyes.
4. The facial feature people are most apt to dislike in themselves is the chin.
5. Men who grow beards may be hiding a weak chin.
6. People with full lips are sexier than people with slimmer lips.
7. Intelligence shows in the shape of the skull.
8. People from the same ethnic group tend to look alike.
9. I can rely on my snap judgments about character from one quick look at a face.
10. I know everything important about how my own face looks.

Face Watching Habits Quiz ANSWERS

1. FALSE. Paying attention to your client's expression sure beats paying no attention at all. But you are more apt to *respond* to her emotions than proactively change them.

To really take charge of a conversation, get on that customer's wavelength. Avoid making the comment that causes a negative expression to display on that face. For instance, learn to read the categories of Eyebrow Shape and Ear Angles.

2. FALSE. What exactly are beady eyes, anyway? The overall impression "beady eyes" could be triggered by any one of these: Small Eye Size, Close-Set Eyes, or Deep-Set Eyes.

My advice? Save beads for necklaces, unless you are also going to discuss rhinestone ears, sequined eyebrows, etc.

3. FALSE. Unwillingness to look you in the eye is not a reliable clue to dishonesty. Reasons for "shifty eyes" include shyness, sexual insecurity, and depression.

In fact, Americans from different cultural backgrounds are sometimes taught to avoid eye contact as a mark of *respect.*

4. FALSE. According to a survey in *Psychology Today,* 30 million Americans dislike their chins, but 60 million hate their noses. Here's a more vital statistic, however:

According to my ongoing survey of client reactions, guess what happens to 99% of people who learn the inner meaning of face data they dislike? They gain a new respect for everything about their physical face, nose included.

5. FALSE. By growing a beard, a man has the opportunity to change the shape of his chin. With face reading, what you see counts. And thanks to free will, our faces change in many ways. Beards are just one of them.

When a man covers his chin with a beard, he transforms it. Inner personality changes accordingly.

6. FALSE. Anybody can be sexy — or not. You have done better some days than others, haven't you?

Here's a more reliable way to read somebody's lips: Learn to read Lipfulness in our Chapter 17. Test the accuracy for yourself.

7. FALSE. Phrenology, which gauged IQ by reading the bumps on the head, was used in Victorian England as a way to brand people as good or bad; its accuracy has long since been discredited.

Just to be clear, Face Reading Secrets is used as a way to add depth to our understanding of people, not take it away; it has nothing to do with phrenology, superstition, or determinism.

Common sense tells you the front of a man's face ought to be a heck of a lot more informative than the back of his scalp, right?

8. ONLY IF YOU DON'T LOOK VERY CLOSELY. Although a few physical traits, like skin color and hair texture, may be enough for stereotyping purposes, ethnic similarities are not a significant part of this system of physiognomy. When you learn to read faces properly, people actually look less stereotyped, more individual.

We have already discussed how Face Reading Secrets® is not about color. As for observations about hair above the forehead or below the chin, you'll have to turn elsewhere for experts about meaning. Might I suggest wherever you get haircuts?

Faces have plenty to keep you occupied without including these details of social obsession.

9. FALSE. Such judgments are usually incomplete, misleading, or self-fulfilling prophesies. Oops!

10. MAYBE. Society teaches us to look at faces in ways that are both limited and limiting. We're programmed to be obsessed by color, complexion, wrinkles, expression.

Power-Packed Reader, as you learn face reading, you will probably find many things about your own face you never noticed before. What an inspiration, discovering that all these new items of face data can reveal gifts of your soul!

5. Practical Advantages

Start off your new skill set for face reading with positioning. Where will you aim your eyes?

It's only common sense. Before you can *interpret* any face reading data, first you must *see* it. So, Power-Packed Reader, look for information in this order:

1. Choose one physical **feature**, like a nose or mouth. One. (So you would choose only one eyebrow, eye, ear, or nostril to read at a time.)
2. Each feature contains several **categories**, like Nose Length, Nose Tip Size, Nose Tip Angle. Choose one category to read at a time.
3. Each category contains one or more different **items of face data**, such as Long Nose, Short Nose, Moderate Nose Length. Identify one of these face reading characteristics. That will have a meaning for you to interpret.

Simply sorting this out gives you the first of our practical advantages for reading the Secrets. Too many would-be face readers check out an entire feature.

They opine "Big schnozz" or "Cute nose" and never notice anything more. This is, of course, the opposite of quality physiognomy.

Power-Packed Reader, I'm setting up this Face Reading Program to make it super easy for you to notice the details that matter most.

Starting with our next chapter, you will be invited to view one facial feature at a time. Within that chapter, I'll present one category at a time, teaching it thoroughly.

On a purely physical level, you will see what you have on your face. Then you will find out what it means in the system of Face Reading Secrets®. Decide for yourself about the accuracy.

Soon, I predict, you will love reading those Secrets. Incidentally, I don't make that prediction because of being a psychic. I'm not a psychic but a teacher of energetic literacy, reading people here and now. And having taught face reading on three continents — more if you count foreign editions of my books — I'm quite certain that you are going to be wonder-struck.

That's like "thunder-struck," only more pleasant.

To help you to become joyfully wonder-struck by reading the Secrets, the rest of this chapter is dedicated to practical tips that will give you a big advantage for learning extra-quickly and easily.

Develop a Face Reader's Curiosity

If you were studying ballet, you would have to work on your turnout. Well, a face reader needs a different kind of flexibility, something less painful to develop.

When you use this particular skill set, **face reader's curiosity** can become a habit. You will grow used to entering into a slightly different pacing, almost like a meditation, with your eyes fully open.

Call it an appreciative, even loving, kind of curiosity. You can turn it off or on at will. Developing this will give you a huge practical advantage as a face reader (and also may help you to evolve as a person).

In previous chapters I reminded you of different ways that you have already learned to look at faces: Checking out stereotypes like a census taker, checking out expression, etc.

All these old ways of judging faces are done automatically by now, given your many years of practice.

By contrast, physiognomy is a different approach. Face reader's curiosity must be pursued with your conscious mind, every face reading, every time, no matter how many years or decades you do face reading.

So here is a list of six new habits to use whenever you read faces.

Six Distinctive Steps

Step 1. The Mystery Step

Reading faces, prepare for awe, a kind of innocence. Imagine how that will feel, being open to mystery even as a very experienced face reader.

A bit later in this chapter I will go into more detail. For now, suffice it to say that being open to mystery is a far cry from old habits of expression watching.

Step 2. Shift Your Awareness

When you read faces, you are not viewing them in the usual way. Shift your awareness into a more thoughtful, appreciative mode.

Will observers think you have turned wacko, with glazed eyes and a weird fangy smile? I sure hope not.

The change of awareness won't necessarily show to anybody on earth… except you.

When reading faces, you will look for physical face data exclusively, so let distractions (like lipstick on a woman's teeth or your favorite old face watching habits) wait until later.

Step 3. Slow Down

No visible speed bumps will stop you, Power-Packed Reader. You must make the choice on your own: Purposely slow down enough to read one item of face data at a time.

None of that quick, "Label the guy as 'hideous honker' and get the job over with."

With experience, it takes just a tiny tad of time to see the data properly. Accuracy depends on taking this private, slow-motion moment.

You know what they say, about face reading — or was it computers? — "Garbage in, garbage out."

Step 4. Asymmetry Alert

Educate yourself right now about this fact of life: The left side of an adult's face contains different data from the right side.

Asymmetrical (ah-sim-MEH-trih-cul) is a weird-looking word. Nonetheless, "asymmetrical" strikes me as way more respectful than "crooked," or "imperfect-bent-hideous-shameful-or-ugly," which are more common labels that non-physiognomists use… at least until they know better.

What's the big deal about symmetry? Most babies' faces have perfect symmetry. Most adult faces don't.

Confusingly, you may find perfect symmetry on most of the adult faces you see on TV, since they are part human, part plastic. Or, at least, since so many are surgically altered.

Personally, I wish that every face reader would make a pilgrimage to England. Just to watch the telly.

Most folks I've seen on British TV wear their original faces. You can find loads of meaningful, very human asymmetries.

Meanwhile, without "Crossing the pond," you can find plenty of asymmetry on all the folks who still don't have their own YouTube channel.

Asymmetry can help you read faces. Depending on which Secrets you wish to read, look at one side of the face rather than the other.

- For business applications, read the right side of the face.
- For relationships, read the left side.

In a future chapter, Power-Packed Reader, I'll explain more about left and right. Meanwhile you can do fine with your mirror and the photo examples provided.

Step 5. VERY Important

Notice if the item of face data you have found is a VERY. This will add finesse to your interpretation. Extreme examples of face data are your most vital clues to character, while less intense versions won't signify as much.

VERY extreme items of face data show in shape or size or proportion. For instance:

- Does Gladys have a Straight Eyebrow Shape or a VERY Straight Eyebrow Shape?
- Is Joe's Cheek Padding biggish or VERY big?

Even for advanced face readers, finding the VERYs can be tricky. So I will coach you about this in Part Three of our Face Reading Program. For now, it's enough to know that face data can be more or less VERY. Notice what you can, without forcing.

In particular, avoid reading the "squinties," which are the opposite of the VERYs. Should you catch yourself worrying this way, please stop trying so hard to see that particular item of face reading data.

Move on to something you can eyeball more easily.

Step 6. Find patterns

When you feel comfortable reading one item of face data at a time, finding asymmetries, seeking the VERYs, ta da! No longer a beginner, you will be a more sophisticated face reader who can seek and find patterns.

Our program with "The NEW Power of Face Reading" is meant to be beginner-friendly. From the very start of your study, however, why not establish habits you can use later?

Are you already an intermediate or advanced face reader? Then discovering patterns will become increasingly delectable.

As you may have guessed, I built both beginner, intermediate, and advanced levels into this how-to program, so you can cycle through the book after reading 100 faces or so and take your skill to the next level.

Whatever your degree of expertise, as a face reader you can seek patterns, comparing and contrasting face data until you put the whole face together in a meaningful way.

This is where you can really show your stuff, Power-Packed Reader. Because you *will* find patterns.

Curious what this will be like? You can find many examples of a professional quality face reading, all for free, at my blog. This is easy to access at www.rose-rosetree.com/blog.

Doing a full face reading is such huge fun. And practical, too. Sure, you can get there. Reading faces for character is a life skill that will only deepen with time, a kind of wisdom to keep your relationships fresh and flowing.

To this professional physiognomist, doing a full face reading for a client takes at least an hour. Patterns that show are deeply meaningful, with insights that wake up the soul.

But even a beginner's face reading, lasting a few minutes, can be accurate, inspiring, practical, fun.

And isn't that plenty? Or maybe you want more from face reading. Hmmm.

Which brings us to the topic of becoming…

YOUR Kind of Power-Packed Face Reader

That is what you can become, YOUR kind of Power-Packed Face Reader. For this, **intention** is our very important Mystery Step #1.

Intention's power is built right into this system of face reading, very necessary to help you to become your kind of Power-Packed Face Reader.

Personally, I have an intention in teaching this system to you. Same as my intention in using it for myself: To open up a heart of compassion.

Face Reading Secrets® is essentially a loving system of physiognomy, designed to help a person grow in compassion and perceptiveness. Both!

Neither a pushover nor blind to enemies, you can gain power by realistically appreciating the good in people, what can be found, here and now.

So many folks care only about spotting liars and crooks. That guarantees a kind of theft in life.

If you focused on spotting the rare bad apples, you would miss all the varieties of Delicious and Jonagold and so many other juicy, sweet mouthfuls of crunch.

So choose wisely how you position your consciousness. Intention can help you to do that.

Now, my personal intention — that opening up a heart of compassion — doesn't have to become *your* intention.

What does matter? Each time you start reading faces, take a moment to set an intention. Why will you be reading that person's face? Choose a worthy intention.

Intention Counts for Reading Your Own Face, Too.

What if that face you are reading belongs to you? Would it be a waste of time to take a whole 10 seconds to set an intention?

I sure recommend that you invest the tiny amount of time it takes to set an intention for your own sake.

That intention of yours can reflect your spiritual or religious values. It can be strictly practical. Intention hinges on whatever matters to you in the moment.

Wise Intentions

Reading people deeper through physiognomy, your choice of intention matters enormously. It will affect how you aim your eyes, your mind, and your heart. Here are some examples of intentions that might be productive for you:

- Communicating better.
- Earning more money in an honorable way, becoming extra helpful to others.
- Have more passion and authenticity in close relationships.
- Improving social skills, making new friends.
- Developing full potential for leadership.
- Making wise choices about dating and marriage.
- Using personal power more effectively.
- Spiritual growth, honoring the specialness of each person you meet.
- Fulfilling your life purpose by making the most of your talents.

Use Intention to Empower Yourself

Any system of face reading coaches you to look at a person's physical face, then interpret what you find. This particular system has you read the person's Secrets because you also look *through* that person's face, all the way to the soul.

It's a kind of bonus, and I don't mean Nose Bonus. This deeper perception will happen automatically, bringing you cumulative growth as a person.

All that's required is a suitable intention, something that motivates you to learn about people in a deeply appreciative way. Plus knowing how to actually use that intention.

Setting an intention means thinking your choice one time, inside your head. Such as:

"I want to communicate better." Or, "This time, my purpose when reading faces is to use my personal power more effectively."

Keep it simple, Power-Packed Reader. One thought. One time.

That counts. Your step of intention setting has been done just fine.

Setting an intention doesn't mean a tortured stance, as though in the throes of constipation. A simple wish does the job. Then trust that your chosen intention will come true.

6. Cast of Characters

Look who is here to help you read faces! Such a treat, this set of photos I have assembled to help you learn face reading... so come and meet our Cast of Characters.

You may recognize these faces from the start of this book. But we can have way more fun than simply referring to "Whoever." Why not have me supply some ways to tell these fine folks apart?

Ultimately this physiognomy how-to will star YOU, Power-Packed Reader. However, I wasn't able to take your picture, posed gorgeously alongside significant others.

So I did the next best thing and substituted this crew of 20. One and all, they are good sports who graciously consented to be in our photographs.

When introducing new face reading data, I will often refer to this wacky group. Everything I write about them — their names, how long they have spent in jail, their confusing and complicated relationships with you, etc. — will be **completely fictitious**.

And, of course, resemblance of any of these folks to real people you have ever encountered, living or dead, is a coincidence. (I don't know about *their* jail time, either.)

In reality, all the folks in this book are simply here as "Practice people" for you as a face reader. So, who are they in our alternate reality, designed for physiognomy practice?

Allow me to introduce you. Just names and a bit of back story. I want you to feel motivated to do detective work on each one.

Speaking of detective work, you can find large, color versions of all these photos in the Online Supplement to "The NEW Power of Face Reading" at my website. Find that at www.rose-rosetree.com.

- **Ava** is your mother's best friend.
- **George** is your father's best friend.
- **Annette** is your favorite aunt.
- **Wayne** is your favorite uncle.
- **Alexander** is a cousin who has always annoyed you.

- **Joyce** is a cousin you have always liked.
- **Anthony** is a cousin who wants to marry you. (Kidding.) He is a family friend.
- **Rowan** is your new boss at work.
- **Matt** is your new client (or customer or employee) at work.
- **Gary** is a potential client (or customer or employee).
- **Cliff** is another potential client (or customer or employee).
- **Madison** is yet another potential client (or customer or employee). (Oh, you are so much more successful since becoming a face reader!)
- **Kathryn** wants to friend you on Facebook.
- **Oliver** has 52 friends in common with you on Facebook. Curious about him?
- **Valerie** is a friend from work who just invited you to a party.
- **Fred** is your new next-door neighbor.
- **Lloyd** is a neighbor you have never known well. (Is it time to get acquainted?)
- **Jesse** is a neighbor who acts friendly, but you suspect it is only to interest you in going to his church.
- **Shirley** is your old third-grade teacher. As a person, she always puzzled you.
- **Helene** is a new yoga teacher in your neighborhood.

Such wonderful faces! Their treasure troves of information await you, Power-Packed Reader.

7. Mirror Skills

Power-Packed Reader, give yourself every advantage for learning this new skill set.

Practice people have been supplied in our previous chapter, but let's include at least one real live specimen. You! Start with your own face, because it is truly magnificent — as you will soon appreciate more than ever.

Of course, you might prefer to sit with a sweetheart or best friend or even a very open-minded parent. Go through one chapter at a time. Supply two mirrors per person.

How delightful it can be to share your responses to each item of face reading data.

Only I do want to warn you against choosing a face reading partner like Cousin Carissa. She prides herself on being "a skeptic." Really she's the kind of cynic who specializes in tearing down whatever conflicts with her massive prejudices.

Don't share face reading with anyone remotely like Carissa. Not now, not later. Not even after you become really skilled as a physiognomist.

I have been there. Based on that dismal kind of experience, I would like to spare you trying to change someone's mind about face reading. Such a colossal waste of time... for you.

For the self-anointed debunker, it's not a waste of time but a sport. The big payoff would come if the debunker manages to wreck your joy and confidence about face reading.

What do face reading cynics have in common? They are losers. At least when it comes to the wisdom available from physiognomy.

Cousin Carissa may be lovely in other ways. When you spend time with her, by all means, enjoy those other ways. Simply don't share this interest with her.

For every person who sneers at face reading, you can find dozens who will find it interesting, helpful, even inspiring. Let those smarties benefit from your insights.

Which Kind of Mirror

As you pursue this program for reading the Secrets, you will definitely need a mirror or two. Mirrors don't have to be fancy. Ideally:

- A hand mirror can be comfortably picked up or put down. Just make sure the mirror is big enough to show your whole face.
- A wall-mounted mirror needs to be positioned so that you can see your face easily on the level. (Or you need to be able to move comfortably into that alignment.)
- If the mirror stands on a table, you must be able to lift the mirror to be on the level with you. Either that or you can move your body to position your face is on the level.
- Your mirror ought to be reasonably clean, so you don't feel discouraged by smudges. (Take the occasional two minutes to shine up your reflection.)
- Choose a mirror bigger than a postage stamp, please. No need to get all squinty in the pursuit of personal truth.
- Avoid cracked or broken mirrors. So discouraging!

Prepare Your Face Physically

Must you scrub up as if preparing for surgery? Ouch, no need to take face reading that seriously.

Power-Packed Reader, "Regular You" can be read just fine, even through makeup.

Probably, anyhow. Are you wearing gobs of really, really gorgeous makeup then might distract you? Then blot away that fourth coat of lip gloss.

You won't be reading expressions any more than makeup, so no need to grin at your mirror reflection.

Fortunately there is an easy middle ground between smiling and frowning. Could be called "My face in repose." Or "Just looking normal."

Worried about whether your face will look "normal" enough? Relax.

Literally. When you hold up that mirror, searching for face data, how about this? Simply stay awake, and not forcing your face into any particular expression.

Cringing and worrying aren't required, not for being a physiognomist anyway. Look forward to seeing your face physiognomist-style.

If it helps, remember that God don't make no junk.

On the Level

As you prepare to read anyone else's face, look from a straight angle. The same applies to how you can best study your own face. As a physiognomist:

Don't look up to people. Don't look down on them. To see the truth, be on the level.

Practice looking into your mirror right now. Is your arm comfortable?

Angle your face like a mug shot, not to one side or the other, neither up nor down. For physiognomy, that's called "On the level."

Adjust as needed, or ask a friend to help. You may have some pretty automatic habits about mirror holding.

- I have seen guys thrust their chins upward, as though preparing to shave under the chin.
- I have seen gals coquettishly dip their chins down, eyes downcast.

But really! Who is being flirted with now, or shaved?

Some of you Power-Packed Readers may be habitual looker-downers, which you mislabel as "On the level." Level with what, your lap?

Please accord yourself appropriate dignity. Hoist up that mirror until you can see yourself easily, head up and not quite screwed off your neck.

Seriously, some folks have the habit of holding the mirror on the level, then looking upwards, as if searching for a UFO suitable for escaping from the entire look-in-mirror ordeal.

Well, you don't have to crick your neck to improve things. That face of yours is perfect, reflecting your soul. Which happens to live right here on earth.

In short, Power-Packed Reader, that mirror can become your friend. Don't give yourself a hard time, twirling like a ballet dancer from the neck up. View yourself at a reasonably straight angle... doing your level best... and you will get accustomed to all that splendor.

Turn the page and see Ciff for inspiration!

Sideways Views

Behold the side of your face. Now is a fine time to take a look.

If you are into something as deep as face reading, chances are that you adore the really fancy Double Mirror Trick. You know, using two looking glasses to create an infinite regress of your own reflection.

Much as I can relate to anyone's longing for infinity, face reading requires a different use of your two mirrors. Settle for one view of your human profile at a time.

The total is two views, in sequence: One on the left side and one on the right. Notice any physical differences yet between them?

Power-Packed Reader, you are so fascinating!

One last technical point. When viewing your face from the side, did you revert to old habits of seeing your face *not* on the level? Let your chin angle provide a clue.

Cliff Learns to See Himself on the Level

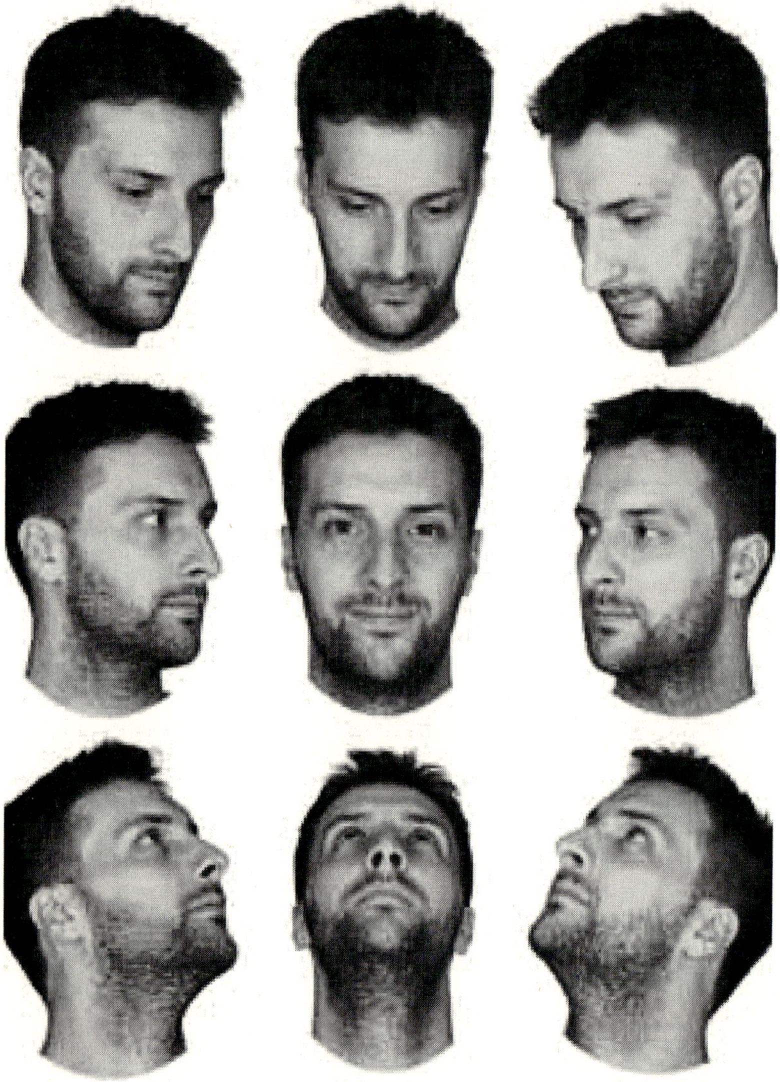

Calm that chin down. No need to stick it up extra high. Compare that chin to your neck. Pivot gently until you can approximate a normal, straight angle.

Hey, I'm 64 years old now. I know something about extra chin. Maybe you do, too. Well, let's be clear. Face reading means reading one's face down to the first chin. Only. However many extras there may be.

Speaking of extras, my system of face reading does not include butt reading. (Although I have certainly been asked to perform this service, read people at nudist events, etc.)

Let's keep it simple, okay? With this Face Reading Program, we will read faces only and read them on the level, whether frontally or in profile.

Beware Multi-Tasking

Power-Packed Reader, your lifestyle may demand constantly checking for texts, playing cool background music, and otherwise staying electronically plugged in.

Whatever! Only don't combine that with physiognomy. While you read your face, simply read your face. Afterwards you will have so much more to tell friends.

Personally, I wouldn't recommend snacking or smoking cigarettes or combing your hair or anything else but reading faces. (At least while you are reading faces.) Even when you are a very, very experienced face reader, you can do your best only while paying attention in the here-and-now.

And when you turn expert enough to read faces for other people, whether as an amateur or a professional, also demand that same respect from your client.

If Joe can't spare three minutes of uninterrupted "face time," why tell him about his fine nostrils?

Hello! Joe doesn't respect what you are doing. Save your breath and wisdom for those who will appreciate them. (Which might even be Joe another day.)

Time, Not Measured by Counting "Big Honkers"

As you explore the power of face reading, ideally give yourself 10 minutes of study time daily. Then consider that you have done plenty.

Okay, you could add on additional 10-minute chunks, but only do that if you feel inspired. We're not talking "Big ordeal," right? You will choose the number of time chunks. And you are always going to be nice to yourself as a face reader, right?

How about pacing yourself during a face reading? Don't save time by giving a quick, impatient glance at Gladys's nose, then proclaiming:

"Gladys has a big honker."

Gladys deserves better. If you are going to focus on her nose, pause long enough to see it properly. Ask yourself, "How is it big?"

Which item of face reading data gave that first impression? "Big" could be any of these:

- Long Nose Length
- Large Nose Thrust from the side
- A pronounced Arched Nose in Profile
- Large Nose Padding at the bridge
- Large Nose Padding right above the tip
- Large Nose Padding all the way down
- A nose with VERY Triangular Nose Padding all the way down its central ridge
- A Large Nose Tip

Soon we can enjoy an entire chapter dedicated to "Nose." Meanwhile, relax. This Face Reading Program is as systematic as could be.

Different physical features, like noses and ears, have their own chapters. Each feature contains several categories, which I'll introduce you to one at a time. Within each category, you will find different choices.

Armed with your trusty mirror, looking on the level, you can start connecting that physical face of yours to inner truths about what makes a person special.

Earlier I joked about how kids see reality so clearly that magic tricks don't work for them. As you see faces more clearly, you will see through illusions too — illusions like "Big schnozz." It's a kind of magic that works on every face, all the better to locate the glorious talents within.

8. Where Will You Read Those Secrets?

Which Secrets will you read where? Here's an overview.

- **Eyebrows** contain categories about thinking patterns, use of your mind and intellect.
- **Eyes** proclaim ways of connecting socially with others.
- **Ears** reveal ways you connect that are deeper than mere social connection. (Facial categories in eyes show *conscious* patterns, while categories in ears reveal *subconscious* patterns.)
- **Noses** contain insights about career, plus patterns with money.
- **Cheeks** display power characteristics.
- **Mouths** disclose communication talents.
- **Jaws** and **chins** bare characteristic ways of handling conflict, making ethical choices, and other practical aspects of everyday life.

Turn the page to see Ava demonstrate some of these categories. After you've had a look at her, let's start doing some serious looking at *you*.

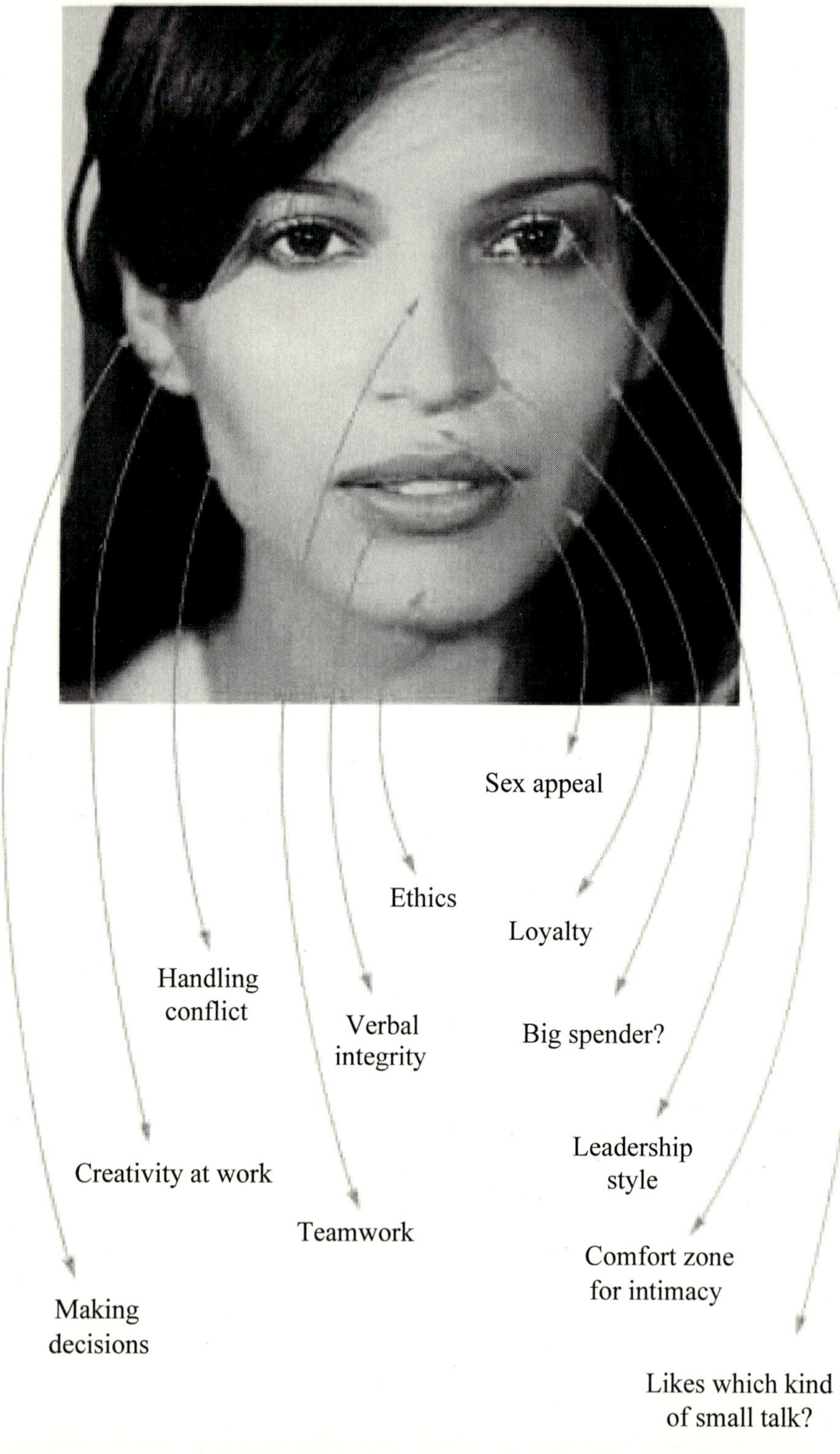
Sex appeal
Ethics
Loyalty
Handling conflict
Verbal integrity
Big spender?
Leadership style
Creativity at work
Teamwork
Comfort zone for intimacy
Making decisions
Likes which kind of small talk?

PART TWO: READ THE SECRETS

9. Starting with Starter Eyebrows

Allow me to introduce you to eyebrows. Face readers find them so informative, it's amazing.

One minute of eyebrow reading can tell an experienced face reader as much about thinking patterns as several hours crammed with small talk. Because **thinking patterns** are the physiognomy specialty of this facial feature.

Remember that eyebrows, like any other amazing facial feature, contain multiple categories. The first category we will research, Power-Packed Reader, is called "Distribution of Hair."

Distribution of Hair

Distribution of Hair in eyebrows is a vital statistic. To read it, start near the nose, then work your way out toward the ear. Examine one brow at a time, because left and right may be different.

- **Starter Eyebrows** come on strong at the start, then fade away. By the end, you will find scanty hair or none at all. See Gary from our Cast of Characters.
- **Ender Eyebrows** do the opposite. However much hair is in the eyebrow close to the nose, that amount increases on the way to the ear. See Matt.
- **Even Eyebrows** display approximately the same amount of hair from start to end. See Ava.

Tip: Read one eyebrow at a time, because that person's second eyebrow may have a different distribution of hair. For instance, in the photo we have available, Ava could have anything going on with the end of her right eyebrow.

If you were reading her face in person, ask her to move her hair out of the way for a moment. Otherwise, don't read that eyebrow at all.

And definitely do not assume that both eyebrows are similar. Sometimes the purpose of a particular hairstyle, or hat, or camera angle is to disguise asymmetries.

Power-Packed Reader, you are becoming way too knowledgeable to be fooled, ha ha!

What if the eyebrows are thick or thin? That's a different category: Amount of Hair in Eyebrows. How about whether the brow looks arched? Oops, that's a different category, too: Eyebrow Shape. As for the darkness or lightness of those eyebrows, that doesn't count, period. Face Reading Secrets are not about color, remember?

Okay, hoist up your mirror, Power-Packed Reader. Remember to look on the level. What do you have regarding Distribution of Hair?

Interpreting Distribution of Hair in Eyebrows

This face reading category reveals how a person handles details. The physical pattern of each eyebrow parallels a behavioral pattern.

Starter Eyebrows correspond to talent for starting new projects, the special kind of enthusiasm needed to initiate something new.

The potential challenge involves losing interest after the project is underway.

Until you learn the life lesson of balancing your drive for creativity with the steadfastness needed for effectiveness in objective reality, here's what's likely to happen:

- If your eyebrows thin out *halfway* across, like Fred's left eyebrow, you are likely to lose interest halfway through a project.
- If your eyebrows thin out *three-quarters* of the way through, as with Anthony's left eyebrow, three-quarters of a project is as far as you may get before feeling too bored to continue.
- If your eyebrows fade out a mere *quarter* of the way across, like Valerie's (also mine, to the horror of Timothy Mar, as described previously), yes, you may have a major challenge with follow-through.

Why does this loss of momentum occur? On the positive side, people with Starter Eyebrows generate more ideas for new projects than other eyebrow types. Once you have done enough of a first project to see where it's headed, you can grow bored. Creativity drives you to explore the next project on your list.

Although folks with these visionary eyebrows aren't the best to depend on for details, turn to them when you need inspiration.

Owners of Starter Eyebrows, you can overcome that challenge, of course. You just have to try extra hard on follow-through.

Or you might consider delegating your follow-up work. And sometimes it's perfectly okay to lower one's standards for completing every detail of a project.

Ender Eyebrows represent a talent for following up on details. The farther you get into a project, the more details you may find to fix.

Can you, therefore, drive yourself crazy as a never-ending perfectionist? Well, yes.

Procrastination can be a problem, too. Now, I don't mean all forms of procrastination, because there are oh so many varieties. Enders specialize in a particular kind of inertia. It's reluctance to start a new project.

Why does this happen? Enders know what they're in for. With Enders, you know there is no such thing as a quick'n dirty job.

One Ender man of my acquaintance took three years before he felt ready to straighten up his bedroom closet. Then it took him six hours. (The job was perfect, of course.)

Even Eyebrows, our last option in this category, would never be omitted by someone who, physically, has Even Eyebrows. Ava, for instance.

If you have this Distribution of Hair, you know why. How well do you handle details? Only superbly!

With Even Eyebrows, the sequence flows smoothly: You get an idea, develop it, and work out all the kinks. "No problem," you think. "No big deal."

Of course, here on The Learning Planet, there is always a catch. Consider a little potential challenge that comes up sometimes when an aspect of life comes so easily. This is just a little problem, a kind of niche problem, so don't be alarmed.

Okay, this is your little challenge: *A lack of tolerance for the rest of humanity.*

With this challenge, whatever the context, the dynamics are standard. We wonder what's wrong with other folks. Why aren't they good at something we consider a no-brainer?

For instance, if you have Even Distribution of Hair on Eyebrows, it's so easy for you to handle details. Therefore, you may assume it's easy for everyone else, too, and find yourself grumbling:

"What's wrong with that lazy slob, Valerie? Is she a space case or what?"

Or "How come Matt is always bogged down with details? A mature person would just handle them and move on, like I do."

Grumble, grumble, grumble... that's a lack of tolerance for the rest of humanity.

Why don't others use *your* talents? Well, because they're busy using *theirs*.

Want a workaround for this Even Eyebrow's version of lack of tolerance for the rest of humanity? Instead of criticizing others for their inadequacies in the Detail Department, give yourself credit for having actual talent. Then, perhaps out of sheer relief, you might practice improving your communication.

Let's Get Practical: Overcome Shyness

Reasons for shyness can run deep, also run amok. Face reading won't fix it all, but how about a workaround? Read Distribution of Hair and speak to the eyebrow owner accordingly.

Let's say that you and a new friend (from our Cast of Characters) are taking a stroll downtown. You pass a construction site. Here are lines I would recommend for conversation, based on Distribution of Hair in Eyebrows:

- To a Starter like Valerie from our Cast of Characters: "What a lot of work. Do you think they'll ever finish?"
- To an Ender like Matt: "I respect people who can tie up all the loose ends on a job like that, don't you?"
- To an Even like Ava: "I hope whoever's in charge of that mess can find some competent people to clean it up afterwards. Have you ever noticed how few people do a decent job with follow-up?"

Perspective, and Not Just About Eyebrows

Congratulations. You have now completed your first category. We used the very same sequence we will follow with subsequent items of face reading data:

1. Learn the choices within the physical category.
2. See the visual examples from our Cast of Characters.
3. Check out what you see in the mirror.
4. Learn to interpret each of the choices.
5. Think about the accuracy for you.
6. Once we're done with a new category, go ahead and check out more faces for real-life examples. There's no time limit. You only have the entire rest of your life.

That simple!

Except let's pause to add a few refinements to your approach. They can make you an extra-perceptive face reader.

Level with Yourself

It would be smart to double check something about your technique. Is looking on the level becoming a habit for you, when reading faces?

Try the following exercise to feel what I mean about holding your mirror properly as a physiognomist. Ingredients are yourself plus your trusty hand mirror. And, please, if you are not going to take the two minutes, skip the following instructions and proceed to our heading, "Tell Left from Right on a Face."

You must actually do the steps of a technique to get a result. Casual reading will just spoil a perfectly good technique.

Okay, ready to experiment, Power-Packed Reader? Read through the whole sequence of steps. Peek at instructions as needed while going through the sequence.

1. Say out loud, "I respect myself."
2. Close your eyes. Take a deep breath and return to normal breathing. Notice how you feel and put it into words. Open your eyes.
3. Place the mirror on top of your thighs. Literally *look down on yourself.* Repeat Step 1. Look down on yourself some more. Repeat Step 2.
4. Hoist your mirror high. Tilt your face upwards. One interesting side effect of this particular viewing angle: You can see your chin but none of the neck directly beneath your chin. Personally, I think that's wacky.
5. Take a long moment to *gaze up at yourself.* Repeat Step 1. Look up at yourself some more. Repeat Step 2.
6. Position your mirror so it is *on the level.* Take a good look. Repeat Step 1. Look at yourself on the level some more. Repeat Step 2.
7. Open your eyes. Technique over.

Well, what did you learn, Power-Packed Reader? Maybe there was a message for you in the tone of voice.

- Depending on your physical position, repeating those same words ("I respect myself") may even have sounded different.
- Maybe your inner imagery changed.
- Maybe you noticed different sensations in your physical body.
- Each of us has an inner language for learning about deeper perception. Using your inner language, didn't you feel different inside depending on mirror angle?

So, which position felt more truthful, with more integrity?

Plus, which of the three mirror angles gave you a clearer view of yourself?

View Photos on the Level, Too.

Now that you have refined your angle accuracy, let's take it further. View people on the level when you are reading their photos, also.

You can always find a workaround. Tilt your computer screen, hoist up your book or reading device. Power-Packed Reader, do whatever it takes to angle that image directly in front of you.

Looking down at people is never nice. Cricking your neck to look up at people, literally holding them higher than yourself? That's awful, too.

Either way, up or down, distorts how you see the face data. Which, in turn, could distort how you read the Secrets.

Here is a related experiment to help you learn to read face data in photographs. Again, this exercise will take just a few minutes. Ready to invest in some good habits as a physiognomist?

I sure hope so. If you are more in a skimming mood, however, skip forward to our heading about "Tell Left from Right on a Face." Save the following instructions until you are willing to actually do them.

With this latest experiment, get an overview by reading through the whole sequence of steps. Then peek at instructions as needed.

Locate a photo that shows somebody's face clearly. (Maybe that nice big picture of Ava in your spare copy of this very book! So I'll use her as an example here.) Now:

1. Say out loud, "I give other people the same amount of respect that I would like to receive."
2. Close your eyes. Take a deep breath and return to normal breathing. Notice how you feel and put it into words. Open your eyes.
3. Place Ava's photo on top of your thighs. Literally *look down* on her.
4. Notice one thing about her physical face. Then notice something else. Then notice a third facial characteristic. Even though you haven't learned about interpretation yet, you're still free to notice, after all! Next, repeat Step 2.
5. Hoist Ava's picture high. Tilt your neck until you can her image clearly. (Your chin will be up and head back, angled similarly to when you did Step 5 in our last exercise.)
6. Take a long moment to *gaze up* at Ava. Look long enough to see the same three items of face data you saw before. Repeat Step 2.
7. Hold Ava's photo on the level and view her *on the level.* Repeat Step 2.
8. Open your eyes. Technique over.

Power-Packed Reader, what did you notice this time? Doesn't it feel more natural looking on the level? More respectful, too?

Thank you for taking the time to do this exercise. From now on, you may think twice before unnecessarily looking down or up at anyone.

When reading faces, definitely, the position you choose will make a huge difference for the accuracy of your results.

What if someone else is way taller or shorter?

Keep more distance between the two of you. This can decrease the neck tilt factor.

Or arrange things so that one or both of you sit down during the face reading.

Images, whether hard copy photos or electronic devices, are the easiest to move into a truly level position.

A worthwhile intention plus an honest, straightforward angle — that's one of the secrets to help you read the Secrets This will allow your whole mind-body-spirit to engage in the respectful art of reading faces for character.

Tell Left from Right on a Face

Already you know the importance of reading one side of the face at a time. The idea was introduced in Chapter 4. Now let's take it further.

- For business applications, you will read the right side of the face.
- While the left side of a face will help you read the Secrets about relationships.

Back at reading Distribution of Hair in Eyebrows, what if you noticed that yours were different from each other?

Not true for our Cast of Characters (except, perhaps, Ava and all the folks shown in profile). Yet this could certainly be the case for you or other people you face read.

Does asymmetry make a person weird or ugly or freakish? Not at all. Asymmetries can inform you about differences between the public and private aspects of life.

Relish this information. Having differences between public and private roles means that a person has depth. When every relationship is given full-out intimacy, all relationships could be called "shallow."

Instead, folks tend to have meaningful differences between formal relationships and the intimate ones. These differences in personal style have a physical counterpart that you will be able to notice as a face reader. For instance:

- If the right eyebrow is an Ender, that personal style applies to career and meeting people socially for the first time.
- If the left eyebrow is a Starter, that personal style applies to dealing with people in close relationships, a different context of life entirely.

No wonder a physiognomist needs to be able to tell left from right.

However, doing so might be trickier than it sounds. Consider: If you look in the mirror, the right side of your face will show on the right side of the mirror. Left side will show on the left side of the mirror.

Simple? Not exactly.

What mirrors do is, actually, weird. No other life situation makes left and right sides of a face so easy to spot.

Of course, that's because mirrors reverse your face. Which sure makes it easier to shave or put on lipstick.

In no other life situation, however, does your right side match up neatly to correspond to another person's right side. Not unless that other person stands next to you, facing a mirror.

Meet Fred Again. And Again.

Fred can help you become more comfortable telling left from right. Here is his face in all its glory.

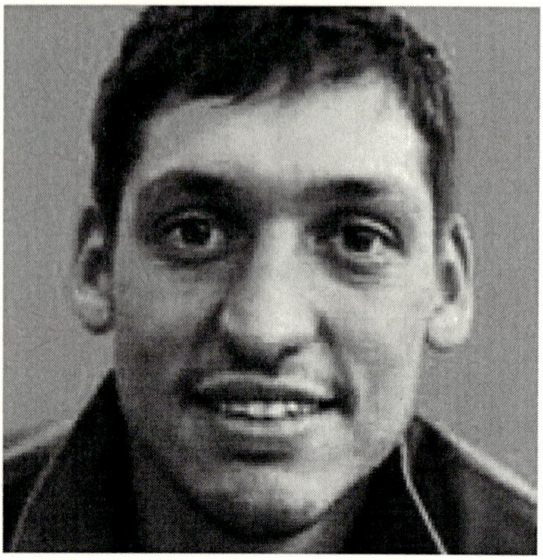

Fred in Real Life

But is this version of his face what Fred sees in the mirror? No, he sees this:

Fred in the Mirror

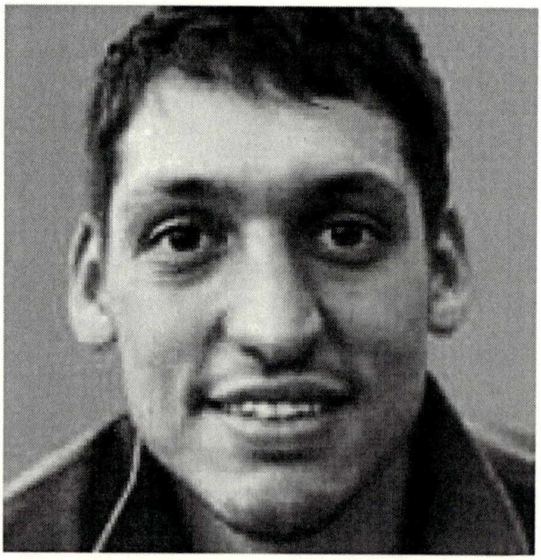

Incidentally, the cute little differences to Fred's collar on either side of his neck can help you to orient your vision. Thoughtful of him to dress that way, wasn't it?

Subtler Asymmetries

Fred has a pretty strong facial asymmetry due to his nose angling. But even subtler asymmetries can make a mirror reflection appear quite different from The Face Seen by Everyone Else But Self Gazing in Mirror.

Take Cliff, for instance. His main facial asymmetry involves both right eyebrow and right eye. These lie a bit higher on the right side of his face, compared to his left. Also, the right corner of Cliff's mouth is higher than the left side. Compare:

Cliff in Real Life

While this is what Cliff *believes* he looks like, based on what shows in the mirror:

Cliff in the Mirror

To See Facial Asymmetries Even More Clearly

All you need, Power-Packed Reader, is a rectangular mirror and a head shot.

1. Place the photo flat on a table.
2. Position the long side of your mirror along the center of the nose in the photo.
3. Angle your mirror up to 90 degrees.
4. Then peek until you find the angle revealing either two left sides together or two right sides together.

Or, of course, you could use Photoshop instead. That's what graphic artist Melanie Matheson did for this book to show how subtle differences can add up.

First check out Oliver as he looks in reality. In a regular head shot, so cute. And pretty symmetrical.

Oliver in Real Life

Except Oliver has subtle differences between the left and right sides of his face. They include:

- A fuller right eyebrow
- A Close-Set Right Eye
- Some forehead wrinkles on the left side only.

Still such a handsome fellow! Those asymmetries aren't just related to gifts of his soul, plus different personal styles with strangers and friends.

Those subtle asymmetries add humanity to his look, seems to me. It's like the difference between a musician who sings on his own, versus the surreal "perfection" created by Auto-Tune.

Facial asymmetries are thus so meaningful to a face reader. Surely it's worth the trouble to notice them.

Just to help you appreciate the impact, here come some contrasting views to wake up your Face Reader's eyesight. With Photoshop, a pro like Melanie can crop half of a photographed face, copy it as a mirror image, and then put the two sides together to look like one face.

Non-physiognomists gloss over "little" differences between right and left. Are they really so trivial?

Oliver, Two RIGHT Sices Together

Oliver, Two LEFT Sices Together

And Oliver, Two RIGHT Sides Together

Go Flippo

So I hope you're convinced, Power-Packed Reader. Telling left from right matters a great deal when you read faces.

Here's my favorite trick. When you're looking at a photo, or someone in the room with you, don't assume it's like looking in the mirror. Instead, "Go Flippo." Switch over, as if preparing to shake hands.

You are adept at that, so your mind knows just what to do. Automatically your right hand reaches out quite easily toward the other person's right hand.

Now, in a more abstract way, your eyes can reach out and cross over as well.

All that practice with shaking hands over the years... how easily this can help you tell right from left as a face reader.

In general, Power-Packed Reader, be aware that left and right sides do have meaning.

Pause to read each side of a face. Don't assume that the first side you see tells the whole story.

Whenever you see and interpret as a physiognomist, unless you're looking in the mirror, remember to Go Flippo. That way, you will correctly provide context for differences to left and right.

10. Eyebrows, Continued

Eyebrows reveal thinking patterns. Whether the eyebrows you read are waxed or tattooed or virginal, guess what? You read them exactly the same way.

Which means reading those eyebrows as they appear right now.

Come to think of it, isn't that how we approach people usually? When was the last time you shook hands with a stranger and demanded clarification:

"Just to help me get to know you better, would you mind telling me? Are you waxed or tattooed, or would you be virginal?"

Eyebrow Hairiness

The Eyebrow Hairiness category means the amount of hairiness overall.

- **Large Eyebrow Hairiness** means oodles of hair. See Wayne from our Cast of Characters.
- **Small Eyebrow Hairiness** means the opposite of oodles, whatever that is. Ah-dles? See Annette.
- **Moderate Eyebrow Hairiness** means half empty, half full, depending on whether or not you are an optimist. Seriously, the hairiness is between full and small. See Kathryn.

Which part of an eyebrow counts for gauging the amount of hair? Look at the maximum amount of hairiness anywhere along the length of that eyebrow.

Fearlessly pick up your mirror, Power-Packed Reader. Remember, this system of physiognomy is based on the principle that "God don't make no junk," Eyebrow Hairiness included.

Interpreting Eyebrow Hairiness

Amount of hair in a eyebrows is such a useful category, revealing how much detail a person feels comfortable handling at any given time (although not necessarily indicative of that individual's extent of patience for sentences that are unnecessarily long) (or convoluted), repetitive, or unnecessarily and unreasonably wordy...just for the fun of it.

Large Eyebrow Hairiness is a highly visible mark of intellectual range. If this description applies to you, aw shucks, you are probably casting your eyes downward and doing the time-honored squirm of modesty.

If it's any consolation, people with Thin Eyebrows can be just as smart as owners of Thickies. It's just that your personal styles are different.

Specifically, Full Eyebrows indicate that you can juggle many projects at once. And if your eyebrows are also Even or Enders, you can monitor details for many simultaneous projects. Masterfully!

Being human, you'll still need to focus on doing just one single project at a time. Only you can successfully track other projects in the background.

Your potential challenge? Aargh, overwhelming people!

Avoid telling friends about all your irons in the fire. Otherwise your buddies/co-workers/employees may seethe with jealousy. Such mental magnificence gone unappreciated!

Another potential challenge is needing to keep things complicated. You may mistrust perfectly good solutions to problems, strategies that you deem "Too simple."

Small Eyebrow Hairiness corresponds to intellectual focus. You can focus like laser light on your project of the moment.

Your potential challenge? Although you can push yourself to juggle a multitude of projects, you might lose effectiveness unless you stick to one task at a time.

Admittedly, that potential challenge may cause you some grief if you live at this historical time, when multi-tasking is celebrated, elevated, to the point where you feel obligated.

These days, pressure to multi-task is crazy extreme, especially for you face readers of a certain age. You might feel oh-so-socially isolated without your mobile phone on red alert for messages, plus music playing in the background to keep you motivated.

It might seem like an automatic reflex, pausing to discharge tension through electronics like playing with your favorite app, countering boredom with Facebook, and following the folks who matter on Twitter.

However, brain research shows that, trend or no trend, chronic multitasking stinks. Okay, scientists put this more tactfully.

For instance, as reported in the Stanford University News, August 24, 2009:

> *"Think you can talk on the phone, send an instant message and read your e-mail all at once? Stanford researchers say even trying may impair your cognitive control."*

In short, people who multi-task do not perform as well as they imagine.

Here's my special face reading caution against multi-tasking for folks with Small Eyebrow Hairiness:

How many heads do you have? Check it out in your mirror.

God has just shown you a sign. The day when you sprout extra heads, arms, etc., that is the day you will become really, really good at multitasking. Before then, perhaps you might settle for being merely human and doing one main thing at a time.

With **Moderate Eyebrow Hairiness** you can focus on one major project at a time. Two or three projects, even, you could manage perfectly fine.

Would multi-tasking be recommended, however? Not unless you have grown that extra head.

Your potential challenge with Moderate Eyebrow Hairiness? You may suffer from… a lack of tolerance for the rest of humanity. This time the challenge involves being invested in many projects at once.

For instance, you discover that Wayne has 14 different projects in progress. (Projects that you know of; maybe he has more.) How do you react?

Until the your challenge is overcome, you might think, "Who does that Wayne think he is, anyway? A man with 14 heads? He does way too much. Why can't he set wise priorities? Like me."

Then, observing Annette, who insists on doing one main project exclusively, you might think, "Poor, limited Annette. She sells herself short. She could be doing so much more in life. Like me."

Let's Get Practical: The Limits of Eyebrow Plucking

Plucked your eyebrows lately? Sure, you could go from Large or Moderate Eyebrow Hairiness to something smaller.

Consider yourself warned, though. Inwardly you would automatically downsize how well you handle details.

Compare that to someone who naturally has the face data of Small Eyebrow Hairiness. For that person, it's no problem, lacking some extra eyebrow hairs. With Small Eyebrow Hairiness, your built-in gift for focusing is magnificent. You are designed to excel with the detail-managing style hardwired into your physical face and soul.

By contrast, what if you don't naturally have this characteristic? Soon as you change on the outside, you will automatically change on the inside. As you may remember, this reciprocal relationship is a universal principle. It underlies all face reading.

So what happens inwardly as a consequence of drastic eyebrow removal? Your personal style around handling details will begin to shift.

Maybe your soul will *welcome* this shift, so it will last physically. Gradually you will develop the full inner gift corresponding to Small Eyebrow Hairiness.

All of us have met folks who plucked their eyebrows on a whim, then were shocked when the hair never returned. Well, now you know why.

Maybe your soul will *fight* this latest eyebrow plucking. Perhaps this different personal style is at odds with the balance of your other talents and potential challenges. Then the eyebrow hairs will grow back.

Keep *repeat-plucking* anyway? You will be stuck going back and forth internally for as long as you insist on plucking those eyebrows.

The resulting zigzag isn't merely a nuisance in terms of tweezing (or whatever). Internally, your personal style is shifting back and forth repeatedly. Dramatic shifts work fine for an accordion, but is *that* the musical instrument you would most like to resemble?

You do have a choice. Even a woman with VERY Full Eyebrows can decide the degree to which those eyebrows must be pruned. Who says your eyebrows must starved thin, verging on anorexic?

Make your choice about Eyebrow Hairiness, Power-Packed Reader. Then take the consequences. Gotta love The Learning Planet, right?

Eyebrow Shape

To read the Eyebrow Shape category, check out the geometric pattern formed by each eyebrow.

- **Curved Eyebrows** (sometimes called "Arched") form parts of a circle. See Fred.
- **Straight Eyebrows** look, more or less, like a straight line. See Kathryn.
- **Angled Eyebrows** contain a hinge, where the hair changes direction. Most (but not all) Angled Eyebrows have their hinges toward the end of the eyebrow. See Shirley.

Tip: Look at the upper edge of the eyebrow, not the underneath part. Mirrors ahoy, Power-Packed Reader!

Interpreting Eyebrow Shape

This category helps you learn about a person's framework for thinking. You have read your own data, right? Now let's read the Secrets.

Curved Eyebrow Shape indicates that you specialize in noticing details about people's feelings. This shape is one of several facial indicators of emotional sensitivity (others include Curved Chin Bottoms, Curved Lower Eyelids, and Large Inner Ear Circles). Sensitivity helps you with relationships, especially when the person you hope to impress is an HSP, a Highly Sensitive Person who can consciously notice degrees of kindness, friendliness, etc.

For nuance as a face reader, notice the degree of curve in an eyebrow. It's directly proportional to the person's intellectual attentiveness to feelings.

Owners of VERY Curved Eyebrows are like magnets for emotion. In their presence, it's not enough to say "I'm fine. How are you?" You may as well come right out with your true feelings. That Curved Eyebrows owner will soon discover them anyway.

The potential challenge? It's being easily manipulated by others who know how to pull your heartstrings.

Straight Eyebrow Shape relates to noticing ideas. It could be devotion to a cause, intellectual curiosity, or a passion for logic.

The potential challenge? Sheer logic may become overemphasized, downplaying other talents that show in your face. Until this challenge is overcome, others may consider you a walking brain, forgetting that you are a complex human being (rather than a cyborg).

Angled Eyebrow Shape reveals a managerial mindset. Part of you is always detached, posing questions like these: "Is this conversation working for me?" "Is this person wasting my time?" "What do I really want from this situation? How can I get it?"

If you have VERY Angled Eyebrows, you won't hesitate to jump in and change the flow of a conversation. Confrontation may even be considered fun.

Scary for other people, though!

Your potential challenge with Angled Eyebrows would be having people consider you intimidating. Here's why I think this can happen, even if you don't say a word.

- Others can feel when they're being watched.
- Your detachment can trigger their worst fears.

Therefore, overcoming that potential challenge simply involves not blaming yourself. Should your problem-solving ways strike others as intimidating, not your problem!

Surely that potential challenge is a small price to pay for such a big strategic advantage. Managers thrive on detachment.

Let's Get Practical: Keep that Expression Pleasant

Remember our Quiz on Face Watching Habits? I suggested that reading expression won't do you much good, once you have made somebody scowl.

Better to *prevent* gaffes by getting on the person's wavelength with a bit of face reading!

Yes, I'm proposing a proactive way to keep other people's expressions pleasant. Just use Eyebrow Shape as a guide to conversation.

For instance, imagine that you and a first-time date are strolling near a downtown construction site. Here are lines of conversation I would recommend, based on your date's Eyebrow Shapes:

- To Curved Eyebrow Shape: "When I see that kind of building in progress, it makes me wonder how it feels at the various stages of doing the project. How do you react, seeing all this construction?"
- To Straight Eyebrow Shape: "What a huge responsibility, keeping all the parts of that project in order. How do you think they do it?"
- To Angled Eyebrow Shape: "I really admire whoever is managing this. Do you think they might have a few problems to solve with a project like this?"

It's amazing, how much better small talk goes when you pose questions related to the other person's thinking style, as related to Eyebrow Shape.

The power of face reading can help you with so many promising relationships that are under construction.

Extra-Special Face Data: Startup Hairs

Power-Packed Reader, you have been working diligently to wake up that power of face reading. Occasionally I will reward you with a special treat. While you are learning to read different facial features, I will point out something unusual but worth noticing.

Interpreting that rare bit of **Extra-Special Face Data** can score you extra success in life.

Will you search for it everywhere, scoring strangers deficient if they don't have it? I sure hope not. Instead, celebrate when you come across somebody with that extra-special something. And then take advantage of your inside information.

Here's our first sighting of Extra-Special Face Data: **Startup Hairs**.

These eyebrow hairs are located on the nose-side of an eyebrow, rather than the ear side. Startup Hairs grow straight up, in contrast to most eyebrow hair, which grows sideways.

Most eyebrows contain a few initial hairs growing straight up. Seldom, however, will you find vertical eyebrow hairs numerous enough to form the definite clump of Startup Hairs.

For an example, see Valerie's left eyebrow.

Visible starts to eyebrows symbolize conscious access to thoughts and feelings at an early stage. Before embarking on a new project, the rooted one will anticipate potential problems that other folks won't notice.

What's the potential challenge? The Startup Hairs wearer risks being considered a wet blanket. If you have this rare gift, you know how, sometimes, people can take your advice badly.

For instance, you'll say, in the friendliest manner, "Hold on. There could be a problem."

The response? Seldom is there anything like a "Thank you very much." Instead, there's more of a "How dare you, Troublemaker?"

Sadly, the fact that you generally happen to be *right* may not win you popularity points. Still, you can adjust to possessing an enviable talent.

Of course, Power-Packed Reader, it matters which eyebrow contains the Startup Hairs.

- For business applications, read the right side of the face.
- For relationships, read the left side.

So, in the case of Valerie, which of her eyebrows has the Startup Hairs? Both, but especially her left eyebrow. Therefore, I would interpret this ability to anticipate problems being a strength especially in her personal life.

Eyebrow Height

While exploring other categories nestled in eyebrow hair, don't miss Eyebrow Height. Do you usually notice the relative amount of distance between eyebrows and eyes? Even the largest Eyebrow Height will be less than two inches. Yet again, God — and a world of fascination — lies in small details.

- Most people have **Middlebrows**, with a space between eyebrows and eyes that you will come to recognize as moderate. See Wayne.
- Owners of **Lowbrows**, by contrast, wear their eyebrows close to the part of that face that blinks. With an extreme Lowbrow, it can look as though eyebrows are tumbling into the eyes. See Lloyd.
- With **Highbrows**, you would show a big distance between eyebrows and eyes.

  At first glance, folks with Highbrows may look as though they are raising their eyebrows. They're not, if the face is seen in repose. Which makes the Eyebrow Height qualify as face reading data rather than expression. See Joyce.

Tip: Use the top edge of each eyebrow as your point of reference, not the bottom edge.

Extra Tip: How can you tell the difference between raising one's eyebrows temporarily vs. the face reading data in repose? Just one photo won't tell you. But real life will.

Highbrows remain uplifted throughout your entire conversation. Middlebrows and Lowbrows relax eventually. This lower position will remain until expression heaves the eyebrows up again.

No flinching before you look in your mirror, Power-Packed Reader. For one thing, that would temporarily distort the height of your eyebrows, wouldn't it?

Interpreting Eyebrow Height

The height of each eyebrow informs you about a person's preferred timing for expressing thoughts.

With **Highbrows** you are comfortable keeping ideas to yourself. Although you don't literally hide thoughts in the space above your eyes, you do employ some kind of inner equivalent, a mental compartment like a safe deposit box for your plans.

Innate discretion helps you avoid blabbing about new business ventures or relationships. Until they are well established, you will keep these glad tidings private.

When an important conversation is coming up, you can rehearse it to perfection. No other Eyebrow Height talent can best you in this regard. Besides, keeping your own counsel has obvious advantages for every aspect of life.

Your potential challenge? It's appearing aloof, inscrutable. Of course, that may be a small price to pay for such a strategic advantage.

Lowbrows correspond to a talent for spontaneous timing. Blurting things out puts you in your power. Think "Forcefulness." Think "Immediacy."

The potential challenge? Not using your talent! My advice is to forget some other advice, the kind called, "Think before you speak."

Rehearsing conversations in advance will make your words sound stale. If you are a Lowbrow, you know your ideas are like bread that pops out of the toaster, best when fresh and hot.

Just don't get yourself fired, divorced, arrested! Most spontaneous talk is a good thing.

For **Middlebrows**, amount of time before you speak is a non-issue. You are flexible. In one situation you will practice beforehand. Another situation, you will tell it like it is, no fuss, no muss, no forethought.

The potential challenge? How many times have you wondered, "What's with these other silly-heads?"

After all, you lack a Highbrow's problem of appearing aloof. Neither do you run a Lowbrow's risk of speaking so spontaneously that other folks call it "Tactless."

No, as a Middlebrow, your only problem would be that perennial affliction of the fortunate, a lack of tolerance for the rest of humanity.

Let's Get Practical: Conversational Pauses

Your timing with ideas is personal. It relates to your personal style as displayed in Eyebrow Height. Complicating matters, Power-Packed Reader, you belong to at least one social group and national culture. Each of these comes with a pattern for what is expected regarding the length of **conversational pauses.**

Conversational pauses? That term means how, typically for that culture, people allow a certain amount of think-time between responses to each other:

In New York City, conversational pauses last mere seconds. In Tokyo, it's only polite to allow a sweet wad of silence.

Power-Packed Reader, once you own the concept of conversational pauses, you can compare your personal style with what's expected of you. Frankly, that cultural expectation may not be a great fit with your personal style.

Well, learning about that could be good news, actually.

What a relief, to stop blaming yourself! Modify your social skills as appropriate. But deep down? In a situation that matters a great deal to you? Value your timing instincts over "What everyone else is doing."

As for understanding friends and family members, what if you discover that some of them are VERY Highbrow or Lowbrow? Then, Power-Packed Reader, you will understand better how they deal with their routine, expected conversational pauses. In the process, more than ever, maybe you will open up your heart of compassion.

Eyebrow Range

This latest eyebrow category, Eyebrow Range, is not a kitchen appliance. Instead you are comparing the sweep, a.k.a. The biggest difference between high and low points on an eyebrow.

As always, read each of your eyebrows separately. Scope out the biggest up-and-down distance between the lowest part(s) of an eyebrow and the highest part.

To help you see this category, imagine taking a ride on each eyebrow as if it were an attraction at an amusement park. What if you were strapped into a cute little car toward the nose, then travelled along the hairy track out toward the ear. How much of a thrill ride would that be?

- **Big Eyebrow Range** means a large, dramatic sweep. Now this is one dramatic ride! See Joyce. A VERY version belongs to Shirley.
- **Small Eyebrow Range** gives you no up-and-down worth mentioning. More like riding a subway car than amusement park thrill ride. See Alexander. A VERY version is supplied by Kathryn.

- **Moderate Eyebrow Range** provides some play, nothing huge. Think of the roller coaster in the kiddie part of the amusement park, suitable for those adults whose adventure threshold is for just a tiny bit of drama.
(Power-Packed Reader, tell me I am not the only grownup who actually prefers this kind of roller coaster in real life! Of course, I am way adventurous about reading face parts.) Anyway, see Matt and Anthony for fine examples.

Now, hoist up your mirror, Power-Packed Reader. Whatever you have is just fine. Remember? This face reading system is based on the premise that "God don't make no junk."

Interpreting Eyebrow Range

What is this range category about? Surely it can't be amusement park rides. But that is close, very close, Power-Packed Reader. Eyebrow Range reveals the degree of emotional up-and-down to be expected from the eyebrow wearer's thoughts.

Some emotion always underlies thinking, bringing a certain emotional charge. The question here is, how much?

When interpreting any face reading category, remember it is just one category. Eyebrow Range adds impact, or subtracts it, from the flow of communication.

That's different from qualities that you would add as a communicator, expressing your thoughts. (For that, read the mouth category of Lipfulness. Then pick up extra nuance by reading Lip Proportions.)

Reading Eyebrow Range on others, you can anticipate the person's usual degree of underlying drama.

This is a basis for communicating in thoughts, whether everyday conversation or writing, drawing, photography, dancing — any art form that communicates thought.

With **Big Eyebrow Range** you might take others on an extreme, sweeping journey. And I'm not even talking about having an argument, more like describing a shopping list for the supermarket.

Even a topic like "Spinach and cheese" might provide you with huge underlying surges of pace and emotion. (For instance, just ask Shirley to read you a grocery list.)

The talent keeps listeners involved in the conversation, prevents snoozing. Might even make grocery shopping more interesting....

As for the potential challenge? Enough already! Can't Shirley's conversation ever be normal, without the big emotional charge?

Small Eyebrow Range can be very soothing for others. No big emotional sweeps of passion during everyday conversation; instead you present a steady flow of ideas.

You might be able to tranquilize others without using pharmaceuticals. Or you might be praised as someone who generates a contagious serenity. Or you might simply impress others with your cool, as Alexander does so commandingly.

This gift can also intensify intellectual rigor. Typically you will develop a sequence of thought based on its own merits. You can report an incident just as it is, not the thrill ride version.

The potential challenge? Soothing your listeners can shift into snoozing your listeners.

To overcome this challenge, listen for sounds of snores or sighs of boredom. Stop immediately and ask a question, shake a shoulder, do something effective (but legal) to wake up your listener.

What if you are more like Anthony, with **Moderate Eyebrow Range**? Don't expect the amount of intellectual drama to be predictable. It's a situational flow.

The potential challenge?

"Honestly, can't those other people present ideas in a mature way? That Shirley can be such a drama queen! While poor Alexander is so one-note!! Why can't they talk the normal way, just like me?"

Same old, same old lack of tolerance for the rest of humanity. Except maybe you have guessed by now, Power-Packed Reader. When you are the one with any particular lack of tolerance, the problems won't feel generic at all but personal… at least until you have overcome your healable challenge.

Let's Get Practical: When to Prepare for Emotional Drama

People reveal who they are through speech and action. Never is face reading meant to be a substitute for common sense.

However, reading the Eyebrow Range category can help you to make predictions of a certain kind. How steep a ride you are in for, handling that other person's conversation?

If calmness and steadiness matter most, surround yourself with talk buddies who possess small or average eyebrow range.

Yet everyone could enjoy splurging on at least one work associate or friend with the drama of VERY large eyebrow range.

Don't hold that personal style against someone like Joyce. Her style doesn't mean "Being weird." It's the magnificence of her soul.

Extra Special Face Data: Unibrow

Talk about thrill rides! Say that the eyebrow you have chosen to ride on, visually, belongs to Frida, a Spanish artist famous for her one long Unibrow.

Frida's Eyebrow Range doesn't start near the middle of the face. To see it, or imagine riding on it, you would have to scoot close to one ear and not emerge from your ride car until you had nearly reached her other ear.

Probably you have seen folks with this face reading data. Maybe you have even noticed Unibrow on Lloyd, from our Cast of Characters. If not, take another look, as he's right at the start of our book.

Take a good look at Lloyd's eyebrows until you spot how two separate eyebrows form one Unibrow.

What's the great thing about having a **Unibrow**? Your one and only eyebrow makes an intellectual statement, indicating talent for active thinking, a nonstop mind at work, and, perhaps, exceedingly long sentences, including a rather lavish, impressive, appropriate, sprinkling of commas.

Your potential challenge? Watch out....

Tricky Facial Characteristics

Power-Packed Reader, let's pause mid-Unibrow conversation. I really must introduce you to a little secret about Face Reading Secrets.

Most of the face data I interpret for you will correspond to a talent plus a potential challenge. However, a very small number of items are really about definite challenge. Not potential challenge but definite.

Sure, talent is also associated with a Unibrow. That's not the big deal, though. Definite challenge is the big deal.

So occasionally, Power-Packed Reader, I will be revealing one of these Tricky Facial Characteristics. This is our first.

Unibrow, Continued

Unibrows signal nonstop thinking. Typically, the mind doesn't turn off. Insomnia may be a problem.

Therefore, a Unibrow is one physical characteristic that I recommend changing. Tweeze. Try electrolysis. Perhaps rent a tiny lawnmower.

Since face data and personal style are interconnected, it could be really helpful to mow down the connecting part of a Unibrow.

Calming down nonstop eyebrows may help a mind to relax. Could even end a certain type of insomnia.

Although I haven't interviewed Lloyd, some of my real-life students have followed my advice about this particular Tricky Facial Characteristic. And it worked.

Calm Down (Even More)

Wow, Power-Packed Reader, you have nearly completed your first detailed chapter about a facial feature, with its many categories and different items of face reading data.

Perceptive and Persistent Reader, you have survived learning about a Tricky Facial Characteristic, plus you have practiced hoisting up your mirror to see what you have got, then putting your mirror aside in order to read the grim news about what your face data means.

Only not so grim, right?

And you are taking it easy, doing all this, correct? I'm going to remind you officially once again that VERY equals VERY, etc. So you don't ever, ever have to give yourself a hard time over reading faces.

What if something on your face is difficult to see? Then it isn't worth reading. Sit this dance out. Enjoy gazing at Fred... or whomever.

The normal sequence to relax into is this:

- You read about physical variations within a category.
- After you finish the bulleted list, it's your turn. Look in the mirror to discover what you have in that face reading category.
- If you are reading this book along with friends, check out each other, too.
- With photo examples, remember to pick the book up to eye level.
- Then consider the identification phase complete. Enjoy reading about the meaning. You might also consider practical ways that you can apply your talents to real-life situations.

It's easy to use the power of face reading. Just consider some problems that have concerned you recently. How will you, personally, use related strengths of personal style to overcome difficulties? Where is your path to excellence?

Wondering about Cosmetic Surgery?

Eyebrows are the easiest part of the face to change, giving us a perfect segue into that popular topic of changing faces through surgery or other means.

Changing faces with a scalpel — of course that topic is important for us physiognomists to understand. So let's clarify what changes and what doesn't change inwardly, as related to cosmetic surgery.

Back at Unibrows, you might remember my mentioning insomnia. I wasn't saying that a person could have insomnia because eyebrows grow a certain way. An outer characteristic doesn't *cause* an inner aspect of personal style, whether talent or challenge.

More accurately, it's a reciprocal relationship. Meaning that if you change the inner person, the outer face changes.

This natural kind of change is by far the most common. But when the outer face changes, through cosmetic surgery or eyebrow plucking or so-called "Accidents," a person changes inwardly. It's automatic.

Recognizing this dynamic is way more important than thinking about cosmetic surgery in purely physical ways.

Most of you Power-Packed Readers will not choose to go under the knife to "clean up" your face surgically. Instead, you will simply continue evolving spiritually.

Due to that reciprocal relationship between inner person and physical face, some face reading data will change over time.

What's an example of having face data change from the inside out?

When I married my husband Mitch, right on the honeymoon, my nostrils changed in a way that suggested a different style of spending money, from VERY Small Nostril Size to Moderate Nostril Size.

(Breaking news on that kind of face data will come in our "Nose" chapter. Although details of all the clothes purchased on that honeymoon will remain secret.)

Another example: After I became a mother, my eyelids changed in a way that reflected a new style of intimacy, from Small Eyelid Fullness to Moderate Eyelid Fullness.

Now that my boy is in his last year of college, our relationship has changed and so have my eyelids. Now I have No Eyelid Fullness. (Check out this category, and other eye characteristics, in our next chapter.)

The general point is that, evolving here at the Learning Planet, your choices and values create consequences over time. As you evolve in certain ways, your face will physically alter in ways that correspond to your personal style.

Not as predictable, perhaps, as buying a new nose from a cosmetic surgeon. Not as predictable but way more fascinating!

Now that you are becoming a face reader, over time, you may notice plenty of changes that out-picture on your own personal face.

Well, congratulate yourself when this happens, Power-Packed Reader. It's the fascinating and sacred story of your evolution as a person. As your personal style alters, so too will your face.

A Second Opinion

How about changing from the outside in? This is what happens with cosmetic surgery.

I know, people are told, "With a nice new nose you look better, people treat you better, you feel better."

But there's more to life than external validation. Thoughtful people care about internal validation more, because we are accountable for who we are within. Other people provide feedback that helps us evaluate what seems right for us.

Important though objective reality can be in this way, thoughtful people do not allow their lives to be ruled purely on that basis. External validation makes a poor substitute for values that come from within.

With cosmetic surgery exerting change from the outside, a patient will alter on the inside… and in ways that can be predicted from reading the Secrets.

A nose job may win social points from people who value a certain style of nose. However, that surgically achieved alteration could also result in a loss. The cosmetic surgery patient might inadvertently pass up the chance to do work that is highly original and important.

Or consider a different popular surgical procedure: Chin implants.

Purchasing this may help a patient to look more imposing. Yet adapting to the inner consequences may be more than the person bargained for, deep down. For a while, it could destabilize a personality or set in motion a cascade of consequences toward inauthenticity.

Even if the physical operation purchased is completely successful, the patient will need to adjust to inner side effects. They're inevitable, due to the reciprocal relationship between the outer face and the inner person.

Cosmetic surgeons have hired me to advise them on how their procedures change people on the inside. These surgeons were worried about litigious patients and unsuccessful surgeries. (The latter are more common than you might think, unless you specifically research this topic.)

What causes so many cosmetic surgery procedures to be unsuccessful? It could be a mismatch between what is requested physically versus what that person's soul will accept, long term.

If you are considering cosmetic surgery, you might want to get a second opinion. And I don't mean from a second cosmetic surgeon.

Find a professional physiognomist to explore consequences of the proposed change. Face readers know better than to treat their faces as if they were made out of Play Doh™.

Any cosmetic surgery will have unintended consequences for the inner self.

Depending on your values, that might seem trivial. You might be far more deeply invested in winning praise for looking good. Compared to that, nothing else matters.

Another possibility is that your values are just the opposite. If fully informed about inner consequences before going under the knife, you might choose to *not* go under that knife.

Keeping an inner-based talent might matter more to you than the social aspect of looks.

One thing's for sure: Cosmetic surgery is a far more complex choice *spiritually* than most folks realize. As a face reader, you will be in a position to understand this more fully.

But if you must change something, why not experiment with your eyebrows? There's good reason why they're the easiest part of the face to change.

As you learned in this chapter, eyebrows relate to thinking patterns, and flexible thinking helps us stay young where it counts, inside.

11. Eyes

Eyes win. Can any other feature compete for popularity? So often eyes win our attention, whether we're gazing romantically at the color, searching for expression, or probing for the soul. Yet have you ever considered that typical ways of looking at eyes are terribly limiting?

For one thing, we're missing the truths we could find if we gazed slightly elsewhere — around the eyes. Skin-covered portions around an eye can tell us a great deal.

Actually the "truth" written all over someone's face with expression may cover up, or even contradict, a long-term truth that could be read with physiognomy.

Maybe it isn't romantic, but if I were single now, I would go shopping for Eyelid Curve, Eye Angle, etc., not just the goo-goo expression emoted by eligible partners.

Regardless of marital status, physiognomists find eyes a perpetual source of fascination. This chapter will show you how to read alternatives to expression in eyes (which people can work hard to control). Power-Packed Reader, you will get to investigate a deeper reality (one that most people can't control at all).

Searching for meaning in eyes as a face reader, here's what all the categories will have in common: Personal style in handling social situations.

How do Rowan, Matt, Gary, and Cliff interact when together at work? Of course, their personal styles could be quite different at home.

These social studies can be so much fun, I'm sure you will enjoy this chapter. Just remember, there's way more to you, or to anyone else, than personality characteristics while being social.

Lower Eyelid Curve

Lower Eyelid Curve is an attribute non-face-readers seldom notice... unless you are a woman trying to make a killer impression by swabbing each tiny lash with mascara.

When you study this underrated aspect of eyes, here is the first thing to learn. Usually **involuntary muscles** contour the shape of your lower eyelid.

However, you can consciously use **voluntary muscles** to temporarily alter the shape.

Grab a mirror now and see for yourself by acting in two short "movies," coming right up.

"The Pride, The Glory, And The Hideous Death"

Movie #1 is a melodrama called "The Pride, the Glory, and the Hideous Death." You, regardless of gender, have been cast as the beauteous heroine.

It's a silent movie and the plot is pretty predictable, so let's skip ahead to the final scene. Alas, you have been tied to the railroad tracks.

Staring upwards, you happen to see the villain who is bending over you, ostensibly to gloat over your plight, but mostly to give you the chance to deliver your final speech.

Emote as you read it:

"You beast! I trusted you. Now I realize how you lied when you said you wanted to use the deed to my property as a dance card. Of course, I refused your proposals of marriage.

"But terrible cad that you are, you ignored my refusals. And then, even worse than confiscating my home and cattle, you did the unpardonable. You read my diary.

"How you will suffer some day, you ink blot upon the penmanship book of humanity!"

There you go. Dainty fists clenched, glare at the villain for all you are worth. Feel the indignation, the rage.

Good.

Now freeze that expression. Stare into your mirror and look (on the level) at the shape of your lower eyelids.

Take a deep breath, shuffle your face parts back to normal. Now prepare for Movie #2.

"Hearts And Flowers All Day Long"

Yes, Power-Packed Reader, our second experiment allows you to star in a different movie. This one is pleasant family entertainment, entitled "Hearts and Flowers All Day Long."

This time you get to have your very own gender and sexual persuasion. Once again, you are the main love interest. And once again the plot is rather predictable:

A meets B. They fall in love. They fight. Now their bubbling passion seems doomed to a low simmer, possibly evaporating to the point where it will burn the saucepan.

Not to worry, here comes the thrilling conclusion. Most unexpectedly, your co-star declares a hidden, hopeless, and passionate love for you.

Oh, did I mention that you get to pick your co-star? Make it someone droolingly adorable. Imagine yourselves together, neatly locked in an embrace.

Now, your film role requires that you stare into your love interest's eyes as you ask the all-important question:

"You say that out of all the people you have known in your life, I am the most attractive, intelligent, generous, kindly, creative, and downright saintly? Tell me, when did you first begin to notice?"

Emote, remember. Emote.

Freeze. Check out your lower lids this time.

Become Your Own Film Critic, Eyewise

These movie scenes informed you well about Lower Eyelid Curve as a *temporary* reaction. Provided, that is, you were able to scrunch up your face a whole lot when acting. Otherwise it's back to acting school for you, I'm afraid.

Under certain circumstances, such as those in Movie #2, you can make goo-goo eyes. Emotions shift your face so dramatically that the English language has a special word for it, "rounding" your eyes.

Temporary emotions associated with this expression include feeling infatuated, curious, vulnerable, or otherwise emotionally wide open. See Jesse, who has just been photographed by his very, very big crush.

If this eye shape were a default expression on your face, your *typical* way of holding eye muscles, then it would count as **Curved Lower Eyelids**.

For example, take Alexander here, posing enticingly for the camera. Or Gary. Or Ava's right eye.

Actually, all the rest of his waking hours, Jesse is such a VERY. That big round curve under each eye isn't available just to his crush.

Under other circumstances, such as those in Movie #1, you can "narrow" your eyes. In detective fiction, characters often "cut" their eyes. How appropriate to the genre!

Your expression in Movie #1 could have reflected wariness, hurt feelings, suspicion, shyness, or other emotions related to a general emotional closing down. Or, possibly, the unique humiliation of being tied to railroad tracks by a diary-snatching villain.

For an example of Straight Lower Eyelids, see Rowan. (If her picture could talk, you would know that the photographer just insulted her makeup job before snapping the image.)

Of course, if that eye shape were a typical way of holding Rowan's eyes, she would have the face reading data of **Straight Lower Eyelids**.

What about an eye expression not appropriate to either movie? That would be a temporary flicker of **Moderate Lower Eyelid Curve**.

See Fred. Sadly, he was doing our Movie exercise at the time of the photo, but isn't as good at acting as he is at cuteness.

Plenty of folks move faces there, part of a good day's work. Neither open nor closed, neither receptive nor self-protective. Sure we can go there!

Your Eyelid Curve, Unrehearsed

What have you learned from our movie experiments? There is a difference between temporary expression and a person's face reading data. The former is temporary while the latter means a habitual way of holding one's face in repose.

Yes, each of us has a default setting for Lower Eyelid Curve at any time in your life, much like having default formats with your favorite word processing software.

Sure you could switch to 14-point type (like the heading you have just read). But probably a more standard type size, like 11-point, will pop up on the screen and stay there until you change the setting.

That's what I invite you to read right now.

My nickname for this face reading category is **The Wariness Index**, as I will explain after you have seen your face data. For now, consider a continuum of curviness where the straightest scores 1, while the curviest scores 10.

Before you hoist up your mirror and apply a number from 1-10 for each eye, here are some useful tips:

Definitely remember to look on the level, because angling the head can really distort Lower Eyelid Curve. (Photographers make use of this trick fairly often, actually.)

Many, many people have a cute little habit when looking into a mirror for more than a second or two. The habit is to round your eyes or otherwise hold your face in a manner that makes you look better to yourself.

Hey, everyone needs a hobby. Besides, we all want to look good to ourselves. This is healthy.

For face reading, however, it matters that you see yourself without distortion. So please, for this face reading category plus all those that follow, avoid that face-fixing kind of habit. Just for now, as you're reading these words, your facial muscles are in default position.

Well, freeze them, Power-Packed Reader. You're coordinated, right?

Show that coordination by not moving a muscle on your face. Simply bring your mirror up to an even angle, then checking out your Wariness Index.

On a scale from 1 to 10, how would you rate the amount of curve in each of your eyes?

- **Curved Lower Eyelids** range from 8-10 on the Wariness Index, with 10 being the VERY version of curved. Besides Jesse's score of 10 on the Wariness Index, Kathryn also scores 10 for each eye. I would give Oliver a 9 on his right eye only.
- **Straight Lower Eyelids** range from 1-3 on the Wariness Index, with 1 being the VERY version of straight. See Rowan, who scores 1 on each eye. Annette would also score 1. And so would Lloyd's left eye, while his right eye would score a 2.
- **Moderate Lower Eyelid Curve** spans scores from 4-7 on the Wariness Index. Matt shows 6 on his left eye. A 5 is modeled for us beautifully by Ava's left eye.

Oliver's left eye has a score of 4. Were you fooled into noticing his right eye only? Plus maybe the cute blond hair distracted you. Non-physiognomists would probably never notice this telling asymmetry of Lower Eyelid Curve.

All Wariness Index scores have meaning. If you didn't research each eye separately, you might want to go back and do the other one. Relatively few people score the same on both eyes.

Interpreting The Wariness Index

As a default expression, your Wariness Index reveals your degree of openness with strangers. How far do you typically extend yourself emotionally?

When interpreting, remember that your score for the right eye relates to dealing with strangers in relatively impersonal roles, like customers and co-workers, politicians, doctors, librarians, teachers.

By contrast, Lower Eyelid Curve on the left eye pertains to your trust level with folks being auditioned as friends, dates, in-laws, etc.

With **8-10 on the Wariness Index**, you demonstrate great willingness to "Be here now" with other people, even total strangers. Everyone is treated as a potential teacher. And you are eager to learn.

So what's the catch with these ultra-curvy lower eyelids? Gullibility, sometimes. Vulnerability, always.

Childlike sensitivity can hurt, of course. Which is why so many people have chosen to grow out of it and develop the next type of eyelid curve.

Scores of **1-3 on the Wariness Index** signal a different talent. Low scores mean high wariness, suggesting that you are superb at judging which people would waste your time.

Typically you will evaluate strangers within seconds. Most become rejects. Why invest emotionally in people who are draining, scatter-brained, and so forth?

This emotional time management comes with a potential challenge, of course. You risk being not only shrewd but judgmental. Some perfectly good potential buddies may wind up in the trash.

Back on the plus side, however, nobody is a more loyal friend than someone who scores 1 on The Wariness Index.

If you have a set of straights, you know why. Given the tough test you ask people to pass, anyone managing to succeed will be a friend for life.

Just for fun, ask the next "Scored 1 on the Wariness Index" person you meet, "How long have you had your best friend?"

"Since kindergarten" is a typical response.

What if you score **4-7 on the Wariness Index**? You have learned some practical skills for self-protection.

Give yourself credit. During the testing phase with new acquaintances, you can stay comfortably aloof-ish. Yet you open up more than folks with higher scores on the Wariness Index.

The potential challenge? Your personal style around wariness isn't really superior to others, just easier on you. So if you are tempted to fall into lack of tolerance for the rest of humanity, pause. Maybe take a few blinks.

Let's Get Practical: One More Way to Keep Friends

How can this face reading category help your social life? Take another look at your own Wariness Index. Then accept the strengths of your personal style.

If you live at the low end of the Wariness Index, don't push yourself to trust strangers instantly. How can someone with 1s, 2s, or 3s do that congruently? Only by falling in love with a fantasy or believing the pitch of a con artist.

If strangers must earn your trust, what's wrong with that? Call it "Smart."

Conversely, if you are at the high end of the Wariness Index, know in advance that you may be a pushover for love, etc.

Slow down the pace; intimacy doesn't have to proceed like a sprint. Also, it won't hurt to check on your inner balance occasionally.

Could you be carrying around hurt from old relationship disappointments? Then get yourself some quality healing. It's no disgrace to need occasional support for that tender heart of yours.

With a mid-range score on the Wariness Index, congratulate yourself on having brilliant social adjustment around handling strangers.

That said, now you can quit expecting the same from anyone else, such as dates or clients at work.

And for all you Power-Packed Readers, what's my advice, whenever you are presented with a potentially important new relationship? Look 'em in the eye... at the bottom.

Each person's Wariness Index score on the left eye is important for you to read. It will help you to pace the relationship appropriately.

Horizontal Eye Set

Ready, set, go. Wait, don't physically go anywhere! Pause at that set part, since I'm referring to the horizontal distance between both eyes.

Warning, Power-Packed Reader, now that you have paused. What follows in this section is one of the trickier, more technical categories in all of Face Reading Secrets. You might want to skip it entirely and move on to Deep-Set Eyes. I won't think any less of you, that's for sure.

What, you're still game to explore the tricky category of Horizontal Eye Set? Hooray! Let's go.

Soon I will ask you to view how close your eyes are to each other. Fortunately you have the dandiest measuring unit for reading this category: The width of one eye.

Whose eye? Yours, if reading your own Horizontal Eye Set.

Otherwise your point of reference would be an eye belonging to the person whose face you are reading. Imagine that extra eye, lining it up as if you were "seeing" three of that person's eyes in a row.

Do they touch? Is there space between them? Or do the three eyes fit pretty well, with neither gaps nor touching?

I call this measuring method the "**Three Eyes Technique**." Before you try it on yourself, here are some examples of what you might find.

- **Close-Set Eyes** live like friendly neighbors, close and comfortable. With the Three Eyes Technique, do the eye corners seem to touch or overlap? Count that as Close-Set Eyes.
- **Far-Set Eyes** are spaced more like distant cousins, one living close to the edge in one direction, the other located on the opposite coast. With the Three Eyes Technique, you could easily fit at least one extra eye.
- Most faces have **Average Eye Set**. Power-Packed Reader, avoid squinting, mumbling, and desperately measuring with your fingers to figure out how many imaginary eyes you can squoosh into that space. If you find, "Pretty much three," count that as good enough.

For examples of Average Eye Set, see Shirley and Kathryn. Neither of them minds your staring.

Asymmetry with Horizontal Eye Set

Now that you have the general idea, Power-Packed Reader, let's refine it. With Close-Set Eyes or Far-Set Eyes, maybe one of the eyes is responsible more than the other.

Very often, there is asymmetry regarding Horizontal Eye Set. Only one of the eyes is close-set or far-set. For instance, many people have one Close-Set Eye plus one Far-Set Eye.

Once you have determined that the three eyes don't easily fit in a row, it's time to add a second technique, the "**Paper Method**." This technique will tell you whether one eye or both is responsible for that close-set, or far-set, configuration.

For the Paper Method, hold a blank sheet of paper lengthwise down the center of the nose. This will showcase one side of the face at a time. Then compare which eye is closer to the center of that face, at the paper's edge.

With Lloyd, for instance, what shows with the Three Eyes Technique? Close-Set Eyes alert! So next use the Paper Method.

This will help explain why that third, imaginary, eye doesn't fit in neatly. Lloyd has a Close-Set Left Eye. While Lloyd has an Average Set Right Eye.

Let's take Valerie for an example. Using the Three Eyes Technique, what if you lined up an extra imaginary eye between the two real ones? You would have room to spare. So on to the Paper Method. It reveals that Valerie has a Far-Set Left Eye and an Average-Set Right Eye.

Unless the closeness or distance seem obvious, go on to a different eye category. Also to a different person, considering that any stranger you have been frowning at this intently would be justified in fleeing the room. It can feel just a bit threatening, receiving a prolonged face reader's squint that you never requested.

Anyway, now that you have been schooled in both the Three Eyes Technique and the Paper Method, consider yourself prepared for some mirror gazing. How about looking at your own Horizontal Eye Set right now?

Interpreting Horizontal Eye Set

Horizontal Eye Set symbolizes width of perspective. Before interpreting, remember, this category reveals personal style, a preference rather than a fixed way that someone must always respond to life.

Depending on the gift showing here, you prefer a certain perspective. Sure you can shift it, just as you're capable of moving your eyes in their sockets.

Defaults still matter, including that non-trivial matter of your innate talent.

Only you know how you have responded — your default — to our latest eye category. Looking into that mirror, were you calculating hard, straining to compute precisely how many millimeters are involved in your Horizontal Eye Set?

This will not win you bonus points for physiognomy. However, you can probably give yourself credit for having **Close-Set Eyes**. As if folks with any other eye set would stop to calculate millimeters!

With Close-Set Eyes, you have a talent for focusing. That means focusing on any aspect of life that matters to you. Alas, you are not omniscient God, even with those magnificent eyes. Merely a human, you can pay quality attention to just one thing at a time.

With Close-Set Eyes, that attention brings details to life, whichever aspect of life interests you. Care about how well the carpet was vacuumed? How about the precise way to knot your tie?

If it matters enough for you to pay attention, nobody else notices details better than you. Therefore you excel at crafts or the technical aspects of singing or any activity where a discriminating focus is required.

The potential challenge? Oh, little things like perfectionism and criticism. Being so good at noticing things, once you start finding fault, you can perform like a champ. Only avoid that. You don't just want to be right. You want to be happy.

Power-Packed Reader, here's some relationship advice if your partner has Close-Set Eyes: Marvel at the surveillance ability. Laugh at the rest.

How about partners and others with **Far-Set Eyes**? Don't expect them to cross every "i" and dot every "t."

Ha, did I just fool you there? More likely if you have at least one Far-Set Eye.

You're doing well if you remember the periods at the ends of sentences. If anything, you tend to space out, especially if you also have Starter Eyebrows. That's your potential challenge, anyway.

As for the talent, it's a broad perspective. Got a problem to solve? With Far-Set Eyes, you will introduce something new, a broader perspective not previously considered. Inspiring!

Romanticism, idealism... these are other aspects of life where it's marvelous to have Far-Set Eyes.

Clairvoyance may be one of your inborn gifts for deeper perception. Every human being has a full set of gifts for energetic literacy, aura reading, etc. Only clairvoyance is the really famous one right now, so enjoy it if you have that eye set.

And another perk of Far-Set Eyes is that you are more likely to get a job on TV or movies. Ever notice what a high percentage of folks on screen have your kind of Horizontal Eye Set? It's a screen thing.

- Well known fact: Cameras distort everyone's face, adding 10 pounds.
- Less well known fact: Cameras make eyes appear more close-set than they really are.

On television, Shirley might appear to have Close-Set Eyes while really she has **Moderate Horizontal Eye Set**.

So let's turn to that face data next. What's the talent if you have this most common eye set attribute?

Congratulations on your flexible range of focus.

In some situations, you take a wide view, as if using a wide-angled lens for photography.

In other situations, you emphasize tiny details, as if zooming in for a close-up.

Generally you go back and forth, adjusting your range of focus at will... no less remarkable a talent for being effortless.

Well, I bet you can guess the potential challenge. That little lack of tolerance for the rest of humanity. What's with Cliff, who keeps seeing the big picture but forgets to wear matching socks? What's with Lloyd? Just for once, could the man relax?

"Why can't other people be normal, just like me?"

Let's Get Practical: Calling All Golfers

Golfers, hear this. Since I began teaching Face Reading Secrets in 1986, I have found only one item of face reading data that links directly to any human endeavor.

That's Close-Set Eyes and golf.

Well, think about it. Golfers must discriminate fine nuances of turf, of slope, of club. The super-fine distinguishing abilities of Close-Set Eyes can pay off at the golf course.

Of course Horizontal Eye Set alone won't guarantee success at golf. You also must be able to hit the ball.

Whenever a world-class golfer has a picture in the newspaper, I head for reading Horizontal Eye Set. So far, every time, I have found at least one Close-Set Eye.

Do you have that right on your own, personal face? Then you might consider picking up a golf club. Consider a personal experiment about Close-Set Eyes and golf. Send feedback over to the Rose Rosetree blog!

Extra Special Face Data: Deep-Set Eyes

While scanning your Eye Set in the mirror, Depth of Eye Set can be worth your notice as well. Actually you will see it most easily from a profile view, requiring a second mirror.

Locate your eyebrow. Beneath it you will find the top of the eye socket.

Aren't you glad that human eyeballs don't need to be changed periodically like light bulbs? I am, and not only because I'm a face reader.

Seriously now, when your eyes were installed, how far in were they placed?

Just to fast-track you to what is relevant in physiognomy, the Depth of Eye Set category has three possibilities: In, Out, and Average. For practical purposes, you only need to read one of these possibilities: In.

Also known as Deep-Set Eyes.

You can see Depth of Eye Set from the front, provided that you have excellent depth perception. But that two-mirrors trick will make it much easier. Depth of Eye Set shows so much more easily from a side view.

Here are the possibilities:

- With **Average Depth of Eye Set**, the eyes are slightly in-angled compared with the forehead area right above the eyebrows. For example, see Helene.
- A rare possibility is having one or two **Out-Angled Eyes**, sometimes called "Protruding Eyes." Not pictured in our Cast of Characters! (When I said "rare," I meant it.)
- While **Deep-Set Eyes** are recessed. See Alexander.

Tip: With Deep-Set Eyes, while you are checking, notice if one eye is quite a bit deeper set than the other. That's fairly common. It's the same deal with asymmetries of Cheek Prominence, a category you will learn to read in a later chapter.

Interpreting any asymmetry with Eye Set, remember the usual rule. Right side of your face equals public type relationships, like work and meeting strangers for the first time; left side informs you about personal relationships, where somebody like Helene knows you deeply.

At least Helene assumes she does. More on that soon.

Regarding examples from of Cast of Characters, both Helene, Wayne, Oliver, and Valerie have Average Eye Set. None of our cast of characters has an Out-Angled Eye; not surprising since this is extremely rare.

As a new face reader, the last thing you need do is obsess over every facial characteristic that is theoretically possible. Instead, spend time on what you are likely to see.

Interpreting Deep-Set Eyes

Deep-Set Eyes are worth learning to recognize at this stage in your face reading career. For context, the Depth of Eye Set category reveals underlying patterns of social engagement.

Let's use Alexander as an example. When participating in a conversation, how involved will Alexander be?

His inner reaction is anyone's guess. Behind a polite smile, Alexander may inwardly be rolling his eyes. Typically, the secret emotion with Deep-Set Eyes can range from cautious skepticism to silent ridicule.

With a VERY version (or simply a VERY horrid relationship), the concealed emotion might be contempt.

If you have a Deep-Set Eye, you know what I mean, right? Deception isn't necessarily involved in this form of social withdrawal. Rather, there's a gap between what is felt inwardly versus what is outwardly acknowledged.

Potential challenge? As they say in the London subways, "Mind the gap."

Avoid letting that gap grow too large. Otherwise you never will be able to have a close relationship with that person in the future.

To close the disclosure gap, say just a little bit about what bothers you: "Joe, do you realize that you are flossing your teeth right in front of me? I wish you wouldn't."

Eyelid Fold

If you were with me in a workshop right now, I would invite you to join me for a break. In my Face Reading Workshops, one of our more diverting entertainments is to walk around the room making faces at one another.

Compared to kids, grownups can be pretty inhibited about smooshing eyebrows towards cheeks; taking full advantage of the 700 or more ways that you can shove out your lips; exploring the special humorous effects created by letting your fingers get into the act of face making.

Plus you could explore a delicious assortment of ways to twist your lips and nose over to one side of your face.

Try making some faces right now, if you dare. It's good for you. Don't believe what you may have been told as a kid, "Stop making that face or it will freeze forever."

However, even the most uninhibited grownups are unlikely to experiment with one face-making trick that is popular with kids.

Next time you are driving with a back seat full of youngsters, watch in the rear view mirror when they start turning their eyelids inside out — not that I would recommend you try doing this with a grownup's less flexible body.

Adults generally ignore eyelids. Many of us haven't yet noticed that eyelid structure for humans comes in two different varieties. To start reading this category, notice how the skin of your eyelid folds down from the brow bone. You will find either:

- A **Double Eyelid Fold**, where the eyelid tucks into itself. As a result of that fold, you will find a crease at the eye socket. (Ladies, in makeup instructions for using eye shadow, sometimes you are asked to brush a contrasting eye shadow color right in that crease.) (Unless you don't have one, which would be the case with a Single Eyelid Fold.)

  For examples of a Double Eyelid Fold, see Rowan, Gary, and Joyce.
- With a **Single Eyelid Fold**, the skin connects directly from brow bone to eye. See Matt.
- Should you find a Centerfold, you are looking at pin-up pictures in some magazine. Honestly! Come back to face class.

Hoist up your mirror, Power-Packed Reader. You don't want to take this vital face data for granted.

Interpreting Eyelid Fold

This category relates to a basic social expectation about how you relate to other people. Who matters more, them or you?

Subconsciously there's a big difference, related to Eyelid Fold. Do your eyelids connect you directly to others? Or you have an ego-boosting pause, or crease, separating you from others?

With a **Double Eyelid Fold**, you come first.

Well, duh! Who else? (You may be thinking.)

No matter how close you feel to family and friends, your life is about me-me-me. Deep down, that's what you expect.

Potential challenge? Could there be just a bit of selfishness?

As a world traveler, I delight in subways. Cities where I have taken subways (as both a traveler and a face reader) include New York, Boston, Washington D.C., Chicago, London, Paris, Frankfurt, and Tokyo. All those Occidental cities have cultural differences between them. But they are trivial, compared to the one subway system I've surveyed in the Orient.

Americans, Brits, French, and German passengers all display plenty of "Me-me-me" attitude. You can observe it clearly in body language, expression, how passengers look at each other, how they talk. Often passengers litter freely. Why not? It's as if the public space belongs to them.

In all of those subways, most of the passengers have a Double Eyelid Fold. So that's the dominant culture.

With a **Single Eyelid Fold**, others come first. What does your family want or need? How about expectations from your parents? What is expected of you socially in each situation? Honor could be at stake, so don't be selfish!

Out in public, consideration for others matters at least as much as your own comfort. Witness the immaculate subways in Tokyo. Witness a new sign I saw in the subways during my 12th trip to Japan, in 2010.

Thoughtfully translated for English-speaking passengers, the sign pictured a dripping umbrella. Words, as I best remember, advised us:

When it is raining, please close your umbrella thoroughly before you enter the subway station. Otherwise you might form a puddle, which would offend your fellow passengers.

To this native New Yorker, could there be a greater contrast? Not wanting to revolt you, no details will follow about what goes on underground, except I will admit that I adore the crazy salad of my homeland, especially those subways. While I'll freely admit...

It sure makes for elegant subway stations, having the majority of passengers with Single Eyelid Fold!

The talent that corresponds to Single Eyelid Fold is a deep, almost instinctive, consideration for others. The potential challenge? Sense of personal identity can take decades or longer to develop.

Let's Get Practical: Question This Offensive Term

In the education of face readers, eventually, an offensive bit of language must be discussed. And I don't mean "subways."

Surely you have heard the term "Slanted Eyes."

Here's the funny part — though typically a discussion of "slanted" eyes is more offensive than humorous if your eyes are the ones under discussion — so-called "slanted" eyes aren't particularly slanted at all.

At least, they're not slanted more than eyes that aren't dark brown and set off by skin with a white undertone.

(As a so-called "Caucasian," I do find the labels about skin color extremely confusing. "White" skin, to me, looks more pink. While "Yellow" skin is more white. Go figure.)

Here's the point, however you see skin tones. Assuming that you are human and own a pair of eyes, they will have an angle or slant. So will your mouth, your eyebrows, and other face parts. None of this is related to skin color.

When we look more at Eye Angle (later in this chapter), you will find that Eye Angle is entirely different from Eyelid Structure.

When you are brave enough to look, really look, past the stereotypes, you will find nothing unusual at all about Eye Angle in people whose ancestors come from certain parts of Asia.

What you may find, however, is a Single Eyelid Fold. If you don't have this, stare discreetly at the next person you meet who does. Skilled physiognomists see face data, not weirdly inaccurate stereotypes!

And, of course, in this melting pot world, you will find plenty of Americans and Europeans and South Americans and Australians with Single Eyelid Fold. Just as you will find Asians with the double variety.

Look for the person, not the stereotype. Willingness to do that will help you to gain the full power of face reading.

Eyelid Fullness

After you read Eyelid Structure, it's important to go immediately to this next category. A balanced interpretation comes only when you supplement research on Eyelid Fold with reading Eyelid Fullness.

Power-Packed Reader, to see this new category, look at the fold of skin directly above the eyelashes.

Anatomists have a cute name for what's beneath the skin here, "Tarsal plate." That previously-mentioned kid trick of turning eyelids inside out involves playing with the plate — an expression which was not designed to be used in the same conversation as "Eyes like saucers."

We adults have very adult reasons to explore Eyelid Fullness. To recognize it, imaginary cosmetics can help. As you stare in the mirror, pretend that you have decided to slather your eyelids with a gaudy blue shade of eye shadow. How much will show when you open your eyes?

- To get your money's worth from the face paint, you would need **Large Eyelid Fullness**. See Jesse.
- Cosmetically, what happens to your investment in eye shadow when you have **Small Eyelid Fullness**? Not much. See Rowan.
- If you have **No Eyelid Fullness**, don't even bother with eye shadow, real or pretend. The glop is only going to show when you blink. See Oliver.
- **Moderate Eyelid Fullness** looks like a small rim encircling the half-circle of an upper eyelid. See Ava.

Tip: Usually eyelids with a Single Eyelid Fold have No Eyelid Fullness, but never say "Never."

Now, Power-Packed Reader, with or without physically putting on any eye makeup at all, hoist up your mirror to find the face data.

Interpreting Eyelid Fullness

Eyelid Fullness reveals how a person defines intimacy. As always, in Face Reading Secrets, there is no right or wrong. Although there sure are different personal styles.

With Large Eyelid Fullness and a Single Eyelid Fold... oops, you are not looking correctly. Large Eyelid Fullness doesn't happen with this type of Eyelid Structure. At least I haven't seen it, not even once. With Single Eyelid Fold, you nearly always would have No Eyelid Fullness.

Of course, there's also the possibility of what I refer to later as the "Double Whammy." So if you do find some Small, or even Moderate, Eyelid Fullness along with your Single Eyelid Fold, skip down to that section.

Meanwhile, let's interpret **Large Eyelid Fullness** along with a **Double Eyelid Fold**. What's the gift?

You tend to get very close to other people. Sure, deep down (given the significance of that Double Eyelid Fold) you define yourself as an independent person, the center of your own world. When with a significant other, however, it's as though you have admitted that other person into total sharing powers for that world.

Congratulations on your talent for closeness. You can learn a great deal through intense intimacy. And that can apply to work relationships (right eyelid) as well as relationships with family and friends and lovers (left eyelid).

The potential challenge? That could be either extreme co-dependence or some degree of confusion between where you begin and your significant other leaves off.

Remember, any challenge related to face data can be healed. No shame in having any challenge, either. You are living on The Learning Planet.

At the opposite end of Eyelid Fullness, how about Small Eyelid Fullness? (And No Eyelid Fullness would be the VERY version.) What if you have **Small Eyelid Fullness** along with a **Single Eyelid Fold**?

Then you have a basic setup, deep down, for feeling connected to everyone else.(That connection relates to the Single Eyelid Fold.)

Given that sense of identity, you still maintain the ability to naturally think of yourself first, in a healthy way. (That's where Small Eyelid Fullness comes in.)

Nearly everyone with Single Eyelid Fold does have No Eyelid Fullness, the extreme version of Small Eyelid Fullness. What if you have it, Power-Packed Reader? If you think about it, aren't you grateful?

Consciously you won't dwell extensively on particulars about what you need, want, desire, etc. When you slow down and pay attention, however, you can access that info just fine.

Mostly you have a gift for paying attention to yourself objectively, noticing how you are dressed, your social standing, how people respond to you in different social situations.

And your social expectation is that you belong. Perhaps you prize effectiveness at doing what it takes to belong honorably, acting in a way that brings credit to your family. Consideration, while balanced with a healthy sense of self, could be your biggest intimacy talent.

The potential challenge? When asked to pay attention to yourself, that might feel weird or hard to do.

Struggling to find that individual self, what if you can't find a clear, obvious sense of self? You may start to worry. The more you seek that elusive inner self, extra worries can be heaped on, as if you were seriously abnormal.

Which, of course, you aren't. Sense of self is abstract for everyone. And there is no such thing, really, as "normal." (Keep reading faces and this will become more and more obvious, trust me. We professional physiognomists have many a giggle over the concept of "Normal.")

With **Moderate Eyelid Fold** plus a **Double Eyelid**, in theory, intimacy style is no big deal. Your actual intimacy in particular relationships, now that can be a big deal! You're so good at this aspect of life.

Overall, the point is that your degree of intimacy does not become a source of torment. You are expert at getting as close as need be, one relationship at a time, one situation at a time.

The potential challenge? Oh, that silly lack of tolerance for the rest of humanity and their big issues around something "so simple"!

By contrast, what if you have **Small Eyelid Fullness** or No Eyelid Fullness plus a **Double Eyelid Fold**? Your intimacy talent requires putting yourself first.

You need time on your own. You need your own space, too. Literally.

Figuratively you also need to put your life first. So you will participate in high intimacy-type conversations only when it feels right.

The potential challenge? Stay away from that scary Country Western Music.

Living in Virginia, I hear it on the radio often and have really come to like it. As you may know, however, this music has some rather weird themes. Most songs will touch on one of them:

- Celebrating the singer's Christian faith and flag-waving patriotism.
- Enjoying a lifestyle defined by sex, getting drunk, unemployment, and/or being in jail. (Also, most shocking to this English major in college, proudly deviating from standard English grammar.)
- Idealizing co-dependent love.

That last part is relevant to face reading, of course.

Any love song you hear in Country Western Music, and believe in, is likely to make you feel really lousy about yourself... if you have Small Eyelid Fullness along with a Double Eyelid Fold. (As will any other music that glorifies co-dependent love.)

You know those songs. The gist is, "You treated me like garbage but I will always love you."

For heaven's sake, find other music if that co-dependent sentiment bothers you.

After you have overcome the challenge, you can listen safely, able to like the soulful singing and the catchy tunes and, also, yourself.

Extra Special Face Data: Anchors

How about non-music-related potential challenges with Small Eyelid Fullness? You might have real-life interactions with other people who have larger Eyelid Fullness than you. They might call you "Selfish" because you are not just like them.

Probably you are not just like them. You simply do not think, speak, and act like a person with Large Eyelid Fullness.

Well, that problem can be overcome quite easily. For instance, you might read this part of our chapter a few times extra, until the basic concepts really sink in.

Or you might own the concept now! Expecting other people to be "just like me" is ridiculous.

Similarly, believing other people when they expect you to be "just like them" is guaranteed to make you feel bad. Constant comparison shopping —after you already have chosen a human soul with its own gifts for this lifetime — is, fortunately, not necessary.

What I find fascinating as a face reader is how many of the most sensitive people you will encounter, folks with a Double Eyelid, happen to have Small Eyelid Fullness. This combo is what I call an **anchor**.

As a physiognomist, Power-Packed Reader, you are developing skill the only way a person can. You are learning to read one category of face reading data at a time.

Yet you know that, long-term, the big physiognomy skill will involve putting an entire face together.

Eventually you will have the skills to spend an hour reading one person's face, interpreting one item at a time and, eventually, building those items into patterns. (Yum, that's the big fun of physiognomy!)

Consider this possibility now, even while you are still building skills.

What if you were to read someone's face and find one item after another related to sensitivity, caring about others, feeling connected to others, giving to others, emotional range, etc.? In short, the face is loaded with sensitivity-related talents.

Suppose further that, after you explore categories within ears, cheeks, lips, etc., (including some not included in this beginner's program for reading the Secrets because, honestly, I couldn't fit in everything I know as a physiognomist into one book), guess what? You might discover that some people have 5 or 10 or 15 or more characteristics that are sensitivity-related.

Still other people have only a few characteristics that are sensitivity related, yet they are VERYs. So that represents a big deal with sensitivity as well.

So think: What is to keep such a person from turning into one gigantic mushball of sensitivity, constantly serving others and having no life at all, prior to the inevitable cry of "I'm meeeeeeeeeeeeelting"?

There is, thank God, an anchor. In one aspect of life, at least, that person is wired to sing, "Me-me-me-me-me-me-me."

Whew! That anchoring characteristic is what keeps this individual from turning into a quivering mushball of sensitivity, useless for helping anybody and also having no personal life.

Aha! You are getting this, right?

I suspect that Rowan is such a person. How wonderful that she has the anchor of No Eyelid Fullness along with a Double Eyelid Fold. This does not make her insensitive, merely sane.

The moral of The Anchor Story is simple. Your face is perfect, as a reflection of your soul.

So is everybody else's face.

Therefore, Power-Packed Reader, when you encounter an item of face reading data that seems different from your usual self-concept, please remember this. You are reading just one item of face data, one little item out of an enormous collection.

Tell me. Did you flinch when you read "Your intimacy style requires putting yourself first socially"? Did you take that to mean, "You horrible, unfeeling selfish person"?

Consider, there is nothing wrong with putting yourself first when making social choices. Calm down. Then contemplate anchors.

Let's Get Practical: Advice to the Lovelorn

Eyelid Fullness could be the most important face category to read if you are single and seriously seeking a mate.

Look at that cute-faced single on the other side of the room. Sure he's attractive but, if you were to dance together through life, how tightly would he hold on?

Or to put it in the universal language of love (which is food, obviously), will he stick to you like peanut butter? Or will he barely hold on, more like spaghetti cooked al dente and flung against a wall?

Every couple has some degree of attachment. This can range from one extreme to another. Some pairs are so fused, they live in a state of perpetual closeness. Other pairs are nearly separate; they do an adult-sized version of children's parallel play.

Lucky you, the Power-Packed Face Reader! To find out if a new date will want to share his castle, you don't have to take him into the sandbox and watch how he plays. Eyelid Fullness will tell you any time, anywhere.

Full Eyelids are rightly nicknamed "Bedroom Eyes," assuming you realize that sex has nothing to do with this kind of bedroom.

The face data means that relationship-wise, when you pair off with such a person, you will be expected to *live* in the bedroom.

No escape for you to the formal living room or the private bathroom. Forget it! Get used to living close in, up front, and personal.

Having Full Eyelids, yourself, means that you both give and demand closeness. Depending on your partner's needs, intense closeness could create a glorious relationship — or a nightmare. Emotional generosity of this order enables you to learn profound lessons about compassion and kindness. (Also learning to avoid co-dependence.)

Regardless of your Eyelid Fold, what makes Small Eyelid Fullness wonderful? The independence. With this inner attribute, you are self-reliant socially at this time in your life.

No matter how much you love, how deeply, how long... you remain your own person. Unless you are with someone whose eyelid characteristics are similar to yours, here is what I recommend. Have a conversation about intimacy style once that love relationship turns serious.

Explain to your loved one that it's not personal. You just need plenty of emotional space — your own things, your own life and, if possible, your own room.

Actually, when you are reading any face category and find major contrast between yourself and your love partner, it can be helpful to have a conversation about your different personal styles. Those who haven't yet learned face reading, or some other form of deeper perception, most likely expect you to be "just like me." Clarify!

Extra-Special Face Data: Double Whammy Eyelids

Sometimes you will find the combination of a Single Eyelid Fold plus Moderate Eyelid Fullness. I call this a "**Double Whammy**." Not only will you see it on plenty of people these days. You might even encounter it in the mirror!

For examples, see Kathryn and Helene.

The associated talent is constantly feeling close to others, then yearning for ever-greater intimacy. Keeps you growing, for sure, Power-Packed Reader.

The potential challenge? You may give yourself a very hard time indeed about whether you care enough.

Trust me, you do.

Finding a strong sense of identity may take a while. And do remember the term "potential challenge." This one can be overcome just like any life lesson here at Earth School.

At the risk of sounding ultra-metaphysical, here's my personal view on being born with the Double Whammy. Your soul has chosen a life contract where you will be given boundary lessons galore. You may even belong to a cohort of souls I call "**East-Meets-West People**."

I'm a member, even without a Double Whammy. Millions of us are in that group, bringing Eastern and Western values into one life. And many East-Meets-Westers do have that signature look.

As an East-Meets-West person, with or without a Double Whammy, you live with a deep commitment to Eastern values, like connection to your family and spiritual colleagues, built-in consideration for others, a strong sense of honor, deep ability to listen to others, and a mystical approach to the Divine.

Simultaneously you have, or are developing, a Western sense of identity, including a strong personal ego. This guides your actions, speech, and thoughts, amplifying a belief that you are entitled to full use of your free will. You can be a caring person and also a me firster, absolutely!

Of course, many people with a Double Whammy are not involved in that East-Meets-West project for human consciousness. Complicating matters, a very popular surgery today is to modify the Single Eyelid look by surgically adding an extra bit of Eyelid Fullness. Supposedly this is a more "Western" look.

As we have already considered in previous chapters, all cosmetic surgery brings inner consequences. That is due to the reciprocal relationship between physical face data and the inner person. Choosing cosmetic surgery is an intensely personal decision, often fraught with concerns about social status.

In no case is this more ironic, to me, than when somebody chooses to surgically create a Double Whammy. Talk about social pressure!

I wish that everyone considering this surgical procedure would learn in advance about the inner significance. Vanity surgery is not makeup. Consequences will follow, even if the enthusiastic patient doesn't believe in them.

Double-strength drive for closeness can bring great spiritual beauty, but the potential challenge is equally great.

Eye Angles

Some of the most unnecessary relationship problems happen because people cannot accept each other's Eye Angles. Consciously they don't know this, of course. Last I heard, Eye Angle hardly qualifies as legal grounds for divorce in any legal courtroom.

Nevertheless, when you find out what Eye Angles mean, you will appreciate how important it is to read this eye category and avoid the related challenges.

First let's get the physical concept. Eye Angle means the tilt of an eye, end to end, compared to the rest of the face. Which is not difficult to spot once you know what to look for.

Frankly, it's easiest to use spots, or dots, to get your bearings. Here's how:

Begin with one eye since asymmetries to Eye Angle are more common than you might suppose. Imagine a dot on the inner corner of that eye, right at the tear duct. Imagine a second dot where the eye tapers off at the opposite corner — and look carefully to see this place. Often it's higher up than a novice face reader expects.

Now that you have imagined your two dots, connect them with an imaginary line. This line will have an angle. That angle, and that alone, is what I mean by eye angle.

So don't get caught up in Lower Eyelid Curve, how cute the eyelashes might be, Eye Set, or color of anything. Consider Eye Angles like every other face reading category, meaningful on its own as a sacred geometry of the soul.

Power-Packed Reader, once you develop your eye for reading this category, you can notice three variations.

- Most people have **Up-Angled Eyes**. See Joyce and Alexander.
- **Down-Angled Eyes** are far less common. See Annette's left eye and Fred's left eye.
- If you're lucky, sometimes you will encounter an **Even-Angled Eye**. Unfortunately, our Cast of Characters includes none. Statistically this isn't the least bit surprising. Because Even Eye Angles are so rare, I estimate that you will find them on maybe 1 in 2,000 people. (And that means one of those eyes, not both. Two Even-Angled Eyes are even more rare.)

To see what you have, look in the mirror now. Research each eye separately. Line up the imaginary dots on each corner, connect them with your imaginary line, then follow the angle.

Interpreting Eye Angles

Ready for a laugh? Your whole life, you have been hearing how eyes are the oh-so-deepest thing about people. Well, hello. The meaning of the Eye Angle category is arguably one of the most superficial attributes in all physiognomy.

Although, of course, the category still fascinates a face reading fancier like me.

Power-Packed Reader, Eye Angles reveal a person's usual degree of optimism or pessimism in social situations.

Preparing to attend that mad tea party? Deciding where to spend Christmas? Must you attend that business meeting? Eye angles help you to understand Annette's initial degree of cringe at the prospect at attending some perfectly nice birthday party.

About 95 percent of human beings, all over the world, have eyes that angle upwards to some degree. The more VERY an **Up-Angled Eye**, more likely that the owner's outlook will be wildly optimistic, even idealistic.

Yes, Up-Angled Eyes correspond to high expectations for a partner, child, parent, boss, or employee.

Power-Packed reader, might there be complications related to various degrees of Up-Angled Eyes?

Such an understatement! Try this quick multiple choice quiz. Where might conflict arise?

A. Between idealists and parents (who must deal with these impossibly high expectations).
B. Between two idealists, with their wildly different (but high) expectations about each other.
C. Within an idealist's own mind and heart, after reality sinks in.

Give yourself a bonus point if you guessed the answer is:

D. All of the above.

And, not to sound unduly discouraging, an even worse potential challenge goes with the territory: Denial.

Here's the most VERY example I have encountered so far of this Up-Angled-style denial. One day my client Joe came home from work. He came home to his wife of 16 years and discovered that, suddenly, she was gone.

Gladys, The Wife, had also taken the kids, the furniture, everything but a little mattress for her husband to sleep on.

"This was a terrible shock," explained Joe and his VERY Up-Angled Eyes. "Far as I was concerned, our marriage was perfect, no problems whatsoever."

Admittedly Joe had some problems beyond the challenge related to his Up-Angled Eyes, but you get the point.

An idealistic outlook goes with adventurous risk taking. "Look before you leap" was probably coined by despairing parents of a kid with VERY Up-Angled Eyes.

Disappointment is most likely when expectations are high, but does that discourage the world's native optimists? Of course not. And the world is a better place for it.

What talent can you expect if you have the opposite attribute, **Down-Angled Eyes**? You are a problem finder and a problem solver.

"That's ridiculous," Gary might say. (The right eye you can't see in his profile shot does happen to angle down.) "What if finding problems is just your job?"

Here's a laugh, Power-Packed Reader. "Finding problems" is probably not required as a big part of Gary's job. Most people, even if they had his job, wouldn't focus on problems the way he does. Although they might be just as successful. Their personal styles would be different, that's all.

Let's turn to an example about you, if you have this talent for solving problems. Think back to the most recent family gathering you attended.

Weren't you one of the first to spot the impending divorce of Aunt Linda and Uncle Pantelis?

Weren't you the one to foresee potential difficulties when your Cousin Josie raved to everyone about her new job selling Happy Fat Cookies, the new brand whose goal is to make cholesterol "a more cheerful, chewy word"?

Admit it, you identify problems where others do not. This makes you a fabulous problem solver. Because you do not have denial (the potential challenge of the Up-Angled Eye majority worldwide), you recognize when other people have problems.

Your significant others need people like you, willing to face up to problems. Also you may have developed exceptional compassion.

Down-Angled Eyes are a Major Compassion Awakener, for me, however. (Flag that term now, because it will be explained later, in our "Nose" chapter.) Problem solving and compassion rank high on my list of Most Valued Virtues.

But here's the problem that anyone — and I mean anyone —with Down-Angled eyes has got going.

Pain, extreme emotional pain! In your history! Experiences of pain that felt soul scorching!

Power-Packed Reader with a Down-Angled Eye, haven't you known such pain here at The Learning Planet?

Deep pain happens to all who live on earth, at least all who are self-aware enough to notice their inner lives.

However, some people like Fred and Annette go through situations in life that are truly unbearable. They feel despair that the agony never will end.

Somehow we endure. Usually, that particular set of circumstances does end. When we have survived, the internal challenge definitely ends.

Afterwards the face is marked. Surviving major inner challenge marks a face... with a Down-Angled Eye.

- When you meet somebody like Fred, with a Down-Angled Left Eye, you can be quite sure he has endured something agonizing in his personal life.
- When you meet someone like Gary with a Down-Angled Right Eye, that person has gone through human-scaled hell in professional life.

Perhaps success or fame didn't bring the expected fulfillment. Both Elvis and Marilyn Monroe developed Down-Angled Right Eyes, late in their careers.

Though rich and famous, neither star lived happily ever after.

Sometimes a life does head north, rather than south. Sometimes a person even does so much inner healing that… the Eye Angle changes from Down back to Up.

I'm living proof. Compare these photos of me at ages 19 and 54. Note the Down-Angled Left Eye that eventually turned up-angled.

Just for fun, check out the author photo on our last page, taken many years later. Even more Up-Angled.

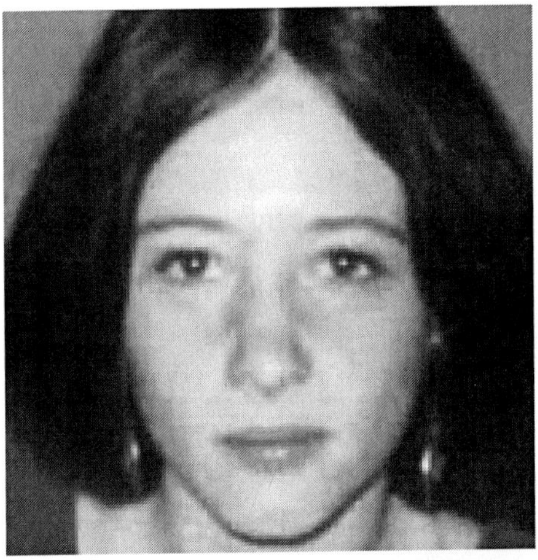

Rose Rosetree at 19

Rose Rosetree at 54

Even if the individual goes on to have a very happy life, that soul remembers how it felt to suffer so much. Extreme, unforgettable, compassion has been earned.

Okay, Power-Packed Reader, you get the point. On to the cheerier topic of **Even-Angled Eyes**.

What if you really have one? Odds are against it, remember. So double check in that mirror of yours. Are you sure that you don't have a very slightly Up-Angled Eye instead? That's what shows in Matt's left eye, for instance.

With an Even Eye Angle, you possess a rare degree of realism. Neither a pessimist nor an optimist, you assess social situations far more accurately than others.

Your potential challenge? That would be a lack of tolerance for the rest of humanity, in all their confused opinionated-ness.

Again and again, you must remind folks you know that a glass of water can be simultaneously half full and half empty.

Reminding them isn't the tiresome part. It's how you handle their typical common response: "That's not possible. I don't get it. You are not seeing things right."

Actually, you are.

Let's Get Practical: Lying

What if your biggest concern when reading eye characteristics is truthfulness? Throughout this chapter, maybe you have been waiting for "The good part" about how to tell from eyes if someone is lying to you.

Does any eye category tell you for sure when someone is lying? How about any category, or any single item of face data?

Not that simple, sorry. If you are willing to do a more complex form of face reading detective work, you can find useful information, though.

Lying is revealed through a combination of face reading and doing research at the surface of life, with speech and action.

Admittedly, aura reading can do the same job and better. But that is a separate skill set. A skill set I would love to teach you another time, Power-Packed Reader.

Actually, becoming a face reader first will make it all the easier for you later if you decide to learn the skill set of aura reading, a.k.a. "Energetic Literacy."

Meanwhile, you can tell a great deal about honesty when a person's self-description or actions dramatically contradict a VERY strong facial characteristic.

What if you were meeting Rowan for the first time? You notice her right eye scores 1 on the Wariness Index, yet she comes across as excessively friendly. I would wonder if she had an ulterior motive.

That wouldn't prove lying in any courtroom, not even the "Courtroom of My Personal Opinion." However, I would test my suspicions in the same way that I would if Rowan flunked a polygraph. I would ask plenty of questions. I'd sure test her a lot before entrusting her with my checkbook or love life.

Same thing if someone's face shows an extreme version of a mouth characteristic that we will turn to later, where personal self-disclosure is about as comfortable as pulling teeth. Wayne has that face data, for instance. So he might have a challenge with self-disclosure.

As described in our Cast of Characters, Wayne is *your* favorite uncle. But what if he were meeting *me* for the first time, and I knew almost nothing about him. We have just met at a business networking event.

What if Wayne were to volunteer loads of highly personal information.

"It's only our very first conversation," I would wonder. "What could be the purpose behind his telling me all that? Him? With that mouth?"

Several years ago a political candidate for Governor of Virginia had a campaign photo that aroused this kind of curiosity. Marshall Coleman's face showed a characteristic related to killer instinct, the deepest level of competitiveness that can show in a face.

This tooth characteristic showed clearly when Coleman smiled. Yet the expression projected in his smile was utterly opposite to the message of his teeth.

"Trust me to do whatever you say" proclaimed his boyish grin. "I'm meek and mild, your humble public servant."

With a different face, I might have believed it. But with those teeth? Never.

During that election, it happened that I was interviewed by a reporter with "The Washington Post." Along with other face reading comments, I couldn't resist expressing my concerns about candidate Coleman, who struck me as the proverbial wolf in sheep's clothing.

Reporter Hank Stuever laughed for a long time.

"I have a friend who covers this guy and he makes it no secret that Coleman loves campaigning. Just yesterday my friend heard him say, 'You know, I love the fight of the campaign more than anything else about it. I love a good fight.'"

Do I recommend that you use face reading to sniff out dangerous people by seeking out contradictions like these? Not particularly. Based on profiling I have done professionally since 1986, consider this advice:

The biggest danger from crime doesn't come from criminals. Suspicion is a far worse enemy.

One of the most common questions people ask me, when they first learn about reading faces is, "Tell me how to spot a liar. Show me the crooks."

What a tragedy! I remember talking to Gladys, a prospective student who was really enthusiastic about finding the crooks.

I countered by sharing the part that makes me enthusiastic, how face reading could help her plumb new depths of human nature, to gain compassion, to recognize her biggest talents.

After I summarized this enchanting world of wisdom, Gladys looked disgusted. "You mean it can't show me the crooks?"

Had I sold burglar alarms — or fear — it would have been so easy to please Gladys. Since I was striving for personal growth, our conversation ended abruptly.

Do you know the concept of self-fulfilling prophecy? What we expect from people is often borne out by reality. Therefore, if we're constantly looking for crooks, we will find them. The best we will notice in others is the degree to which they are terrible crooks.

Conversely, what happens if we choose to probe faces for wisdom or talent? We can find that, too.

In reality, your chance of being attacked today by a criminal is... relatively small. With a suspicious attitude, however, you are guaranteed to find evil lurking in every corner.

To protect your quality of life, therefore, the best way to use face reading is NOT to go out of your way to look for liars.

Keep your wits about you, of course. Then seek the truth about who each individual really is. Everyone has a sweet(er) side. Aim for that and you will receive the best that person has to offer.

Chapter 12. Ears

Psssst... Power-Packed Reader, when you are ready for deep and useful secrets, turn to ears. No other facial feature speaks more eloquently about how a person designs reality. These profound patterns are largely subconscious, which makes reading these Secrets all the juicier.

Okay, here's a related secret. Ears are my favorite part of face reading. Every category within ears reveals something deep about your way of interpreting feelings, thoughts, and the rest of your life experience.

If you ever thought reality was "One size fits all," ha! Read this chapter and you just might laugh loudly enough for your ears to hear.

Ear Length

As we start listening to ears as physiognomists, let's begin with Ear Length.

How on earth can you gauge such a relative thing as Ear Length? Start with yourself in the mirror, naturally. (You will look at your face on the level, remember? Position that mirror neither higher nor lower than your face. Because Ear Length is one of those attributes that can be easily distorted by angle of view.)

Ear Length is relative to your face itself. Compare the length of your ear to the length of your face:

Spread two fingers to measure the length of one ear. Instant "**Handy Ruler**"!

Start at the hairline (or where the hairline would be, if hair remained). Then move your Handy Ruler to gauge how many how many ears could be lined up, end to end, before running out of face space.

Stop at the jawline. And the number is...?

- Did you barely fit in three ear lengths? Then you have magnificent **Long Ears**. See Rowan. Note that Lloyd has VERY Long Ears.
- Could you line up more than three of the cute little things? Then you qualify as having fabulous **Short Ears**. See Jesse, Fred, and Matt.
- Did you fit in three ears? Then you have awesome **Medium Ear Length**. See Kathryn, George and Helene.

Guess what, Power-Packed Reader? If counting imaginary extra ears seems too complicated, you are also allowed to take a wild guess. Given the rest of the face, does the Ear Length look Large, Medium or Small? What do you think, huh?

Now is as good a time as any to remind you that face reading is intuitive, even the part that requires assessing the relative size of visage parts.

Reading Ear Length doesn't have to feel like you are in the shoe store, stepping into their strange, guillotine-like device for measuring foot size. Lighten up!

Approximate size will do. Anyway, the more ears you read, the easier you will find your way around this category.

Interpreting Ear Length

Ear Length whispers how much information a person subconsciously prefers to receive from other people and the environment.

This amount, like Ear Length itself, is relative. Not One-size-fits-all at all, but complex! Here's a hint: This category reveals how much information feels comfortable to receive at any given time, plus personal style for handling all that input.

Long Ears correspond to exceptional listening ability. Lloyd constantly picks up facts, stories, general knowledge, specific details, excellent words to use for tricky crossword puzzles (if Lloyd ever does crossword puzzles), etc.

Readily soaking up information of relevance to personal interests — that's the talent.

What could possibly be a challenge for someone who soaks up information the way that dry sponges slurp up water? Getting soaked, that's what.

Maybe you are familiar with this challenge. Even after you have heard all you want to, somehow you can't resist taking in more.

Eventually, you may become confused about what you, personally, think... as distinct from all the info that has seeped in from various sources.

Still, the advantages of Long Ears are many, including skill at crossword puzzles. Or any activity that draws on general knowledge.

By contrast, folks with **Short Ears** don't just collect information, they take it seriously, even personally.

Overload alert, if you are in this group! Your potential challenge is to fill up faster than others. Then you shut down and stop paying attention, no matter how hard others are thumping their chests and doing the rest of a noisy chimpanzee imitation.

(It may be hard to admit to yourself that you might shut down in this way. If curious, ask for a second opinion, someone who knows you well.)

Potential challenge aside, what is wonderful about your cute Short Ears? How well you use what you take in before shutting down. Quality matters in life, not just quantity, right?

In your case, depth of listening counts for a lot. Taking things to *heart* can be more tiring than taking things just to *mind*. So cut yourself some slack, Jesse and others.

As for Medium Ear Length, wow, you can be flexible at listening! Sometimes you will take in data like crazy. Other times, you will choose to turn off.

Overwhelm at a subconscious level doesn't weigh you down much, does it?

Nice flexibility, Power-Packed Reader. Your only related challenge is that teensy problem, a lack of tolerance for the rest of humanity.

Why does Fred stop listening so quickly, then start defensively texting? Why does Rowan exhaust herself, being so darned available as a listener?

When will these sillies have the decency to be more like you?

Brace yourself. The answer is, "Probably never." Can you hear that?

Let's Get Practical: STUFF

Power-Packed Reader, it's time I introduced you to STUFF.

"**STUFF**" is my hopefully unintimidating name for stored-up emotional and/or spiritual problems.

STUFF can always, always, always be healed. Just find a competent practitioner and permanent healing can happen quite rapidly.

You see, STUFF can get into anyone's aura and subconscious mind. Frankly, STUFF can cause any talent that shows in a face to be underused.

This is more likely with ear categories than with face reading categories from other parts of the face. So beware, Power-Packed Reader, as you learn about Ear Length and all the other ear categories you will learn to read in this chapter.

Why is STUFF so relevant to personal styles that show with ears? Remember, ear categories are about subconscious specialties. Other facial features reveal personal style with conscious functioning.

The sheer quantity of STUFF carried by an individual can make it impossible to use, or recognize, any personal talent at all. Until some of that STUFF is released, it might even be hard to use one's ear-category talents.

Mostly you will find Face Reading Secrets to be a really, really accurate system. However, Power-Packed Reader, here is where you receive gentle warning. As you use face reading on people besides yourself, sooner or later you will encounter folks who are way out of touch with themselves, whether that be caused by huge amounts of STUFF or disdain for noticing anyone's inner life in depth (perhaps being busy looking for liars and crooks, etc.).

How can you spot these naysayers? Face reading won't warn you. Aura reading or skilled empath merge (deeper forms of energetic literacy) can make this abundantly clear.

But hey, you don't have to take precautions before reading faces, other than simple politeness. If you are going to read your buddy Joe's Ear Length, you don't have say what you find out loud.

If you do want to share your face reading, it's only polite to ask first. For instance, "Joe, I do face reading. I wonder, would you would be interested in having me tell you something about your ears?"

Receiving a yes, go ahead. What's the worst that can happen? Well, if Joe suffers from loads of STUFF, you will get a clue rather quickly. Everything that you tell him, he will respond by saying, "No. Nope. Wrong. No. No. Never." etc.

Well, don't read Joe's face any more.

Or, at least, stop reading his ears.

As someone who works professionally as a healer of STUFF, I can tell you that Joe (and everyone else) is really, truly able to release STUFF permanently. Assuming that folks choose to, they can make it their business to find appropriate help. (Whether they make this choice or not is, of course, none of your business.)

When someone like Joe clears out major amounts of STUFF, he will turn way more aware. This would help him to actively use every gift of his soul. He might even enjoy receiving face readings.

Regardless, you can keep reading faces for yourself. And don't feel discouraged if you run across a naysayer like Joe.

It's highly unlikely that you, personally, are so STUFF-ridden yourself that all your ear talents are clogged up for now. Folks with that much STUFF usually run away shrieking from any form of deeper perception.

However, what if you do find that any of the categories you read in this chapter don't resonate for you? Consider a session of healing with a STUFF-removing, mind-body-spirit healer of your choice. Could be, your quality of life is about to improve.

Ear Position

Most people think of ears as having only one possible position: Attached to the head. A Power-Packed Face Reader like you can, however, look for something more informative. That would be Ear Position.

This category is more sophisticated than whether ears stay stuck on your face or, whoops, not.

Where, relative to the rest of your face, do your ears hang out?

To see this category, you will need to line up a couple of mirrors so that you can inspect yourself in profile. You also may need, temporarily, to rearrange your hairstyle.

That goes for all the rest of the ear categories in this chapter. By some strange, hairy coincidence, covered-up ears are hard to read.

Prepare to read Ear Position by drawing two parallel imaginary lines from a profile view. One extends horizontally, starting at the end of your eyebrow. The second horizontal line begins at the lowest part of your nose, whether that be your nostril or the nose tip.

- Occasionally you will find **High Ears**, with the top reaching above the eyebrow, while the earlobe doesn't reach the tip of the nose. Examples are both of Oliver's ears, Lloyd's left ear, both of Kathryn's ears (her left ear being a VERY).
- More common are **Low Ears**, with earlobes below the tip of the nose. The top of the ear may not reach as high as the eyebrow. For examples, see Joyce's right ear, also Helene's ear in our profile shot.
- Most common of all is **Middle Ear Position**, fitting neatly between the highest part of the eyebrows and the nose tip. Who has that face data? See Jesse, Rowan and Fred, plus Anthony in profile.

Tip: Why not try to read Ear Position from the front? You will certainly see something. Only that something could be distorted based on how the head is angled.

When you look up or down, that changes the appearance of Ear Position. Which is why I recommend that, when reading your own Ear Position, you make the experiment easy by keeping your face on the level. Grab a second mirror and look from the side.

Even in profile, when reading Ear Position you will always need to check that the face angle is straight, not tilted.

For instance, with our Cast of Characters, Madison's chin is lifted. Helene's head is a bit tilted, too. And whatever are we going to do with that mischievous Gary, leaving his ears off entirely?

With real-live people, it's easier to read them in profile than from the front. You won't need to hold even one mirror. So take advantage of every opportunity you get, Power-Packed Reader. This is such a useful face reading category.

Soon you can become really comfortable at reading Ear Position, by which time your discernment will be well developed. Even then, you may prefer reading Ear Position in profile. I do.

After so many decades of reading this category, I still use the two imaginary lines. It's so helpful to have those reference points. Using them for perspective, Ear Position won't change when someone tucks a chin downward or turns towards a 3/4 view. Actually, those reference lines alert me when face position deviates from straight up-and-down.

It is always preferable to read a face from that straight up-and-down angle. Usually I refuse to read a photograph if I have to tilt my neck like crazy. Why work so hard to unscramble images sent to my brain?

Face Reading Secrets is a system that allows you to take it easy; it's supposed to be different from doing extremely advanced yoga asanas.

All that said, Power-Packed Reader, take out your mirrors and check out your own Ear Position.

Interpreting Ear Position

Ear Position reveals speed and personal style for making decisions.

Sales people take note. This is one of the most practical face reading categories you can read.

With **High Ear Position**, information processing speed is fast. So you can make your best decisions quickly.

Once upon a time, at a party, my attention was flagged by a man with the highest-placed ears I have ever seen:

"Hello," I told him. "You have the highest ears I have ever seen. Do you learn things unusually fast?"

"Well," he returned without skipping a beat. "I do speak 18 languages."

In many social situations, people will assume you think smarter just because you think faster. Enjoy it!

Not to mention the fun of sitting in a movie theater. A joke is made. You laugh. Then you get to relax while listening to others in the audience who eventually get the joke and laugh.

What's the downside of up-hoisted ears? Impatience can be a problem. You get the point, already. Why doesn't the person who's talking to you? (Answer: She doesn't have High Ears, so her mind doesn't move as fast.)

Another potential challenge involves your need for closure. Although you make good decisions at top speed, stalling can drive you nuts. Sometimes you may rush into a decision based on incomplete data; you feel too squirmy to stand waiting another minute.

Such a problem is not likely with your opposite ear type, someone with **Low Ear Position**. You have a different talent much celebrated in *siang mien*: Thorough, deliberate processing of information.

Wisdom can result, especially when a choice is highly complex. Sculptures of the Buddha vary a great deal but he is usually shown with VERY Low Ears.

The potential challenge? Unlike statues, real people have different processing speeds. With Low Ear Position, your most comfortable, wise, default speed could be relatively slow, bringing potential disadvantages.

For example, Joyce (with Low Ear Position) may have a slower speed of intelligence than Anthony (with Middle Ear Position). While Anthony is almost certain to think more slowly than Kathryn (with High Ear Position).

So Kathryn might get in more words as a pundit on a Sunday scream-fest talk show. However, that speed of intelligence has nothing to do with her degree of intelligence or other intellectual talents.

Speaking of talents, Low Ears relate to personal style for making decisions. To understand how this might affect you, remember to use the context corresponding to the side of your face with that Low Ear Position.

It is very common to have asymmetries with all of the ear categories. So remember: Right side relates to career while left side relates to personal relationships.

In that context, congratulate yourself if you have one or two Low Ears. Even if nobody asks you to model for a Buddha sculpture, what you have is fabulous.

More than anything else, Low Ears mean that your need for wisdom is greater than your need to get a decision over and done with.

To put this a fancy way, you have enough ego strength to delay closure. Here's how I think you operate, at your best:

- First you gather data. That research phase may last for years, if you have your way.
- Second, you evaluate — a word that should be spelled evalu-wait — because waiting is exactly what you unintentionally make others do while you make up your mind.
- Finally you arrive at your decision. It had better be good because odds are that you are never going to want to change it, not after all you have been through.

Yes, some might consider it a challenge that once you have made a decision you are about as flexible as the rock of Gibraltar. But here is what you can tell any grumblers about this potential challenge:

In making my decisions, I value wisdom over getting things over with. Don't you?

As for you lucky readers with **Middle Ear Position**, no such problem for you, only the usual lack of tolerance for the rest of humanity, specifically the hasty and the dawdlers.

Challenge apart, your flexible intellectual pace can be an entirely positive asset.

Let's Get Practical: Wavelength Alert

Power-Packed Reader, how can knowledge of Ear Position improve your relationships? First pay attention to what you have got.

Then adjust to your friend's wavelength.

Is your Ear Position *lower* than that of your friend? You might want to provide some friendly reassurance that you are, indeed, listening.

"There's a lot to think about here," you might say. When mulling over a decision, praise your buddy's patience.

Or just add a friendly, "Hmmm."

What if your Ear Position is *higher* than that of your friend?

Show mercy. Slow down the lightning speed with which you leap from one edge of thought to the next, possibly leaving in your wake the rubble from a marathon of mixed metaphors.

With Middle Ear Position, enjoy your deft pacing. Don't take it for granted in somebody else, though. Otherwise you might need to practice the dreaded Tolerance for the Rest of Humanity.

Ear Angles

How far do the ears stick out from your head? There's another valuable clue for each Face Reading Detective.

Don't make reading this category harder than it has to be. I have seen many a student try chasing his own Ear Angle by pivoting his neck around like an owl wannabe.

You can do something way easier. Read one ear at a time. Look from the front on the level.

- From that full frontal perspective, you can discern **Out-Angled Ears** pretty easily. Because you see quite a bit of the ear's shape. See Fred. And Rowan has a VERY version.
- From the front, some ears simply don't show. However, that doesn't mean "No ear." That means **In-Angled Ear**. Cliff, for instance, owns two of them.
- **Moderate Ear Angle** happens when you see some of the ear sticking out, not as much as Rowan but more than Cliff. For examples, see Alexander and Matt.

Tip: Ear Angles don't necessarily remain constant from the top of the ear all the way down to the earlobe. Base your decision on the biggest stick-out for any ear. Hence, you would count Lloyd's right ear as Out-Angled.

Interpreting Ear Angles

Ear Angle informs you about personal style with social conventions. Imagine that the airwaves in this room are filled with messages from society:

Dress casually to show you're cool.
Dress formally to show you're sophisticated.
Undress to show you fit in with the rest of us nudists.

So confusing!

Social scientists can (and do) have a field day studying all the folkways and morays and just plain wacky social messages that affect people like us.

These are subconscious expectations, where we can intuit the truth about what is expected before being told.

Sometimes the spoken words can be total contradictions, such as "Make yourself at home" in a household where the social rules are so rigid as to be practically military, with family members who barely stop short of saluting each other.

Social rules can be so complex. For instance, have you ever heard of **proxemics**? This is a specialty within sociology.

Proxemics explores a culture's unspoken rules about how close is too close. When people stand near each other, will that be interpreted as normal, friendly, or insulting?

Middle Easterners expect to get physically close, while Germans and Swiss need plenty more distance, preferably sticking an Alp or two between each individual.

Through it all, ears stay attached to each person's head! Informatively!

Back at understanding the Ear Angle category, Power-Packed Reader, you don't have to study proxemics. Simply realize that, regardless of where you were born and raised, you have a default sensitivity to following social rules.

That default sensitivity, or talent, applies to your personal style with how others around you prefer proxemics. You have a subconscious comfort zone, regardless of whether your in-laws eat meals quickly or slowly.

This personal style impacts you at work, too, whether or not corporate culture dictates that your hair must be neatly arranged at all times, etc.

Out-Angled Ears signal independence. Instead of following other people's rules, you prefer to make your own.

This can be especially useful for entrepreneurs but, really, that form of leadership in everyday life is useful regardless of how you earn money.

Your potential challenge? It's damage control. Sometimes you may have to explain why you did that shocking thing you just did.

Just remember, what matters most, long run, is that you showed leadership in the first place.

A lifetime where you never annoyed anyone? Ridiculous! That would count as a life wasted.

Unless, of course, you have **In-Angled Ears**. This corresponds to a talent I call "Social radar." In any social setting, new or familiar, you subconsciously note all the expected behaviors, even the subtlest of nuances when it comes to manners, dress, and other ways that people display their Manners IQ.

Even when you choose not to conform, the choice is made consciously.

In work situations, you will benefit from your ability to fit in wherever you go.

Fit in? Hey, you can melt in... like butter on fresh hot corn.

So what's the potential challenge? How deeply can you respect people whose manners are terrible? Even if you work at being non-judgmental, admit it. When you see some weirdo acting out at a party, doesn't your respect for that person plummet?

Until your challenge is overcome, sure you will cringe. When the life lesson is learned, you are more likely to shrug.

Maybe the real problem with those In-Angled Ears is that your own good manners come so naturally, it's hard to consider them a personal achievement.

Reading the Secrets can bring perspective, Power-Packed Reader. Other people aren't necessarily idiots. They simply lack your gift.

For additional consolation, know that your ability to fit in can greatly help your career, especially if you work in professions that are traditionally conservative.

With **Moderate Ear Angles**, you are free as a well-trained bird. When it pleases you, social expectations will be noticed and followed. When you don't care, you won't care.

Either way, it's unlikely that conformity issues will carry a heavy emotional charge for you.

No worries, unless you count that potential challenge of a lack of tolerance for the rest of humanity. How can Shirley act so stuffy? Will Rowan once, even once, act the way you expect?

Why can't these people fit in perfectly? You know, "Just like me."

Earlobe Size

Now here's a simple category. Unless you have been living in a cave (on Mars) you recognize earlobes already. Reading this category can be easy, too.

Push aside scarves, hats, collars, and floppy hair. If you can't see an earlobe clearly, don't try to read it. Nifty though echolocation might be for bats, it won't help you here.

How about frame of reference for measuring Earlobe Size? Your overall gauge is the rest of that person's ear. (What, you thought this Face Reading Program came complete with a measuring Q-tip?)

- **Small Earlobes** are short or narrow or cause you to make a frowny face trying to find them at all. See Madison and Anthony.
- **Large Earlobes** are chunky, whether you notice length or length plus width. See Fred's left earlobe and both of Wayne's.

- **Medium Earlobe Size**? That's what's left over after you have discarded the possibilities of Large and Small. See Helene and George.

Interpreting Earlobe Size

This category whispers secrets about how the earlobe wearer notices physical reality. Subconscious preference is meant, of course, not the equivalent of wearing horse blinders.

Courtesy of your conscious mind, you can force yourself to pay attention to physical reality or strive to pay attention elsewhere. But how about when you don't try or force?

The Earlobe Size category reveals your default style for paying attention... innate habit... and, as usual, a gift for personal excellence.

Small Earlobes signify that you are more interested in metaphysical reality than physical reality. You care such a lot about what things mean that you are not necessarily going to pay a lot of attention to how they physically look.

Think philosopher. Think absent-minded professor... rather than art professor.

Your potential challenge? You may give lousy driving directions. Instead of telling Wayne the correct street signs and turns leading to your home, you might settle for something quite vague.

Frankly, details like driving directions don't matter to you that much. Deep down you may believe that details are why God (or somebody) invented GPS. Now if your guest, Wayne, wants to discuss the *meaning* of home, you will have loads to say.

With **Large Earlobes**, you are so observant that you could be a detective. Say you are visiting your cousin Anthony, having drinks in his office.

While you take a trip to the restroom, that prankster rearranges his desk. Returning, you would notice.

Okay, probably you would notice, depending on what kind of drink you'd been imbibing, and how many of those drinks — which isn't the part related to personal style.

Your potential challenge? Are you tempted to respect, or disrespect, other people depending on how physically observant they are? Uh-oh. That could be such a mistake.

Suppose that Cousin Anthony gave you terrible driving directions to his new apartment. Terrible, terrible directions.

Does that mean he is irresponsible, stupid, unlike The Buddha?

Tip: Speaking of The Buddha and earlobes, maybe you have heard the most famous tidbit from *siang mien*: Supposedly big, fat earlobes equate with big, fat wisdom.

Given what you know by now, Power-Packed Reader, doesn't that notion tell you a lot about cultural values in China long ago? People were considered wise if they were innately down-to-earth, paying close attention as they serviced their rice paddy or helped invent gunpowder.

Living on earth today, whether China or elsewhere, human consciousness has evolved greatly since then. Today, it is also possible to respect the wisdom of someone who loves abstract thinking. Go figure!

What about **Medium-Sized Earlobes**? Being observant is situational, where you note different types of detail based on your particular circumstances.

For instance, you might notice every landmark while driving to Cousin Anthony's house, but once there indulge freely in discussing the meaning of life.

Your potential challenge? Aw, shucks, it's just that silly lack of tolerance for the rest of humanity.

What makes Anthony so spacey? Will Wayne ever develop a teensy spark of imagination? It's so obvious to you, how things ought to be done. Surely the Buddha, and other wise people, are "just like me."

Hey, are you ready to graduate from this particular potential challenge? Just write a short essay based on this theme: Which type of Earlobe Size gives someone an advantage at face reading?

Let's Get Practical: Earlobe Fixation

Beginning face readers often care most about a different earlobe category than the one we just explored. What about Attached versus Detached Earlobes?

For some not-quite-face-readers, there is practically a Freudian-style fixation on this characteristic; others are simply proud of themselves that they have noticed the distinction and figure the meaning must be a big deal.

- **Unattached Earlobes** flap away from the head. See Joyce.
- While **Attached Earlobes** seem more connected to that person's head. See Rowan.
- Earlobes that attach to a completely different, second person's head might be interesting… but are beyond the scope of face reading on this planet.

About the significance of this category, first a small warning. All ear categories are about subconscious patterns and, therefore, relatively abstract. Well, the category of Earlobe Attachment is the most abstract of them all.

Earlobe Attachment relates to a choice people have as they evolve spiritually within a state of enlightenment or self-realization.

With **Unattached Earlobes** (as the Buddha is often portrayed), an enlightened person's inclination is to worship God through every little detail of life on earth. Each detail is glorious, infinite joy added onto eternal bliss. Details of life are the emphasis.

With **Attached Earlobes**, an enlightened person tends to worship God as though none of the little details of life matter particularly. Sure, each detail is glorious, infinite joy added onto eternal bliss. However, the source of it all matters more.

Important to note: The full meaning of this description will only resonate properly when you have followed your path to enlightenment and arrived at the goal. Never confuse the path to living the goal. Most people are still on that journey, not yet arrived at the destination.

Extra technical point: Enlightenment is no static goal, or state of consciousness. It is a just a beginning for new spiritual evolution in other ways.

Along that journey to enlightenment, you might go back and forth, sometimes emphasizing God more and other times finding details about life more interesting.

Think about how your own physical face evolved prior to age 18. Some days looking more like Mom, other days looking more than Dad.

Until you reached 18, you hadn't yet developed your personal face. Which is why, as you may remember, physiognomy doesn't apply to folks under 18.

Similarly reread the significance of Earlobe Attachment after you have attained Enlightenment. By all means, send me feedback via email or my blog.

Ear Circles

How good is your sense of proportion? Let's apply it to ears, for a change. Naturally we will start by identifying the two different semi-circles you have per ear, plus a fleshy border in-between.

Use the two-mirror trick, of course, for seeing yourself in profile.

- Your **Outer Ear Circle**, at the top and side of an ear, may be something you never noticed before. Yet this loyal face part has stayed with you nevertheless.
  Notice, part of this Outer Ear Circle lies right above the earlobe… and to the side.
- You may have to do a double take before you recognize the other structure, your **Inner Ear Circle**. This is an indented area that includes the earhole. This Inner Ear Circle is located right above the earlobe… straight up. Also it curves around the hole that leads to your inner ear.

Tip: Pinch yourself gently to familiarize yourself with each of these Ear Circles. (Also, perhaps, to make sure you are not dreaming.)

Unless you have very Out-Angled Ears, use the hand on that side of your body to push that ear forward until much of the shape shows. A gentle tug and sideways bend of your ear can help you to see most of your ear structure in a single mirror.

Pinching the Outer Ear Circle is easy. Simply use your other hand to squeeze on the outer edge of your ear. Pinch it gently all over, just to get acquainted.

To gently pinch your Inner Ear Circle, start close to the ear hole. Your entire Inner Ear Circle is quite a bit bigger than the part near the ear hole. This ear structure could be as big as, or larger than your Outer Ear Circle. Or smaller. Explore away.

Incidentally, the Inner Ear Circle has a different texture, as you may notice during that exploratory self-pinching.

Now let's add more nuance to what you are discovering about your Ear Circles, Power-Packed Reader.

Ear Circle Proportions

Which is bigger, your Inner Ear Circle or the Outer one? To evaluate with a face reader's finesse, you will need to take one other part of ear structure into consideration.

Have you noticed the raised ridge of flesh between your Outer Ear Circle and your Inner Ear Circle. Anatomists call it the "Antihelix," but why not the "Uncle-Helix"? Doesn't seem fair!

Seriously, not being a big Latin speaker, I like to call this an "**Ear Border**."

Inner and Outer Ear Circles are separated by a fleshy Ear Border, a curved ridge where the skin folds over like pastry at the rim of a well-made pie. This border can be clear and well defined. Or the reverse.

When you pinch it delicately, again, you may notice a new ear sensation. Not quite thrilling but interesting....

Because of the folded-over aspect, each Ear Border is the hardest part of your ear structure (along with the outermost part of your ears, the edge of your outer circles).

Got all that? It can be fun, exploring the various parts of your personal ear structures above the earlobe. Of course, I hope you understand that the Inner Ear Circle is next to, but not the same as, the hole that leads to your true inner ear.

Ear Borders are especially fun to observe while you're at this. See if you can follow yours with a fingertip, beginning at the bottom of the Inner Ear Circle, then moving upwards and around as your Ear Border curves to separate Outer and Inner Ear Circles.

Nothing in face reading is harder to grasp than the proportions of Inner and Outer Ear Circles, especially which way the Ear Border angles in three dimensions.

This angling helps you decide whether to consider an Ear Border as part of either the Inner Ear Circle or the Outer Ear Circle.

Yes, Power-Packed Reader, I'm asking you to choose one over the other. Every ear. Every time.

At this stage in your face reading career, while reading yourself, please take it easy making your choice.

Or bring in a friend, and not just any friend but the slightly weird and simpatico kind of friend who is willing to help you figure out which part of each of your ears is bigger, the Inner or Outer Ear Circle (with Ear Border included appropriately).

While your friend is there, helping, use two mirrors to view each of your ears in profile. Now that's easy, checking out Ear Circles as though you were a fish with both eyes on one side. Except, oops, if you were any kind of a fish you wouldn't have ears at all. Sigh!

Tricky research sure. But once you develop the knack for comparing Ear Circle Proportions, you will never lose it.

Photographs in our Cast of Characters may help you to develop that knack. Start to compare the proportions of Inner and Outer Ear Circles on some of our Cast of Characters.

- **Inner Ear Circle Is Larger** when that person's Outer Ear Circle is relatively small. Easy to say, right? See Helene.
- Conversely, **Outer Ear Circle Is Larger** when the Inner Ear Circle is relatively smaller. After all, there is only so much ear space to go around. See Jesse's right ear.
- Or perhaps you will find **Equal Inner and Outer Ear Circle Proportions**, as with Madison.

Tip: When you are very experienced at reading Ear Circles, sometimes you will be able to discern their proportions from the front… if the person has Out-Angled Ears or it is a 3/4 camera angle.

Despite all my years of experience, I don't consider this "Sense of proportion" reliable, merely approximate.

On a real-live person, rather than a one-time photograph, you can usually find a way to peek at ears from the side. Discretely, of course.

I would never try to read Ear Circle Secrets officially without making that short journey sideways. However, I have approximated with Jesse, just to provide a likely example, since extra profile shots were not available from our Cast of Characters.

Tip: To compare Ear Circles, you aim for an approximate sense of which Ear Circle covers more space on that particular ear. For instance, how many M&Ms, laid side by side, would you need to cover Outer Ear Circle territory, then the Land of Inner Ear Circle?

Please don't use actual M&M's, Power-Packed Reader. Otherwise you might lose some in the ear hole. This would not win the same victory cheer as sinking a putt during miniature golf. Save real M&Ms for eating.

So that's settled, I hope. Approximate the size of each Ear Circle. Comparing them, are both circles about the same size? Or does one cover more candy territory?

Understanding Ear Circles

By now you may be wondering, is this face reading category worth the trouble it takes to see the data?

I think so. Actually, it's one of my favorites. Because Ear Circles Proportions reveal something fascinating about how a person sorts through reality.

Before interpreting those proportions, let's start with the significance of each of the two Ear Circles.

The context involves being human. We make reality manageable by specializing in different layers of it. (People who don't do this automatically live in a state of chronic overwhelm and may even be diagnosed with autism, developmental disorders, or other highly specialized ways to spend a lifetime here at The Learning Planet.)

Most folks, however, sort through reality in a pretty consistent manner. Usually we're consciously unaware of the sorting process, yet we do it well enough. In fact, we sort so consistently that most people assume there is but one possibility, theirs, The One True Reality.

Power-Packed Face Reader, you have the privilege of uncovering which of these "True Realities" drives Helene or Jesse or Madison. Amazing but true! Just from interpreting Ear Circle proportions!

For interpretation, first let's clarify the symbolic significance of each type of Ear Circle.

Outer Ear Circles symbolize paying attention to objective reality:

- What people say and do.
- What is measurable, like time and temperature and money.
- Who did what, when it happened, and where.
- The front section of most major newspapers attempts to report on objective reality.

Inner Ear Circles symbolize paying attention to subjective reality:

- Your emotions.
- Your theories and interpretations about what people say and do.
- Your beliefs about what people don't say and do.

- Your current belief system around religion, spirituality, psychology, sex.
- The feature section of a newspaper covers news of this sort, profiling celebrities and their Inner Ear Circle worlds. (Although this face reading term is seldom mentioned directly.) (Okay, maybe never mentioned directly.)

Now that you know the basic significance of each of your two Ear Circles, can you guess what it means when one is bigger than the other?

Interpreting Ear Circle Proportions

Most commonly, the proportion is **Equal Ear Circles**. This represents a talent for balancing inner and outer experience.

If you have this, friends may have praised you as a sympathetic listener who makes use of what you understand in a practical way.

Your only potential challenge is a lack of tolerance for the rest of humanity. Deep down they hear life differently. Until you have overcome this challenge, you may wonder what is wrong with these people.

What world do they think they are living in?

By contrast, you might have **Larger Inner Ear Circles**. Then you would fit in with many of the world's poets, artists, and philosophers.

Are you one of these wonderfully creative people? Then admit it. For you, events in objective reality tend to be metaphors.

You grow extra fast. Because when things go well you say, "Thank you, Belief System." When things go badly you say, "Belief system, help me now."

Your potential challenge? It's being too self-involved. You may not believe in "reality" much, apart from how you interpret what's happening around you.

Your current, cherished belief system had better help you if you ever work for a boss with **Larger Outer Ear Circles**, especially the VERY variety.

Nowk what if that person is you? What if Ear Circle comparisons reveal that you have Larger Outer Ear Circles?

What a talent you have. It's marvelous, being that relatively rare personification of ultra-practical.

When determined to get things done, you won't be stopped by little things like other people's personal objections.

So subjective, those are. So silly. (Seemingly.)

Admittedly, your Larger Outer Ear Circles may signal a challenge with sensitivity. Everyone has some potential challenge, of course. Regardless, you can enjoy tremendous career success because of your grip on objective reality. Practical, scientific, organized — these are just some of the compliments you may have received.

Let's Get Practical: Don't Translate Backwards from Behavior to Face Data

Recently I overheard an adorable conversation while walking down a street in London.

A young couple of lovebirds, in back of me but clearly audible, were having a very earnest conversation about Their Relationship.

Quietly Joe announced that he didn't want to hold Gladys' hand right now. He explained why, taking elaborate care not to hurt her feelings.

After a brief, tense pause, Gladys explained even more elaborately why she understood perfectly and her feelings weren't possibly hurt in the slightest.

Given where this eavesdropper was positioned on the street, I couldn't check out Ear Circle Proportions on either lovebird.

Nor did I think it would work for me to pointedly stop them both on the street and inspect their ears. This was, after all, England, The Land of Manners and Decorum.

As a professional physiognomist, could I guess that Joe had Larger Outer Ear Circles while Gladys had Larger Inner Ear Circles?

Definitely not. Plenty of factors could have been involved. The short list includes Ear Circle Proportions but also Eyebrow Shape, Lower Eyelid Curve, Eye Angles, Lipfulness, Ear Angles, Priority Areas, Cheek Proportions.

Horrors! No, "Horrors" is not a face reading category we didn't get to yet.

Horrors! is my reaction to anyone who attempts to translate backwards from a person's behavior to that individual's face data.

Oversimplifying, confusing, and ultimately disrespectful: That is my short list of why it would be foolish to do a backwards face dance.

But the simplest reason not to go there... How would you feel if this were done to you?

Yes, how would you feel if somebody took a tiny sample of your behavior — perhaps overheard while you had a bad headache and were bickering with your sweetheart — then made a decision about your character and your soul — and then went on to extrapolate how your face ought to look?

No, that would be only a more sophisticated version of the face judging that runs rampant on London streets and elsewhere. Power-Packed Reader, you deserve to do better.

Extra Special Face Data: Protruding Ear Borders

As for the rare talent of a *Protruding* Ear Border, as you know, Ear Borders mark the separation between Inner Ear Circles and Outer Ear

Circles, with a bit of a tilt that helps you to decide which way to call it, part of Outer or Inner.

The cartilage always sticks out somewhat. Well, with a Protruding Ear Border, it sticks out significantly.

By contrast, most Ear Borders just lie flat, so face readers do that special Ear Border Stare to assess whether to count it as Inner or Outer Ear Circle.

A 3-D Jumbotron Ear Border is rare. But when you find it, this symbolizes fascination with the boundaries between what is public and what is private, turning each into the other. Think Oprah.

Let's Get Practical Politically: Vote Smarter as a Face Reader

Politics is one life area where it is important to overcome the potential challenge related to your Ear Circle Proportions. Voting has very real consequences in objective reality, regardless of your innate preference for objective-subjective balance.

Fortunately, it can be relatively easy to transcend that innate preference. Politicians aim to impact objective reality. Elected officials propose legislation and vote on other people's proposals.

Therefore, you can look up what a politician has actually done, researching objectively. Then evaluate within your comfort zone, as related to Ear Circle Proportions.

So anyone *can* research responsibly before voting. But *do* you?

If you have **Equal Ear Circles**, you might go either way about paying attention to objective reality. It's situational for you.

Usually you get it right: You will pay objective attention to the everyday things that require it, while leaping into subjective reality for other important matters where inner considerations matter more.

Only what if you are used to taking only the most casual interest in politics, maybe no interest at all?

What if you have never taken voting seriously, so you ignore elections in favor of your more favored activities? Or, perhaps, you listen to news sources that make you feel good without providing two sides to a story.

Sure you are really capable in other aspects of life, since you take pride in accomplishing what matters most to you. Regarding silly politics, why would that be worthy of your attention?

In my opinion, every election matters. Don't miss a single one, Power-Packed Reader. Use your excellent innate ability to research candidates objectively. Sprinkle in some face reading. Stir. Vote!

What about your political habits if you have **Larger Outer Ear Circles**? Your potential challenge might tempt you to vote without using your heart.

For instance, you might cast a vote based on what you, personally, stand to gain financially from one candidate over another.

Ethically, voting can't be based only on personal profit. Voting is a sacred social responsibility that we citizens ignore at our peril. Voting thoughtfully, or not, is a chance to bring major shifts to objective reality. Each choice you make when voting can make or break quality of life (including subjective reality) for many people, not you alone.

Therefore, take some time every election to give the process all due respect. Preparing to cast your vote, research the human implications of a candidate's positions. What will happen to quality of life for others, not only yourself?

If you have Larger Inner Ear Circles, it's important to assess your voting habits... for a different reason entirely. Avoid basing your precious vote on subjective feelings about politicians or parties.

Before voting, can you can name three things that particular politician has done in objective reality? Have you looked at position statements from that politician?

Search engines make that easy. Unfortunately, in the Age of Internet, we can watch our favorite news sources exclusively. We can favor media that claim to present balanced views while, in reality, doing just the opposite.

Things have gotten so bad in American politics that websites are devoted to counting the lies. Prominent politicians will shrug off not being "factually accurate." Especially if you have Larger Inner Ear Circles, I urge you to find an impartial website that tracks political lies. Then take heed.

Political lies disrespect objective reality, and they're not trivial... even if you feel that all objective reality is kind of trivial.

For entertainment, or any subjective pursuit, it can work fine for you, focusing mainly on feelings. Politics is a serious exception. Before you vote, inform yourself objective reality.

How about using face reading to help choose politicians? Sure, I recommend it. But only after reading about actions taken by candidates. What are their records and their positions? How do they aim to solve problems?

Of course, face reading can help you vote smarter. At a time when politicians are expertly handled and poll-prepped and packaged and surgically altered, it has never been more important to learn who any politician authentically is.

However, I don't recommend face reading (or any form of energetic literacy) as a substitute for informing yourself about objective reality. Never fail to check facts for yourself, Power-Packed Reader. And never, ever waste your precious vote.

Chapter 13. Smiles

Let's pause for a smile interlude. Power-Packed Reader, as you become more comfortable with reading faces, I want you to avoid becoming too comfortable... with smiles.

Around this stage in your development as a physiognomist, you may find yourself getting really comfortable with zooming in for the particular face reading category of the moment.

You have stopped generalizing about the face as a whole.

Nor do you automatically get pulled into someone's expression. Excellent!

Sometimes expression or camera angle may still fool you, though. That can happen around this stage in your development, just because you see face data so much more easily than you did back in the eyebrow reading stage.

Pursuing a more sophisticated level of skill, what can help? Pay attention to **face in repose**.

Face in repose means there is no strong, or outwardly directed, facial expression.

Seek that kind of photo image. Or emphasize that kind of view with a real-live face reading subject.

Soon as a person smiles or winks or offers you a head tilt, all of the face data can change. It can change more than you might expect.

Power-Packed Reader, George from our Cast of Characters is going to demonstrate how much a smile can change face data. Just turn the page.

Smile Quiz

Compare the two views of George below, his familiar photo in repose and then this gorgeous snapshot of him smiling.

How many changes to his physical face data can you count?

George in Repose

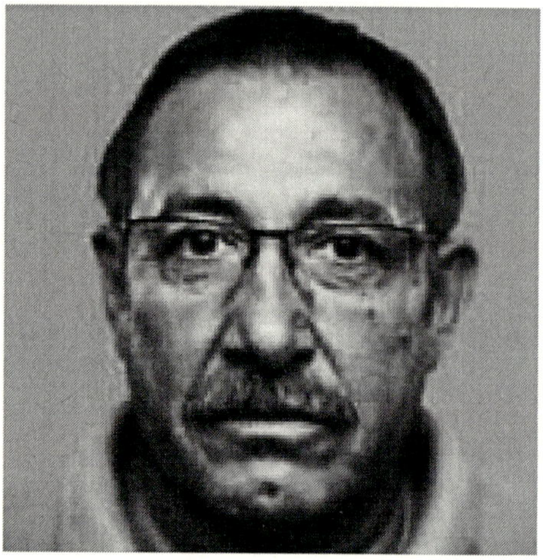

George Smiles

Smile Quiz ANSWERS

So many changes from one smile! This introductory face reading book can help you to understand all 11 of the face changes listed after George's comparison pictures.

1. Eyebrow Shape goes from Barely Angled Eyebrows to VERY Angled Eyebrows.
2. Eyebrow Height goes from Middlebrow to Highbrow.
3. Ear Angle on his left ear goes from VERY Out-Angled to even more VERY Out-Angled.
4. Wariness Index goes from 10 to 1.
5. Eye Angle on George's right eye goes from up to down.
6. Eyelid Fullness on George's right eye increases, and is no longer cut off halfway across his eye.
7. Nose Padding increases for George.
8. So does the relative size of his Nose Tip.
9. Cheek Proportions shift dramatically
10. Big Change to the Dimple situation (We'll get to that next chapter.)
11. Jaw Width changes. (More on the meaning of that later, too.)

The Problem with Reading Smiles

What's the problem with reading smiles?

For starters, the bigger a smile, the more shift to a person's face data. As a person (not as a face reader), I love how George smiles. It lights up his face.

Wow, does it ever change his face data, though! Smiles change face data far more than you might suppose.

When a smile shows something different from a face in repose, the truth of your findings will apply only when that person is acting social, putting on his best face.

Is that really how you want to know him? To me, the beauty of face reading is the depth, how it shows more than people are trying to convey socially, putting on that "Best face."

Another problem with reading smiles is that you may be led back into the separate art of reading expression. This makes it way easier to manipulate viewers than if you choose to do face reading.

Which way do you think folks try harder to appear kind, honest, gentle, generous? When they're alone, with nobody to manipulate, or when donning a fine social smile?

Even when you insist on using your skills as a face reader, smiles can complicate and distort your work.

Observing **smile structure** is a good way for face readers to avoid that.

Authentic Smiles

What is an authentic smile, anyway? This has been studied extensively, and not just by me. Body language experts often refer to a **Duchenne Smile**, thanks to the French researcher who spent a lot of time grinning. I mean, researching a certain facial expression.

Here is what happens in an authentic, Duchenne Smile:

- Lips open.
- Mouth corners go up.
- Cheeks raise.
- Crinkles develop around eyes.
- Eyes flash or twinkle.

Many smiles flunk the Duchenne standard. Not George's. It's for real.

If a real smile, like George's, distorts his face data, how about a semi-smile, a slightly fake smile, etc.?

What would a face reader notice about them, in contrast to an expression reader?

How to Interpret a Smile

If you really want to interpret a smiling face, as a face reader, I can't stop you.

Add this factor to your interpretation, however. A face in repose reveals character in the most authentic form available to any physiognomist.

Soon as a person smiles, interpretation of everything differs. You're interpreting that person in a primarily social context.

George, for instance: When he warms up to friends, he shows himself with that gorgeous big smile. He becomes that kind of person.

When he is in a good mood, at least. Or thinking expansively.

But how about all George's other moods and contexts for living?

For instance, how does George deal with money when nobody is looking? How close does he get emotionally to his girlfriend when she is not in the same room as him, grinning back?

I won't call it a complete waste of time, reading faces on folks who are smiling. I just advise you to do other things first.

Read auras. Learn to do skilled empath merge, if you can, for the very most in-depth knowledge.

Otherwise simply do a whole lot more face reading. On those folks when they aren't smiling.

Learn to Detect Fake Smiles

Several members of our Cast of Characters are smiling, not just George. However, every one of them except George is doing a fake smile at best.

That's why I allowed these particular photos to be included in our official Cast of Characters. It wasn't easy, I assure you, finding appropriate photographs for this honor. I spent hours choosing among the pictures available. Eventually I was able to find many acceptable photographs for our purposes.

Acceptable?

Yes, acceptable. Because the smiles would seem pleasant to you (and other readers) at the start of our book.

Living today, all of us are soooooo used to seeing smiling faces in ads, Internet photos, TV, etc. To have supplied only faces in repose would have turned you off subconsciously and, maybe, consciously too.

So I provided you with a mix. So many of our Cast of Characters have been wearing fake smiles. Have you noticed?

Let's check out every one of those smiles, just to develop your eye. Remember the five points on our checklist, all five required for a Duchenne Smile?

Lips part, mouth corners raise up, cheeks lift, eyes crinkle and flash. All heaven breaks loose!

All the folks in our photos are models. Maybe you have guessed this already about our Cast of Characters. (You know, in addition to their being your neighbor, your third grade teacher, etc., as described in Chapter 6.)

Well, models often practice posing with a fake smile. Why? It keeps them looking friendly by keeping their eyes large and un-crinkly.

Take a good look from this perspective. Who scores points for what?

- **Rowan** opens her mouth. 1 Smile Point.
- **Joyce** opens her lips, then allows mouth corners go partly up. 1 1/2 Smile Points.
- **Kathryn** manages to loosen up her mouth a tad. 1/2 Smile Point.
- **Shirley** is really an accomplished expert at fake smiling. Lips open, mouth corners go up. Instead of raising cheeks, she squishes her dimples extra hard, then crinkles up her eyes just a bit. 2 1/2 Smile Points.
- **Valerie** opens lips, raises mouth corners slightly. 1 1/2 Smile Points.
- **Ava** reveals four teeth. 1/4 Smile Point.
- **Annette** twirls up her mouth corners very slightly, like a pinwheel on a day with no breeze. 1/8 Smile Point.

How about our guys?

- **Matt** barely lifts up the left corner of his mouth. So cool! 1/8 Smile Point.
- **Fred** opens his mouth but can't raise up the corners. (Maybe too heavy?) 1 Smile Point.
- **Jesse** isn't going to let a smile keep his eyes from looking way big and sumptuous. No way. Therefore, 0 Smile Points.
- **Wayne** lifts up mouth corners somehow. 1 Smile Point.
- **Oliver** achieves a petite-style mouth corner lift, nearly acrobatic in its restraint. 1/4 Smile Point.
- **Alexander**, smile for no good reason? You kidding? 0 Smile Points.
- **Lloyd** digs in with his mouth, cheeks, and eyes as if to say, "What me, smile?" 0 Smile Points.
- **Cliff** twists his mouth corners upward a bit before doing the really exciting thing to him right now, moving his head. 0 Smile Points.
- And, of course, we can enjoy **George** in our original Cast of Characters photograph, bravely posed with 0 Smile Points, while his smiling photo wins him all 5 Smile Points.

Can you spot a real smile in profile?

Sure. Only don't expect to find one from our carefully posed models. Real smiles raise up cheeks and just might crinkle a nose or change its proportions (as you have seen with George). Horrors!

- **Madison** makes no attempt to smile, so she receives the appropriate smile score, 0 Smile Points.
- **Gary**? Likewise! 0 Smile Points.
- **Helene** manages to part her lips slightly. Cute. 1/2 Smile Point.
- **Anthony** provides a rather adorable smile for a profile shot, definitely smirking one mouth corner upwards. 1 Smile Point.

Moving past fake expressions, viewing the physical face as it is, can help you so much reading faces. Should you ever feel confused about the degree of smile in a photo, copy the expression in front of a mirror.

Duchenne or not? Part of the face in repose or not? Being able to tell the difference helps you to employ the power of face reading.

Chapter 14. Cheeks

Do your cheeks show you are powerful? Hello! Only it's a matter of how, not if. The varied cheek categories reveal different talents for power.

Considering power, what do you really want: Is it political clout? High social status?

Go for it!

Hey, you can even use your power gifts to joust, except that the required equipment is hard to come by these days. At least the cheek supplies you have been issued are totally up-to-date and of the very finest quality.

You will need them, of course. This chapter reveals the splendor of your cheeks.

Dimples

Everybody loves cheek dimples. Ever wonder why?

Sure makes sense when you know the significance of this cheek category. But before we delve into these tiny face caverns, let's learn to distinguish the four major kinds of dimple.

What will the mirror reveal about you? At times like this, the thrill of face reading can rival the power of face reading! To investigate, team up with your mirror to use this three-part sequence developed especially for Dimple Detective Work.

- Do you find dimple activity when your face is in repose? Is there a circle or curvy line on your cheek?
- Flash out your biggest smile and look again, face still on the level. Do you see dimples now? Maybe one dimple? (Often dimples are often positioned on one side of the face only.)
- Now look once more. No smile, face on the level. Yoo-hoo, dimples?

Whatever you did or didn't find, no worries. Your face is perfect as a reflection of your soul.

Soon enough, we'll get to the advantages of having (or not having) dimples. Meanwhile, have you ever noticed the four different varieties of cheek dimples?

- **Peekaboo Dimples** have a circular shape that pops out with a smile, disappearing before and afterwards. Rowan has one on her left cheek.
- **Permanent Dimples** rivet attention, regardless of whether or not you happen to be smiling. Circular like the Peekaboo variety, these dimples work full-time. If you have one or two, it showed during all three steps of the research you just completed. Shirley, for instance, always shows those cute little circles on each cheek, whether smiling, fake-smiling, daydreaming, anything.
- **Powerline Dimples** look more like a crease than a circle. Such dimples appear when you smile then vanish. Not circular, these dimples are shaped more like parentheses.

((Some faces even have a couple of parallel Powerline Dimples on a cheek.))

(Even one of these line-like dimples would qualify you as a Powerline Dimple Owner.)

(((Should you have two or more on one cheek, consider that you have a VERY version of Powerline Dimples.)))

See George for an example, but note that his dimples display only when he is smiling. In other words, when he presents himself in public, playing his social part in his social group.

Of course, a cheek could have creases or wrinkles that don't count as powerline dimples because they're on your face all the time. For a grand example, find a photograph of the great artist Georgia O'Keefe. In her later years, both cheeks were gloriously cross-hatched with lines.

- With **No Cheek Dimples**, you will simply see perfectly fine cheek contours ***!— unpunctuated --!***

Everyone without cheek dimples could be considered as a VERY regarding the No Cheek Dimple face data. Such as Ava, Wayne, Madison.

Interpreting Dimples

Cheek Dimples are an asset for charm, with the type of charm related to the type of dimple.

Peekaboo Dimples symbolize talent for helping others to laugh. When situations grow tense, you see the funny side, then make a wisecrack to break the tension.

Deservedly, this type of sanity can make you popular. Nothing manipulative about that joking behavior, either. Your funny bone is tickled. So, naturally, you make the sarcastic comment, joke, or whatever.

Notice, we may have just solved the mystery of where the funny bone is located. For you with a Peekaboo Dimple, it's right on your cheek.

Your potential challenge? Peekaboo Dimple wearers, though popular, may not be taken as seriously as their sterner-cheeked friends.

That challenge goes triple if you are female and attractive. "She's so cute. Really, isn't she adorable? Such fun to have around the office. Shame that her brain is so tiny."

Power-Packed Reader, do you think it sounds intense, having Peekaboo Dimples? That's nothing compared to the intense talent-and-challenge combo with **Permanent Dimples**.

Your willingness to charm others seldom goes away, enduring beyond all reasonable expectation, much like the smile of the Cheshire Cat in Alice in Wonderland.

Your personality prognosis is that you will win love more easily than others but may also have more trouble earning trust.

Trust is just part of your potential challenge, unfortunately. The more serious problem involves becoming a professional charmer.

The job is so tempting. If you have one or two Permanent Dimples, ever since childhood, haven't you been praised for extra cuteness? You know, being told things like, "You are just so adorable."

Unlike those with Peekaboo Dimples, your highly visible emblem of cuteness never goes away.

During your growing up years and, definitely after you turned 18 (the age at which you became officially eligible for face reading, of course), you surely figured out that, compared to others, *you are a Prince or Princess Charming.*

You might profit as a celebrity because show business rewards performers with dimples. Think of Betty White's career, for instance: Still sought after and adorable at age 90, with Permanent Dimples intact.

What about living as a regular person, not a celebrity? How do you adjust to being so obviously adorable?

Overcoming that potential challenge requires that you stop dwelling on all that adorableness.

Overcoming also demands that you avoid manipulating people just because you can get away with it. Instead, you actively choose to earn popularity in the ways that other folks do, with qualities like integrity, loyalty, and dependability.

However, the Permanent Dimple challenge can prove irresistible. For a while, at least. You might want to find out what you can get away with. So you might intentionally play up the charm factor, acting self-consciously popular.

This can work, if you have Permanent Dimples. You can enjoy a manipulative sort of popularity. Only it might ring hollow, as if you stayed forever in high school. If that ever bothers you, of course, you can overcome the Permanent Dimple challenge. Plus you still get to keep your cute dimples!

A **Powerline Dimple** embodies graciousness. When you hold a position of power, what does your manner suggest? Instead of flaunting your one-up position, you help your social inferiors to feel good. This debonair style, downplaying your specialness, can help you win friends and influence owners of faces.

Your potential challenge? Just a four-letter word: Fake.

Regarding that humility, you could just be pretending. And, really, who's to know?

Only you, on the inside. Plus God, Santa Claus, and everyone who gets to know you long enough to find out the truth....

Until that challenge is overcome. Which would be another inside job.

So, how do you manage charm if you are among the **No Cheek Dimple** majority of human beings? Extra allure isn't available but you still can win friends and influence owners of faces.

Speech and action add up to reputation. So does auric modeling, the message you broadcast subconsciously to everyone you ever meet.

Your talent with No Cheek Dimples? It's being yourself without the social padding of obvious, effortless charm.

Your potential challenge? The same.

Sure it is possible to endure life without a great deal of social padding. That is the glorious opportunity for people with No Cheek Dimples.

Cheek Prominence

Cheek Prominence is a 3-D category, referring to how far cheeks stick out.

- At one extreme stand **Prominent Cheeks**, eye-popping physical structures that grab attention and make onlookers go, "Wow!" See Joyce, Rowan, Annette,
- Most people, by far, have **Modest Cheek Prominence**. Those round apples on the face are more like dried apples: Quite flat. Alexander provides our first example of many. Just look through our Cast of Characters.

Finding Modest Cheek Prominence doesn't make most physiognomists say anything comparable to "Wow!"

You are unlikely to say — or notice — much at all. Not usually. Not unless you are purposely looking for Modest Cheek Prominence (like right now).

Chances are, you will find it way challenging to find any part of your cheek that sticks out much from the rest of the face. At most, you might be moved to say, "Huh?"

Well, consider that a victory cry. It means that you have identified Modest Cheek Prominence.

Interpreting Cheek Prominence

The meaning of this category may be easy for you to guess. Cheeks in general contain categories about personal style with power. And a practical definition of power is saying and doing things, in objective reality, among other people, in order to get what you want.

If that's power, what do you think it means when somebody's power area (cheeks) are exceptionally prominent? (Or not.)

Prominent Cheeks correspond to a high profile style of leadership. The personality, not just the cheeks, can stick out in a crowd.

Your potential challenge? Oh, the potential jealousy!

If you have those cheeks, you have an intense way of pursuing your goals. Among other people, you are more likely to speak up, to take action, even "Take up arms against a sea of troubles and, by opposing, end them."

Those words, famously spoken by Hamlet, were easier said than done. Language snobs might explain his inaction by the grotesque mixed metaphor. Dramatists might adore the nuances of pain acted out by The Confused Prince of Denmark.

While we face readers might simply say to the character:

"Dude, stop trying so hard to act as though you have Prominent Cheeks. You are like most people. Get over yourself, with the Modest Cheek Prominence. Find some un-dramatic way to seek vengeance. You know, like unfriending your stepmom on Facebook."

Modest Cheek Prominence does signify power styles that are less "in your face." Maybe you collaborate with others to get your way. Only you collaborate relatively quietly, not drawing so much attention to yourself.

Maybe your power style involves asking other folks for opinions and advice. Call it humility or simply intelligence, this encourages people to trust you.

Your potential challenge? If you value certain kinds of social prestige over getting real-life results, you may undervalue what you really accomplish. Maybe it's time to set some new standards for what you consider important.

Let's Get Practical: Develop More Inner Power

How about **inner power**? Students of metaphysics know that obvious displays of power tell only half the story. Human beings have access to masculine energy and feminine energy, both.

Usually men have 60% masculine energy and 40% feminine energy.

While women typically have the reverse.

Everyone definitely has a full 100%, whatever the personal ratio.

Personal power for **Masculine Energy** shows outwardly, in speech and action. You say and do whatever it takes to get results in objective reality.

While the power of **Feminine Energy** is more about inner power, subjective life, being. Who you are inside? What you feel and think and believe? This attracts what you desire.

Does Cheek Prominence inform you about a person's inner power, or feminine energy? Nope.

But remember, power doesn't have to show only in cheek characteristics. Qualities of inner power express themselves all over the face. That includes some categories we have read already, such as Ear Circle Proportions. Larger Inner Ear Circles correlate to a form of inner power, right? Think about it.

One way to grow as a face reader is to relax about how important any one category on the face might seem. Definitely, cheeks contain categories about social power. Yet, if you are reading a face for personal power, you can find more power-related face data in every single major facial feature.

Plus, of course, we're just getting started with physiognomy characteristics within cheeks.

Here's my advice. At this stage in your face reading career, don't make any one item of face data the big make-or-break Big Cheese among all face parts. For one thing, human faces are not made out of cheese.

If you have Modest Cheek Prominence, rather than the sticky-out kind:

- You still can have a fabulous career.
- You still can earn a good income and save money wisely.
- You still can win friends and influence owners of faces.
- You still can pursue your heart's desire in life, working hard and accomplishing real-time results.
- You still can have your 15 minutes (or more) of fame.

Keep reading the Secrets and you will find new ways that you, personally, can achieve all this and more. Prepare to get results in your way, not somebody else's way.

Whether or not your personality displays an obvious kind of social flash for "Look at me, everyone," that counts as just one possible, obvious, personal style. It is one talent that some people have, just one facet of power, correlating with the Prominent Cheeks power style.

Power-Packed Reader, enjoy owning that larger concept. You are still learning how to read faces, and I'll bet you are doing beautifully. Skimmers don't make it as far as the cheek chapter.

Well, now that you have come this far, don't over-generalize about any one facial characteristic, not even a VERY.

Instead, practice reading one category of face data at a time. With interpretation, remind yourself as needed which category you are reading. That is your context.

Your context for interpreting Cheek Prominence, or any other item of face data never needs to be "Make-or-break everything."

Putting all the bits of info together shows your skill, reading faces. You can get there, Power-Packed Reader. You can become a fully skilled physiognomist. It just takes some patience.

Doing justice to the sacred spiritual alphabet called "The face" is exactly the opposite of books like "*The Art of Speed Reading People*" or "*Assertiveness Training and How to Instantly Read People.*" Glad you are reading this one. More long-term power to you!

Cheek Padding

Even kids past the age of four hate it when Granny comes over, pinches a wad of cheek and says something like:

"Aren't you the sweetsiest-neetsiest, cutsie-wootsiest little love boffin?"

Well after your cheek pinching years, cheek flesh still poses a problem — at least if you are sensitive about America's most dreaded condition. Would that be tooth decay, moral decay, lack of fulfilling your potential in life, or an outright disease?

Heck no. We're scared to be fat. For so many folks, flesh on the face means that automatically the rest of that person must be fat.

Well, surprise! The Cheek Padding category isn't necessarily related to obesity, not physically and not inwardly. When a figure grows fuller, the face may not, and vice versa.

I have read skinny clients with big Cheek Padding (like Matt), slender clients with Moderately Large Cheek Padding (like Ava), and hefty clients with small cheek padding (like George).

Sometimes extra weight goes onto the face, while other times it doesn't. Sometimes extra weight goes onto the face and *accentuates* Cheek Prominence. Other times, weight pads those cheeks, *removing* Cheek Prominence.

However Cheek Padding configures on a face, guess what? For face readers, this isn't about "fat" but "meaning."

Once you calm down about this emotionally-charged face data, you are ready to start reading the Cheek Padding category.

Now, how can you tell how you rate, Cheek Padding-wise? So far, we have ruled out measuring the flab at your waist and other points south. Go directly to one of your upper cheeks (i.e., above your waist). Grab hold like a besotted grandma and pinch away.

Then behold that chunk of flesh in the mirror.

- If it's a lot, yes, you have **Big Cheek Padding**. See Matt, Joyce, Rowan,
- If the effort hurts and, perhaps, those grabbing fingers don't pull away at much flesh, admit it. Either you do a sadistic imitation of Granny or you have **Small Cheek Padding**. See Ava. While Alexander has a VERY version.
- Most folks have **Moderate Cheek Padding**. Hey, don't bother to read it. For one thing, you'll turn all squinty face, which is not what this professional physiognomists recommends.

Either you notice big-deal Cheek Padding or lean-faced "Where's the meat?" Otherwise, nearly everyone's face falls into that moderate Paddington-Bear-Without-Cheeks-middle-ground. And if the meaning of Moderate Cheek Padding were a big deal, I would say, "Squint away." But it's not.

So check out as many of the following examples as you need to calm down about this choice within the Cheek Padding category. Ignore the Moderate Cheek Padding belonging to faces of Cliff, George, Fred, Valerie, Oliver.

Interpreting Cheek Padding

You could call Cheek Padding "Power cushions." The softer and fluffier your cushions, the less threatened others feel by your power plays.

Big Cheek Padding corresponds to a talent for gaining support, loads of support from others for your team-building efforts. The larger your power cushions, the more support you tend to receive. So you just might want to rejoice in that.

Big Cheek Padding marks a conciliatory leadership style, making everyone on the team feel important.

Your potential challenge? Say that it is a glorious Sunday afternoon. You would love to be outdoors, doing any one of a dozen delightful things. Only nooooooooooo.

There you are indoors, sitting politely and trying not to grimace. Because you are attending a friend's daughter's flute recital.

This young musician isn't exactly talented. Neither are any of the kids you hear during this music lesson ordeal. And that friend who invited you, she isn't even that close a friend.

Only you found it so hard to say no. Because, until this Cheek Padding challenge is overcome, you would generally find it difficult to say no.

That agreeable attitude of yours is the underlying cause of receiving so much social support. You like to give, not just get.

However, until you overcome the challenge corresponding to Big Cheek Padding, you may not be doing a super-great job, socially, at balancing give and take. Well, take heart, for starters. You really can learn to say no when it pleases you, yet remain a good friend.

Small Cheek Padding reveals a completely different style with power. Socially you are self-reliant. You may even thrive on going it alone. Even if others help you sometimes, you don't wait for that; you get started just fine on your own.

Well, more power to you! Specifically more Small Cheek Padding power!

Your potential challenge? With those tiny power cushions, you may have difficulty with delegation, probably because you believe deep down that you can do a better job than anyone else.

Actually, you are probably right. Still you might want to learn how to delegate.

What are High Cheekbones? Is that a kind of cheek padding?

Not necessarily. You are moving into the category of Cheek Emphasis, which can be tricky to see at first. But I know you will be up to it. Or down to it. Or sideways....

Cheek Emphasis

Sometimes cheeks show a definite emphasis. Often they don't. Having wisdom to tell the difference, and maintain serenity, is your latest challenge as a face reader.

Reading Cheek Emphasis means discerning whether or not somebody's cheeks stick out a great deal in one area when compared with the rest of that person's cheeks. If you do find that kind of emphasis, where is it?

To read this category, answer this question: "Where, if anywhere, do this person's cheeks stick out most?"

Take a deep breath before you hoist up your mirror. Regardless of what you find, you will remain a Power-Packed Face Reader.

Read one cheek at a time, of course. View with a 3-D kind of emphasis.

- Does the cheek you're inspecting have its greatest padding beneath the eye sockets? In that case the person has **High Cheek Emphasis**. See Jesse.
- Or does extra fullness incline towards the opposite direction? Some cheeks bulge out amazingly far down the face, closer to the mouth than the eyes. I call that **Low Cheek Emphasis**. See Annette.
- Another possibility is **Far-Set Cheeks**, most commonly found when the cheeks are also prominent and unpadded. Yes, these are the same cheeks that folks who aren't yet face readers mistakenly

call "High Cheekbones." But take a closer look. See Rowan's left cheek, for instance.

- Or you could be blessed with **Close-Set Cheeks**, where the greatest fullness is near the nose. See Valerie's left cheek.
- Having a hard time finding any Cheek Emphasis? For most people, the mysterious name for what you're encountering now is "**No Cheek Emphasis**."

That's short for "No significant, easy to find, Cheek Emphasis." As you may remember, reading the Secrets does not require that you use equipment like a magnifying glass or squinting.

From our Cast of Characters, who has No Cheek Emphasis? Alexander, definitely.

Maybe you're wondering, do cheeks stick out extra because of bones or padding or muscles or what?

Anything counts, except chewing gum wadded inside the mouth. As a face reader, you are not in biology class, dissecting. Simply notice if any cheek area has bigger bulgy-something compared to the rest of that person's face.

Interpreting Cheek Emphasis

Cheek Emphasis reveals the thrust of a person's power. Oomph shows in different directions, figuratively as well as literally. In certain life situations, those with a particular Cheek Emphasis are especially likely to succeed.

High Cheek Emphasis may be sought after in popular lore, but don't be too eager to go for cheek implants. The corresponding talent can be hard to live with.

With these cheeks, you use all available clout to fight for your values. If someone you know, socially or at work, is doing things you believe are wrong, Pow! You will say so.

That scolding or screaming or legal action may surprise you just as much as others. This gift of yours might contradict loads of other components of personal style. You might have loads of face reading data suggesting that normally you just hate conflict.

With this Cheek Emphasis, you stand up for your ethical values. Even if normally you wouldn't say "Boo" to a goose. But some situations aren't just any old goose. The perpetrator could be a peeping tomcat in your neighborhood or some loon stealing paper clips from the office.

On behalf of society, I commend your honesty, your having social standards that won't quit, your courage. Every culture needs some brave souls who will take a stand for what's right.

Your potential challenge? Don't expect to be thanked by anyone. Quite the opposite.

Even when legally protected, business whistleblowers can have a hard time. Ethical spunk can make for some tough consequences. But would you choose otherwise than to stick up for what's right? I hope not.

What if your Cheek Emphasis lies at the opposite extreme, so you have **Low Cheek Emphasis**? Then you're likely to display a differently beautiful characteristic, a certain kind of tolerance. Graciously you allow other people to make their own choices.

By the way, this doesn't mean you have no morals yourself. It's more that you figure, here on The Learning Planet, the whole point is learning. Therefore, you will advise people you know about what might help them. Afterwards you let go.

Deep down you believe that choices are personal, not to be thrust upon anyone.

Your potential challenge? Enabling.

Besides, there is such a thing as having too much patience with people in your life who keep making the same mistake over and over again.

Far-Set Cheeks are relatively rare, conveying the potential to accomplish something long-term and important, a goal that requires the persistent use of personal power.

Your commitment, loyalty and strength of character can help in support of a big cause, even if work toward that noble cause takes years.

Think Nelson Mandela or Clara Barton. History counts 27 years for Mandela, in and out of South African prisons, fighting to end apartheid. For Clara Barton, long-term courage meant 20 years between her first tending to wounded soldiers to many years after the Civil War, when the American Red Cross finally gained official standing.

History or no history, acknowledge yourself. If you have Far-Set Cheeks, you also possess enduring courage that will only grow stronger over time. Your magnificent leadership gift is especially pronounced if your cheeks are also prominent and unpadded, as in the cases of Nelson Mandela and Clara Barton. Another example is Mother Teresa of Calcutta.

Your potential challenge with Far-Set Cheeks? If you can't find a cause to work for, your life will feel empty.

Or, to be more precise, since everybody can have a challenge that sounds pretty similar… with Far-Set Cheeks, if you cannot find a worthwhile cause, your life will feel way more empty, unsatisfying, and hollow than it would feel for other people if, similarly, they were unable to find a worthwhile cause.

Weirdly comforting for you to know: Everyman's form of misery is smaller than what you would show on a Pain O'Meter that measured your anguish with Far-Set Cheeks.

My advice, if you haven't yet overcome this challenge? First, you might need to re-define "Cause."

"Cause" can mean political or social activity. Or "Cause" could involve handling day-to-day problems for years, raising an autistic child or dealing with your own severe health problem. Angels and saints in human form may not give themselves credit for what counts spiritually as a noble cause.

For inspiration, it might be useful to remember the words of Mother Teresa of Calcutta. When helping her charges, she referred to them as "God in his distressing disguise."

Mother Teresa helped so many people. Whereas you might be helping just one very difficult and annoying person. That counts, even if you will never be canonized by the Catholic church.

However, my second piece of advice applies to you Far-Set Cheekers who still don't feel that you have found a cause.

Just pick something. Choose any cause that seems reasonably worthwhile, any project where you might make a reasonable contribution. The momentum will follow.

Close-Set Cheeks relate to an altogether different talent. If you have such cheeks, admit how great you are at handling life's short-term emergencies.

Maybe you have never admired (or even noticed) this emphasis to your physical cheeks. But aren't you proud of how well you perform under pressure? When there's a crisis, you are the one who will come through every time.

What is the related challenge? Avoid putting yourself in situations where you will have to use this ability. Just because you come through every time doesn't mean that high-pressure effort is good for you.

Health can suffer, long-term, if you keep burning yourself out short-term.

No Cheek Emphasis doesn't mean you lack physical cheeks. Neither does the absence of obvious Cheek Emphasis mean that you lack talent. You are reading the Secrets, remember?

Your talent with this rather common face data signifies a natural versatility with power circuits. You are not especially prone to do just one of the specialized uses of power that you have read about with this cheek category.

As needed, you can use any power play, surprising everyone like a Jewish magician who pulls a rabbi out of a hat.

Free will being what it is — the most powerful force in human life, for power or anything else — anybody can muster up needed power characteristics and make them work. However, that can take huge resolve and determined follow-through.

Except for you, of course, wonderful you with the wonderful No Cheek Emphasis! You find it relatively easy to pick and choose how to muster big power. You are a situational power packer.

Your potential challenge? Only that little thing, a lack of tolerance for the rest of humanity. Until you have overcome this particular challenge, it may drive you crazy: What is wrong with sillies like Jesse, Valerie, etc.? Why can't they be "normal" and "perfect"?

You know, "Just like me."

Extra Special Face Data: High Cheekbones

"High Cheekbones" is one of the garbage terms of unofficial face reading. People can use "High Cheekbones" to mean everything from Prominent Cheeks to Unpadded Cheeks to overall attractiveness.

Bringing in ethnic stereotypes full force, some will say High Cheekbones come from being Native American or Mongolian — but they might as well say being from Peoria or The Bronx or any other place under the moon, as if that caused a person's face data.

Save conversations like that for gossip, please. Unless you are a physical anthropologist.

Today's physical anthropologists agree that all of us live in a melting pot world. **Ethnic purity** works for those nostalgic for bygone days, lovers of certain kinds of fantasy, and political wackos. Otherwise, question the notion.

This is the gist of what physical anthropologists will tell you. Admittedly they won't necessarily use the term "Political wacko." And you might find the occasional anthropologist who adamantly defends labels like "Caucasian," perhaps while staunchly maintaining that there is no global warming.

Rather than dwelling on ethnic stereotypes, or emphasizing bone structures on cheeks or other face parts, guess what? This physiognomist prefers to look at emphasis, where one part of the face sticks out more than other parts. Flesh or fat on the face matters way more than innate bone structure.

Emphasis is one of the main ways that free will sculpts the human face, which I consider a sacred spiritual symbol of each adult's soul.

Proportions within a face convey more than mere skeletal structure. The latter could be linked quite clearly to heredity. The former? It shows in all the free willish shifts to a face, inscribed with flesh and blood.

Back at the example of Mother Teresa of Calcutta, she had High Cheekbones but the emphasis of her cheeks wasn't high but far-set.

To see more, check out the face reading of her at my blog. Or go online to find images until you can see her from a good, face reader's straight-on, camera angle.

And the next time you're tempted to think of High Cheekbones, ask yourself, which is it? Are you viewing Cheek Emphasis, Cheek Padding, or Cheek Prominence?

As a result of your asking, the face data will be seen more clearly and, with that, Power-Packed Reader, your readings will become more informative.

Let's Get Practical: Setting Deadlines

If you are a manager, or self-employed, here is a practical way to use face reading. Take Cheek Emphasis into account when setting deadlines.

This approach will work especially well with employees who have either Close-Set Cheeks or Far-Set Cheeks.

Leave the three-year or thirty-year causes to your Far-Set Cheeked, long-term runners.

Give the three-day assignments to your sprinters with the Close-Set Cheeks.

For everyone else you manage, apportion tasks, deadlines, and consequences into more moderate segments. Set weekly goals, for instance.

A smart manager takes into consideration what each person does best. Nobody on the job really needs to be just like you. Except you.

Cheek Proportions

"Prominence-shominence" you may have muttered, staring at the mirror in vain, as you searched for the facial equivalent of mountain peaks.

As for Cheek Padding and Cheek Emphasis, yours may be neither here nor there. But not to worry. You definitely have readable Cheek Proportions, most vital among all cheek categories.

The term "Cheek Proportions" refers to the horizontal proportions of your face. Using cheeks as a reference point, which part of your face is widest?

Power-Packed Reader, this category is going to be fun. Not only does everyone have interesting Cheek Proportions. Often a person has two very different versions, one for each side of the face.

To see the data clearly, examine each side of your face separately. You may find it helpful to use a sheet of blank paper to cover up half of your face at a time.

And remember not to smile, as this distorts Cheek Proportions.

While staring at your reflection, you might ask, "Mirror, mirror on the wall, where is my Face Width greatest of all?"

If a voice from the mirror answers you, watch out. You are trapped in a fairy tale. Make a run for it!

- More likely, your own voice will answer. Perhaps it will say you have **Cheeks Widest**, where your face thins out below the cheekbones. See Joyce. A VERY version belongs to Rowan.
- By contrast, **Under-Cheeks Widest** means the opposite. On the way down past the cheekbones, your face grows wider. See the right half of Jesse's face.

- **Forehead Widest** is the relatively rare kind of proportion that is widest at the forehead. Cheeks don't look especially wide because the top of your head is even wider. See Valerie, plus the right side of Lloyd's face. Who VERY much has Forehead Widest? Kathryn.
- **Even Cheek Proportions** are the most common finding in this category. Is the width of your face pretty even, going from cheek to jawline?
  For this to be the case, it doesn't matter whether the overall width is narrow or wide. Either way, the width stays constant. See the left half of Lloyds face, the right half of Fred's face, the left half of Oliver's face. And see Annette for a VERY example on both sides.

Interpreting Cheek Proportions

First a confession. As a practicing physiognomist I seldom use the names I just taught you. Instead I prefer certain nicknames. For years I have referred to each of these four cheek proportions by a nickname because, really, how fun is it to peg somebody as "Anything-Widest"?

Seeing Cheek Proportion requires a certain sophistication. It's no accident that I have waited until now to teach you this category. Given how much effort you have made so far, training your eyes, the least you deserve is being stuck with clunky names like "Under Cheeks Widest."

So why didn't I offer up my favorite names initially? They give strong clues to meaning. However, Power-Packed Reader, you have dispassionately observed your face data. You are ready. Now I can share my pet names along with their full interpretations.

The Cheek Proportions category reveals your personal style with leadership, how you attempt to get what you want from other people.

Everybody has a talent for leadership, at least when defined in this way. Sure enough, each variation of Cheek Proportions signifies a personal style that can lead to greatness.

My nickname for Cheeks Widest is **Leader-Like Cheeks**. This cheek style signifies a talent for acting "like a leader."

Notice those quotation marks? Acting "like a leader" is meant to convey irony, since there are plenty of other effective ways of being a leader in addition to this one. (Personal styles that we will cover soon, actually.)

Power-Packed Reader, learning about Cheek Proportions can help you to debunk a common misunderstanding. So often, people assume that true leadership means one thing only: A highly visible, aggressive, in-your-face, interpersonal style.

Sure, that kind of style shows in physiognomy. It correlates with the biggest cheeks possible: The most prominent, the least padded, and definitely the widest part of a face.

Even then, note that leadership oomphies don't mean the same thing as how a person *speaks*. Therefore, verbal leadership — persuasive and effective speech — differs from claiming leadership status in real life. The latter requires action, social skills, taking responsibility.

Later you will learn about mouth categories, which will refine your appreciation for chit-chat compared to the cheeky reality of what a person actually *does*.

Although common, it's silly to mistake tough talk for leadership that walks the talk. Even more ridiculous is believing that obvious standing out in the crowd is the only form of true leadership.

Don't worry about your leadership potential, then, as we keep on interpreting the Cheek Proportion Category. Every other power style we consider can be just as effective as the Leader-Like style that proclaims, "Here I am, the big cheese."

Wise physiognomists aren't fooled by appearances, physically or socially. This doesn't mean we ignore appearances. Instead we look through them, seeking a bigger truth.

Granted, you're fortunate if you have Leader-Like Cheeks. You will always have an advantage when it comes to making a memorable first impression.

The talent registers subconsciously, like any face reading data. With Leader-Like Cheeks, you will be considered a natural leader. It's almost comical how this can work. If you are in this category, you don't have to say a word. Followers will find you regardless. Somehow people sense that you take responsibility; you'll do the work.

Your potential challenge? There you are, say, at a meeting of your favorite club. Nominations are being taken for president — a position of responsibility that you have never sought. You have barely been paying attention, way more busy dreaming about a special relationship. Yet suddenly, heads turn. Fingers point and faces nod and are you ever in the spotlight!

Dealing with that kind of unsought attention can, indeed, be a challenge.

Some leader-like folks welcome their talent for commanding attention; others may spend years fighting it. Frankly, you may as well face it/cheek it.

Should you possess VERY Leader-Like Cheeks, nothing short of a bag over your head will prevent your facially broadcasting a commanding presence. Even with the bag, I might add, your aura probably shows the same thing. However, a bag over your head could act as a pretty effective deterrent to unwanted presidencies.

Under-Cheeks Widest are associated with a contrasting leadership strength, the **Pacifist Power Style**. If you have this, have you noticed? The longer people know you, the more they respect you. Also they have the cutest way of showing it. They will dump their problems on you. It's as though you have become an honorary mother.

Mothers, you know how young children will wait until mommy appears before they vomit all over her nice fresh shirt. Definitely a compliment!

Mommy or not, take it as a cosmic compliment when you have the Pacifist Power Style. Even strangers will approach you with their troubles. Grousing and grumbling — though usually not vomiting — these folks will expect you to listen.

Remember, please, to take this as a compliment. People know you can handle their grumbling because, for any group to which you belong, part of your leadership talent is that you are the stabilizing force, the most mature grownup, the rock.

What is your particular way of using that talent, when called upon? Maybe you will extend a hug or a sympathetic ear. Maybe you'll make a sarcastic remark, which will be gobbled up like candy.

Eventually, the grumblers will leave. Radiant smiles may shine upon their faces. Their hearts will be lighter, their memories hold an ever deepening respect for you.

Gee, can you guess one potential challenge with having that Pacifist Power Style?

Maybe you would like a vacation from receiving all that wonderful respect.

But there's an additional potential challenge. What happens when *you* are the one who needs to dump? Folks with the Pacifist Power Style care so deeply about keeping harmony in relationships. Therefore, you may be assertiveness-challenged. Here's an example:

Suppose that you sell chairs at a Bad Back Store. When your best customer slaps you on the back, not knowing that you happen to have back problems, your first reaction is to say, "Lay off. That hurts." But that might mean hurt feelings, even hurt business. So you suffer in silence.

Next time this customer slaps you on the back, you grit your teeth a tad harder but still say nothing. Why rock the boat?

This habit of your customer's may continue for years, with a growing annoyance on your part. Finally the day comes when you simply lose it. Pat! goes the customer. Pow! go you.

Explosions like these are inevitable until you learn the life lesson about asserting yourself before a big emotional charge develops.

An even more intense power style belongs to folks with Forehead Widest. I call this the **Passion Power Style**.

Ideas are real for you, more real than obstacles that deter other people from reaching their goals.

Thus, you are likely to accomplish more in life than others. Your potential challenge? You'll risk burning out anyone who works with you.

At the opposite extreme of apparent intensity, meet the faces that are, cheek-wise, incognito. Even Cheek Width relates to a **Polite Power Style** that is, similarly, inconspicuous.

But don't sell it short. If you are in this group, you know how to work the system. Results matter more to you than touting your awesome specialness.

With such a style, your only challenge is fading into the woodwork. Remind your boss or partner, occasionally, that you are the one who produced those magnificent results. Only fair!

Let's Get Practical: Do This Favor

In any relationship, one of the biggest favors you can do is to value that other person's power style. Each of us deserves to feel important. We crave to be given our share of the spotlight.

What you have learned about Cheek Proportions can help you acknowledge how others function socially, rather than thinking that your power style is the only version that deserves respect.

Personally, I'm not a fan of today's crazes for texting and Twittering. In particular, I'm concerned about the parallel play style of friendship where, after 10 minutes of direct contact, the partners spend the rest of their time "together" by texting other friends. I call it "**Social Attention Deficit Disorder**."

The disability is self-inflicted. To avoid it, use the power of face reading. You'll succeed more socially, whatever you do electronically.

Simply acknowledge the power styles of yourself and your friends, be it the Polite Power Style, the Pacifist Power Style, the Leader-Like Power Style, or the Passion Power Style.

Nuances only grow clearer when you remember to read right-half of face for work and left-half for social relationships.

Unrelated practical suggestion: Avoid choosing a spouse with your identical power style, as shown by Cheek Proportions. Same thing with hiring an employee to work directly for you. Otherwise you'll be competing. Constantly. For the same share of attention.

Which of the four power styles is best, generally? The Leader-Like Power Style brings the quickest, most obvious social clout. (Notice how common it is among performers, for instance.)

However, if you want to earn your reputation outside show biz, you can succeed just as well with any of the less conspicuous power styles. Simply value your personal style. Then work it.

Doing is different from talking, of course. More about doing when we read the lower portions of the face. After a tech upgrade in our next chapter, that is. Let's pause to assess your progress so far as a physiognomist.

PART THREE: SUPERB PHYSIOGNOMY SKILLS

15. VERY Interesting

Power-Packed Reader, your skills are developing nicely. So let's pause to add a new face reading app.

Way back in Chapter 5, you were coached about a vital skill of Face Reading, Step #5. By now you have had considerable practice. You know how important it is to notice the VERYS, ignore the "squinties," and generally take it easy while hunting for face data.

Now you are invited to pay more attention to what those different VERYS mean inwardly, adding new flair to your interpretations.

Each physical characteristic that you research can be extreme or not. Which can become extremely frustrating until you calm down enough for the process of reading faces to become fully informative.

By now, you have read enough faces to notice if you have been straining to see all the data. Hopefully, you haven't been straining at all.

Maybe you still can add a bit more effortlessness. Or take away some efforting.

While identifying face data, more than ever, you can let easiness be your guide. Any face reading characteristic will be spotted most easily when it is a VERY.

Luckily for you, Power-Packed Reader, this easiest-to-spot facial item is potentially your most important as well.

Why are physiognomists so lucky? More extreme physical characteristics mean a stronger inner significance.

Again, why? The ancient art of physiognomy is based on a reciprocal relationship between the inner person and the physical face. For thousands of years, face readers have used this rule:

VERY extreme physically = VERY extreme inwardly

For short, that's:

VERY = VERY

In my system of Face Reading Secrets, it's important to use that principle, plus two related rules:

Somewhat visible physically
= somewhat important inwardly.

For short, I call these characteristics the "**Somewhats**." Plus, for all practical purposes:

Only slightly visible physically,
squinting needed = no big deal inwardly.

Personally, I call these characteristics my "**Why Bothers**."

Easy Does It Best

In terms of easiness, how convenient for you! As an experienced face reader, you will mostly choose VERY characteristics for reading the Secrets.

Easiest to grab, this info will help you most. Ease, grace, flow, and accuracy are directly related to using the power of face reading.

What about helping others? If you share your observations about VERYs with a friend, your friend will benefit most from this type of information.

Sure, you can include face data that is a Somewhat. Do that occasionally, as time permits.

This extra data will be somewhat important, neither quite as Aha! producing when you give someone a face reading nor quite as useful for your own benefit, reading faces on your own.

For instance, say that you are reading the Cheek Prominence category and what you see is a Why Bother, a sort of, a maybe. Possibly that cheek sticks out pretty much but perhaps not. In mild confusion, you may feel as though you are starting to channel Hamlet.

Why work so hard? Trying to cram that Cheek Prominence data into its proper part of the category is tricky. Inadvertently you might slow down your pace of learning.

Struggle will not help you progress. For any Why Bother face data, your inner comfort and ease will suffer, not just the accuracy, when compared with your reading a VERY.

So, please, skip reading those Why Bothers. And, for your peace of mind, here are some specific recommendations for reading a Somewhat.

How to Handle a SOMEWHAT

Here is what I recommend:

Don't blame yourself. A Somewhat is not your "fault."

Don't go all squinty face on yourself.

Avoid twirling your head around like an owl (Although I would be impressed if you could actually do this.)

Accept the obvious: This particular item of face reading data is just a Somewhat. The significance will be, at best, somewhat insightful.

Whether you have been face reading yourself or somebody else, be sloppy. Face readers, of all people, need a sense of proportion!

What if the worst-case scenario happens when you are reading the Eyebrow category about Distribution of Hair? Say that you find a naughty eyebrow that barely belongs to any choice in this category. Even then you are not entirely sure.

Don't send your subject off to get eyebrow implants.

Never whip out a pink lip liner pencil to fill in the blanks.

Never, ever feel discouraged about yourself as a face reader.

Power-Packed Reader, please consider physiognomy to be an art. Like any art form, it goes best when you follow your bliss. Do the parts that are easy; ease up on the rest.

This book has a noble Cast of Characters, chosen expressly to help prevent your giving yourself a hard time.

If rumors of your struggling reached them, oh the pain. Alexander might even cry!

Instead, be kind to yourself process-wise, allowing for even more ease and grace than you have allowed so far. Go through each remaining chapter and gently practice reading each item of face data. Read the photo example(s) provided. Read your own face, too, always gently and easily.

If what you see in the mirror is not a VERY version, but a Somewhat or a Why Bother, note that.

No repining! Some face reading data is just not worth reading, nothing personal. Power-Packed Reader, this is physiognomy, not engineering school.

Eye Angle Quiz

Let's turn these examples into a little quiz, just for fun.

Remember Eye Angles? Let's review. Check out the following members of our Cast of Characters. Is that angle up, down, or even? After you name that Eye Angle, note if it is a VERY or a Somewhat. If it's a Don't Bother, ha ha! Add no label.

1. Jesse's left eye.
2. Joyce's right eye.
3. Joyce's left eye.
4. Lloyd's left eye.
5. Matt's left eye.
6. Matt's right eye.
7. Ava's left eye.

8. Rowan's left eye.
9. Annette's left eye.
10. Alexander's left eye.

Skip to the end of this chapter for the Eye Angle Quiz ANSWERS.

Develop Your Eye for the VERYs

After years of coaching face readers like you, Power-Packed Reader, I have learned a few things. I have learned to solve problems for developing physiognomists, preventing strain and inaccuracy as part of the face reading process.

This experience has, of course, shaped the Face Reading Program presented here. At this point in your training, it's appropriate to further develop your eye for the VERYs, the Somewhats, and the Don't Bothers. So here's the plan.

From now on, whenever possible I will search through our Cast of Characters to supply more examples than ever before for each item of face reading data. There will be Somewhats galore, plus VERYs. I still won't usually bother showing you any Don't Bothers.

Ambitious? You can always comb through the whole Cast of Characters, seeking the unmentioned folk. They might well be "Don't Bother" about that particular face category.

For practice with VERYs and Somewhats, investigate your own face data, too. Be sure to hold this book on the level, as you were invited to do way earlier. Otherwise you would compromise accuracy with sloppy positioning.

Brain processing is involved in physiognomy. However developed your skill level, you will always have a very human brain.

Once you eyeball the face provided as an example, you may agree with me. Or maybe you won't.

That's okay. I'm not God. I didn't co-create the faces belonging to Annette, Wayne, Jesse, or Matt. And I'm not Annette, Wayne, Jesse, or Matt... who did have a share in co-creating their faces, using free will over time.

So all I do is the best I can, and that has to be good enough.

Same goes for you, right? Power-Packed Reader, just see the face reading data as clearly as you can. Trust your self-authority. With practice, your accuracy will improve. Be patient with that.

Bring on More Sophisticated Visuals

Initially I gave you these VERY examples for Eyebrow Hairiness:

- Full Eyebrows, see Anthony.
- Small Eyebrow Hairiness, see Annette.
- Moderate Eyebrow Hairiness, see Kathryn.

All these folks are VERYs. Here come some extra examples, illustrating those same characteristics, only now we've got Somewhats:

- Somewhat Full Brows, see Oliver.
- Somewhat Small Eyebrow Hairiness, see Valerie.
- Somewhat Moderate Eyebrow Hairiness, see Joyce.

How about examples that would qualify as Don't Bothers? Of course, I don't recommend reading them. Yet I know that some inquiring physiognomist minds want to know anyhow. In your honor....

Our First Example of a Don't Bother

- Don't Bother Full Eyebrows, see Shirley.

Just how much makeup is stuck in those eyebrows? Have they perhaps been tattooed, then faded over the years?

Ordinarily, I would just read eyebrows as they look, makeup and tattoos and all. Only Shirley's strike me as such an obvious and confusing mess of physical-plus-enhanced, I would have to try hard.

No, not that! Not when identifying face data! This experience of overcoming effort alerts me: Don't Bother.

By contrast, how about Shirley's Eyebrow Range? That's different, undisguised under all the fixing. Shirley has VERY Big Eyebrow Range.

Now that's more like it.

Another Example of a Don't Bother

- Don't Bother Small Eyebrow Hairiness, see Alexander.

On close inspection, those eyebrow hairs have probably been combed upwards to look as full as possible. Plus Alexander's brows are too pale to read easily unless you are standing very close or have a way to enlarge his photograph.

(Working from hard copy photos, this face reader does sometimes use a magnifying glass. As for enlarging pictures online or in ebooks, you have probably figured that out long ago.)

Back at Alexander's Eyebrow Hairiness, here's the clincher. What happened when I tried reading this item of face data?

Enlarging his photo or not, I found myself going all squinty face. Which triggered my "Don't Bother" alarm.

Alexander has a face full of VERYs. Why push myself to read something relatively inconsequential like his Eyebrow Hairiness?

How About One More Example of a Don't Bother?

- Don't Bother Moderate Eyebrow Hairiness, see Matt.

Looking at him, I might rack my brain. Is the outer edge of each eyebrow scattered along a moderate degree of fullness?
Or perhaps that segment of eyebrow is simply quite thin and positioned higher up than the rest.

Sure, I could piece things together, even extrapolate from his side views. But why bother? Matt has loads of other facial attributes that can be read more easily.

Such hard work it would be, reading that particular category on that particular face.... Well, skip it.

Don't read Don't Bothers on Matt or anyone, not unless you want to put yourself through the heavy lifting I just described in these examples featuring Shirley, Alexander, and Matt.

My professional opinion? It is ridiculous to fret over facial characteristics of an iffy nature.

Only slightly visible physically = not worth reading.

Really.

Each face includes some characteristics that are more extreme than others. Read only what comes easily, no forcing. That's the best use of your valuable time, Power-Packed Reader.

But Very WHAT?

Shape is one kind of VERY. To spot this kind of VERY, compare two people who have the same item of face reading data, say Curved Eyebrows within the Eyebrow Shape Category.

Eventually you will see a face across a crowded room and it will thrill you. Not because it's some enchanted evening and you have fallen in love at first sight. Thrill will happen because you have found a second person in the room with Curved Eyebrows.

Therefore, you can start comparing this person's amount of Eyebrow Curve with the amount of Eyebrow Curve on the first person.

For example, take another look at Fred's curvy eyebrows. Compare them to Annette's. Whose Eyebrow Curve is more VERY?

The winner of this particular VERY competition would be Annette.

Do Fred's eyebrows still curve more than Joyce's. I think so. Hers are just a few eyebrow plucks away from being angled.

So I would still tell Joyce she had Curved Eyebrows. But mentally I would consider them of the Somewhat variety. Talking to a client, I would express my interpretation accordingly.

Some Curved Eyebrows are extremely curved, while others that fit into the curved category... now that you start comparing... curve only slightly.

Bingo! Sooner or later, the realization will hit you how a shape can be a VERY.

A Different Kind of VERY

Size is another kind of VERY. Tracking this aspect can make you dizzy at first, as if riding backwards on a subway.

Regarding size, you won't just be looking for big versus small, but focusing on VERY big versus somewhat big — or VERY small versus somewhat small.

Still, once you get the knack, researching size is no biggie.

To distinguish size nuances, just follow the proportions within one face.

For instance, say that you are researching the Earlobe Size category. And you have found two people who appear to have Small Earlobes. Whose are smaller?

- Don't compare Helene's earlobes to Oliver's. His features might be larger all around.
- Instead compare the size of Oliver's earlobes to other proportions within his own personal ears.
- Yes, Oliver has are VERY Small Earlobes.
- While Helene has Somewhat Small Earlobes.

You get the idea. The effort of learning now, refining your face reading skills, is different from straining to scope out size characteristics — an effort like mushing your brain, concentrating so hard your eyeballs feel in danger of popping out of their sockets, or otherwise frowning yourself into a headache.

Instead, with Face Reading Secrets you are allowed to be The Cool Physiognomist.

Any form of deeper perception works best with ease and grace. If you ever study aura reading or how to do Skilled Empath Merge, your habits with face reading will serve you well.

If ever you facilitate any form of mind-body-spirit healing, same deal. Ease and grace: They're definitely allowed.

Eye Angle Quiz ANSWERS

1. Jesse's left eye. Up-angled. VERY. (Same as Jesse's right eye.)
2. Joyce's right eye. Up-angled. VERY.
3. Joyce's left eye. Up-angled. Somewhat.
4. Lloyd's left eye. Down-angled. VERY.
5. Matt's left eye. Up-angled. Somewhat.
6. Matt's right eye. Up-angled. But Don't Bother!
7. Ava's left eye. Up-angled. Somewhat. (And slightly more up-angled than her right eye. Which is also a Somewhat.)
8. Rowan's left eye. Up-angled. But Don't Bother!
8. Annette's left eye. Down-angled. But Don't Bother!
10. Alexander's left eye. Up-angled. VERY.

16. Noses

Pop quiz: Draw me a happy face. You know, the symbol for "Have a happy day." Whether you happen to feel perky or not, those insufferable little yellow faces grin at you. Go ahead, draw one.

Now, as an up-and-coming face reader, you can help me answer this. What is wrong with this picture?

No nose, that is wrong! Is nose-lessness a coincidence? I think not. Do you remember what noses represent?

A happy face symbol contains only eyes and mouth. By now you know that eyes mean having an outlook, socially. Although we haven't reached the mouth chapter yet, I'll bet you can guess what mouths represent... communication.

Symbolically, then, a happy face has an attitude and can talk. No listening to others (ears), nary a thought (eyebrows) disturb the blissful experience. Possibly worst of all, from this face reader's point of view, is the one very central omission.

How about the face part that represents work and dealing with money? So we're just going to put that part off until tomorrow, are we?

Bah! Noses are central. They're serious face.

And you thought noses were merely hard to draw?

After reading this chapter, you still may not want to draw them. However, you will know much more about noses than ever before, including many reasons to be thrilled with your own version, not just what it represents but how it physically looks.

Let's Get Practical: The Limits of Work

Nose categories toward the end of this chapter will inform you about personal style handling money, but most nasal data concerns your personal style with work.

And "work" means what, exactly? For our practical purposes, "work" will refer to activities in the big, wide world, hopefully for money but not necessarily.

Volunteer work is noble and counts as well, due not so much to nobility as to your possibly having serious impact on people beyond your home.

By contrast, how about carrying out the garbage, washing your underwear, or weeding the garden? All of us know that is work. Even supervising several maids, plus a laundress and gardener, who do the actual work... would still take work. Alas, none of these sorts of labor will count as "work" in face reading. Sorry.

How can face reading supply relevant information about your personal style with these non-work-type-works? Just go elsewhere, reading your face. Other facial features can inform you about personal style in personal life, such as cheek categories, eyebrow categories, eye categories, mouth categories, chin and jaw categories.

Of course, these items of face data indirectly impact your work style, out in the world. But your special excellence at work can benefit from additional factors, the ones I am teaching you to read in this nosey chapter.

Nose Length

Which kind of Nose Length is supposedly aristocratic, long or short?

Long, of course — but did you ever wonder why?

Are noses with generous length transmitted like a family name, along with write-ups in the Social Register and silver spoons. Can you tell an Old Money Nose at a glance? Sorry, life isn't that simple. At least seeing physical nose length can be simple.

- **Short Noses** are short. See Anthony and Rowan. A VERY version belongs to Joyce.
- **Long Noses** appear long, compared with the rest of the face. See Helene. While Gary and Madison have the VERY version.
- **Moderate Nose Length** is the label that physiognomists give the sort of nose that Goldilocks would have preferred, pretty much in the middle, lengthwise. See Jesse and Valerie. And a VERY version belongs to Ava.

Tip: What's your point of reference for making this comparison? Simply the length of the person's whole face. How much real estate is taken up by The Nose Shoppe?

Sometimes it can help to view the nose in profile, too. So if you are unsure about your Nose Length, take out your second mirror and assess from that different angle.

Interpreting Nose Length

Here is how I view the meaning of this nose category. Breathing is a basic human job. Everyone must obtain the same amount of breath through the allotted equipment, enough to live. Some noses are designed to get this work done directly. These no-frills models are the short, get-down-to-business noses.

Other breathing machines are designed to do the work more decoratively. Style counts. Accordingly, certain workers are set up with the longer, more ornamental variety. Work habits correspond. Less rush, more style.

Thus, **Short Noses** reveal talent for hard work.

Granted, this old-fashioned value doesn't happen to be trendy today. What once was praised as industriousness is often looked on now with suspicion. It's called being a "workaholic." Yet Malcolm Gladwell has made a pretty good case for hard work, a minimum of 10,000 hours of it, in "Outliers."

Whether you think hard work is good or bad, know that it is a specialty of people with Short Noses. They march into the workplace and produce like crazy. They can follow a routine. They don't merely talk a good game but actually do the work.

I challenge you to search any organization. Regardless of job title, social lineage, or pay scale, the ones who work hardest, day in and day out, are the ones with the shortest noses.

Your potential challenge, with such a nose, is being taken for granted. "Of course Rowan will do it. That's her job." Or "No need to thank Anthony for all that overtime. He's a workhorse."

Should you be one of those hardworking short-nosed folks, here's my recommendation. Drop hints. Likewise drop memos and requests for pay raises. Even better, don't hint at all but speak directly. "Sure, I'll take on that extra project for you. Incidentally, will I be paid in comp. time or overtime?"

What about **Long Noses**? Forget expectations they might go with aristocratic trust funds.

The related work talent involves planning and strategy.

Does that mean a short-nosed person can't be creative or use strategy? Of course not. Everyone has creativity. Nose length relates to creativity with handling the full scope of a project.

The short-nosed version is to find ways to keep yourself efficient and motivated. You race against the clock. You race against yourself. Producing a big pile of widgets, customer invoices, and so forth can become a justifiable source of pride.

By contrast, the long-nosed version of creativity is to envision the entire project, designing it as one-of-a-kind; then you follow it through from beginning to end. Abstract designing is a source of pride, with ingenuity running a close second.

Got a Long Nose? Then imagine a job where you punch in at 9:00 and out at 5:00. Your goal is to produce, produce, produce. Half the time, your boss never even tells you the big picture about what you are doing. The amount you get done in one day is fantastic.

Sound good? Sure, if your nose is short. This type of job may be very familiar (except your boss is more appreciative, I hope.) However, if you have a Long Nose, I have just described your version of Job Hell.

Ahem, in milder language: Handling such a job would be your potential challenge.

You can start to overcome that challenge right in your job interview. Explain that you need to see the whole picture, that this overview helps keep you motivated. Do what you can to find employment where you can use your talent, not ignore it.

How about those blessed with **Moderate Nose Length**?

Lucky you, to have such flexible timing about scope of work. Short-term projects, long-term projects — you can excel at either and both.

Because scope of work isn't an issue, that doesn't necessarily mean you slide by with no potential challenge. Ever hear of "Lack of tolerance for the rest of humanity"?

Until you get over yourself (and the talent symbolized by your moderately sized breathing organ), you may readily judge your co-workers as bums and drudges. Although, when it comes to noses, that's hardly the scariest way to be judgmental. Consider...

Noses in Profile

I dedicate the next section of face reading instruction to the world's grumpy nose haters. (In America alone, we have an estimated 60 million of them.)

Power-Packed Reader, if you don't already adore that part of your face, I consider it my personal mission to act as a sort of marriage counselor between your nose and the rest of you.

Partly the reason we're such a nation of nose haters is our peculiar pop culture, with its assumption that, supposedly, the only good nose is straight and short. If you have been brought up on classic Disney cartoons, you received the full download. Your subconscious "knows" that virtue and sexiness are inversely proportional to the size of a person's nose.

And how many movies, of all sorts, did you watch before you got the message from profile shots? Why do they almost always star nice Straight Noses? Obviously it must be because "Other nose shapes aren't attractive enough for a self-respecting movie star."

Ridiculous! Physically, the Nose-in-Profile category means the *shape* of your nose in profile. It is not about how straight your nose looks.

Let's at least reconsider this cultural conditioning. I invite you to summon up full resolve and bravery. Then straightforwardly (side-forwardly, two-mirror-edly) approach the delicate issue of your Nose in Profile.

Take a deep breath, preparing for a good look. Nosing around this way may only be easy if your nose shape is perfectly straight. Otherwise remember that the force of American culture, not to mention the nation's vanity surgeons, may be pulling against you. Keep reading until you find your own true Nose Shape in Profile!

Of course, there can be many variations from the bridge of your nose all the way down to the nose tip. Overall, which is the main shape you notice?

- A **Straight Nose** means straight-ish, not necessarily like a ruler-drawn line made flesh. See Helene.
- A **Scooped Nose** shape deviates from straightness by curving *inward*. The curve could be VERY or somewhat. A scoop counts wherever it occurs, which could be any part of your nose from the bridge to the tip. See Madison.
- The third possibility for nose profiles is an **Arched Nose** shape. Your nose deviates from straightness by curving *outward*. That curve could come anywhere between the bridge and the tip and still count as an arch. See Gary. And a VERY version belongs to Anthony.

Is it a coincidence that the word "Nosology" is a scientific word for classifying *diseases*? What's with all this negative nose stuff? Why can't we make up more positive words, like "Nosetalgia," a longing for the times that make you feel really good, like the last time you saw the center of your face in two mirrors for that fine profile view?

Interpreting Nose Shape In Profile

The nose profile category reveals your most distinctive preferences for getting work done. It's like carrying a business ID card.

So which kinds of personal style could position you to get a raise?

A **Straight Nose** says, "Checklists done here." Working systematically, you are in your element whenever you can start at Point A, then continue down through your list, ticking off points until you get all the way to Point Z, a.k.a., "Mission accomplished."

Lucky you! Typically work positions, with their emphasis on procedures, are designed by people with Straight Noses... for people with Straight Noses.

Consequently, your only challenge is that silly business of lack of tolerance for the rest of humanity. You know, "the slobs" who work with you.

By comparison with your exacting standards, nearly everyone who works with you could be found lacking, except for other Straight-Nose types. Unless, of course, you learn to appreciate different personal styles for getting work done.

Especially if your nose is VERY straight and long (what I call a Relentlessly Straight Nose), like Oliver's, your standards for rigor can be exceedingly high.

Scooped Noses accompany a different style. "I need intuition breaks," could be the slogan on your business card.

To excel at your job, you'll need to pause occasionally. Feel how your work is going. This could bring up emotions or hunches or brain-surges. This can point you toward subtle or big-deal ways to tweak your work.

Herein lies your special excellence as a worker. Just as your nose scoops inward somewhere along its length, you are wise to occasionally let attention turn inward as well.

What, nobody at work has encouraged you to do this? That's likely. You happen to have the least common of the Nose Shapes in Profile. And your workplace was probably defined in terms of Straight-Nose style: By and for people with Straight Noses. Remember?

Also, your current place of employment may not hire professional physiognomists to help all employees do their best. (Pity!)

So take it from me, your consulting physiognomist. While doing your official job in the approved manner, it pays to indulge an occasional inner whisper:

"Yo, feelings! How is this job going? Does anything about it seem not quite right? If so, how could I fix it? Or do I have a hunch about how to make what I'm doing even better?"

Then follow your bliss. Or your nose scoop.

What happens if you *don't* indulge in the occasional intuitive check-in? That could be even sillier. Of course, my official term for this wouldn't be "Silly limitation" but, rather, "Your potential challenge."

With a nose that scoops inward, here's what happens when you don't let yourself take intuition breaks. You procrastinate like crazy before finishing projects.

Don't call that self-sabotage or some other kind of weakness. Such a challenge occurs for you because your soul has stalled you on purpose.

Consider. The totality of yourself, gift included, doesn't want you to end a job before you can show your real talent. Which would require that you listen to that still small voice within, assess how you are doing so far, then tweak away.

With an **Arched Nose**, your business card might read "Creative person reporting for work." That's right, the deeper the outward curve in your nose, the stronger your talent (and need) for working creatively.

Just how would you define "Creativity"?

This need not mean playing the accordion or making sculptures. Creativity means finding a unique solution to a problem.

- You see the resources available.
- You know what you want to achieve.

- With creativity, you find one-of-a-kind ways to use what you have got. Or turn new things into resources. Or use old resources in new ways.
- And, altogether, you create a unique way of solving the problem.

Economists might call it getting more bang for your buck. A physicist might prefer to call it "Elegance."

Actually, each nose shape goes with a particular kind of creativity. And remember, this Nose in Profile category only applies to your behavior at work. Other aspects of creativity show in your eyebrows, your hairline, your lip proportions, and other places as well.

So why have I singled out Arched Noses as especially relating to creativity? If you have this face data, you *need* to work creatively. Not optional, not if you want to be happy and productive when working.

While the more VERY that arch in your nose, the stronger is your need to work creatively.

Creative Interlude

Look, Power-Packed Readers, I know the topic of creativity is ultra-sensitive. So here's more clarification about creativity at work.

What kind of workplace creativity goes with a Straight Nose? You apply creativity to gathering momentum as you systematically follow that procedure.

How quickly and thoroughly can you go through that checklist? How many times can you do it each day? Creativity of that sort is used to keep yourself motivated.

With Scooped Noses, creativity involves discovering ways to plug your intuition into reality. For instance, what if you feel that the pace of a chapter is bogged down with the need to address sensitivity of readers about creativity?

Say that you feel — okay, I, Rose Rosetree, with my Scooped Nose, feel — that unless I clarify how every Nose Shape in Profile can have a creative work style, many of you Power-Packed Readers are going to have your feelings hurt.

So I seek a creative solution. And before I know it, on this bright Sunday morning a week before Christmas 2011, as I have put off first-drafting this chapter for a really, really long time by my standards. (Four days, by the calendar.) Bam! Out from my keyboard comes the weird heading, "A Creative Interlude."

This isn't logical. It doesn't fit my official template in this book for chapter headings. But who cares? It speaks to the heart. (And now, thank God, I'll be able to go back to finishing this chapter without further procrastination.)

By contrast, creativity with Arched Noses involves paying close attention to the resources available outside yourself.

Which people, talents, materials, or concepts can be combined in an unusual manner? How can you perform your task in a way that has never been done before? Musicians devote their creativity to ways of producing sound, choreographers to elements of movement, and so forth.

Noses that move "out there" seem to go with a special sensitivity to whatever "out there" can contribute to the artist's medium.

Your potential challenge? With an Arched Nose, there is only one way to describe what it's like having zero scope for creativity in your job. Job Hell!

Really, the easiest way to overcome this challenge is to quit that nightmare job and go live off your trust fund.

What, you don't have a trust fund? Then you might hunt for a new job. Or officially redefine the scope of work for your existing job. Perhaps you might sneak in some creativity unbeknownst to your boss, ha ha!

As a last resort, you can do creative projects after work.

Stay up late, perfecting that needlepoint or broadening your scope as a yodeling artist. Why not?

Or get up before work. Milk those cows but do it differently every time. Why not?

Oh, you don't own any cows, actually? Draw them. Then draw yourself milking them. You get the idea.

Extra Special Face Data: Bumpy Noses

What does it mean if your nose really does have a bump, not an arch?

Probably it means that you need to take a deep breath, pick up two mirrors, and take another look.

In my clinical experience — ooh, that makes me sound so dignified. Except, of course, I am not a physician but a physiognomist, so I don't work in a clinic or doctor's office of any kind. It won't have the same, nice, professional cloutey ring, but here goes....

In my work as a professional physiognomist, in public school classrooms teaching adult education; in workshop spaces at Tokyo superstores for seminar companies; at mega-millionaire mansions reading faces for parties; and in my little pink office doing face readings for individual clients, etc... never once have I, personally, encountered a student or client with a bumpy nose.

But oboy! Have I ever encountered a lot of folks who told me their noses were bumpy.

Please understand the difference: An Arched Nose curves outward for a portion of its length. The arch could begin near the bridge (like

Gary's) or move out most strongly along the central ridge (like Anthony's), or spring out most towards the nose tip (possibly the case for Jesse, but I can't be sure without seeing a profile shot).

The arched portion of an Arched Nose could be short or long. By contrast, a bump looks more like a marble stuck someplace underneath the skin. It is a very, very short outward curve.

Occasionally a person does have one. Much more likely, that person has an Arched Nose and makes the mistake of calling it "Bumpy."

Could such a person be you, Power-Packed Reader? If you have mislabeled your face data, calling it "Bumpy Nose," don't blame yourself. Realize that the world includes millions of grumpy nose haters, plus millions of folks who have surgically altered their noses to get rid of anything remotely like an arch or bump.

You, however, need not belong to either category. You could instantly become a sophisticated, physiognomy-savvy, proud owner of an Arched Nose. Where you know what your face data means and you rejoice in your talent.

Alternatively, if you really do have that rare thing, a Bumpy Nose in profile, you can have a great life too, loving your nose and knowing what it means in terms of Face Reading Secrets. Here's the talent:

Your work flows in fits and starts. With each project you take on, you will have at least one burst of outrageous creativity.

Your potential challenge? During those bursts of creativity, you may come on so strong that other people have trouble accepting you easily. But there's always the chance that others will call you a genius!

Let's Get Practical: Better Bossing

What if your job involves managing noses? Also the people who belong to those noses....

How can face reading help you become a better boss?

Most important, read (or reread) your own Nose Shape in Profile. Celebrate your special excellence in the workplace.

Then get over yourself. Repeat as needed, "I do not expect everyone I work with to be just like me."

It is to your advantage if employees spice up your workplace by adding variety.

What kind of variety?

With each person you supervise, steal a look at his or her Nose Shape in Profile. If you feel weird about stealing anything while at work, good for you. Get yourself mug shots of all employees, both front views and side views. Then you can peruse at leisure.

Supervising a Straight-Nosed worker like Helene, value that checklist approach. Compliment Helene for being so reliable and efficient.

Or praise the system itself, and how Helene makes that system work smoothly.

Supervising a Scooped-Nose worker like Madison, appreciate that emotions matter a lot to her. Madison won't need to be coddled, necessarily. But praise will fuel her best performance. Sincere appreciation from the heart to the heart could motivate her more than if you were to double Madison's salary.

No worker, whatever the Nose Shape in Profile, functions well when constantly criticized. However, it is extra-counterproductive to criticize a worker who has a Scooped Nose. Find a way to give feedback without making it sound like personal criticism.

Supervising an Arched Nosed, let a team member like Anthony do things differently each time. It matters so much to him. Provided that results are effective, why would his (appropriate) creativity be any of your business?

Employment goes best when each worker uses personal talents. Soul-squelched employees can't do their best work. Even if they would prefer to please you by cranking out work like perfect little machines, that cannot be.

Really, in what business have you ever seen a machine or computer equipped with a nose?

Nose Padding

What's in a nose?

Whatever response just popped into your mind, I'll bet it wasn't this highly practical nose term: Nose Padding.

Sure, people sometimes refer to broad noses or wide noses or narrow noses or slender noses. But that's not going to work for face reading. Terms like these are too emotionally charged.

Besides, terms like these are actually imprecise. Nose Padding refers to the amount of flesh around the nose, from bridge to right above the tip, as seen from a front view. As a physiognomist, you can find plenty to notice.

- Is that nose equally padded at the bridge as at the tip?
- Does this extra nosiness, this padding, increase or decrease on the way down? That matters.
- **Small Nose Padding** means the nose bone is highly visible all the way down the full length of the nose. See Jesse. (Don't let his VERY Large Nose Tip distract you.) And a VERY version belongs to Matt.
- **Large Nose Padding** means that you don't see the bone and, instead, see nose width all the way down the full length of the nose. See Valerie.

- What if a nose gathers a fleshy kind of momentum? What if you see the central bone clearly towards the bridge but then the amount of padding increases? What if, right above the nose tip, that nose is two or three or more times more padded? Then that's **Triangular Nose Padding**. See Fred and Wayne. Joyce has a VERY version.
- For **Moderate Nose Padding**, see Oliver and Shirley.

Some faces, Nose Padding looks dramatic; other faces, it appears less extreme. By now you are growing comfortable at noticing VERYs, right?

Many people have been taught to expect Large Nose Padding to correspond to dark skin. How ridiculous is that? Look again at the examples provided in our Cast of Characters.

Face reading is not skin reading, not for people who live now. Since you have come this far as a face reader, I would like to treat you to a science-based way of banishing the myth of "Race" in today's world.

Why Race Matters Less Than You Were Raised to Believe

Physical anthropologists are the world's biggest experts on race. One such scientist is C. Loring Brace, a professor at the University of Michigan who was interviewed for a PBS Program, "Mystery of the First Americans."

According to Dr. Brace, "The word 'race' has no coherent biological meaning."

For example, "Although Europeans and Chinese are obviously different, in skin color they are closer to each other than either is to equatorial Africans. But if we test the distribution of the widely known ABO blood-group system, then Europeans and Africans are closer to each other than either is to Chinese."

Nadra Kareem Nittle, a widely published expert on race, has written an essay for www.about.com on, "What Is Race? Debunking the Ideas Behind This Construct."

In support of her argument that race is fluid and thus difficult to pinpoint scientifically, Nittle gives this example:

"Skin color remains a primary trait Westerners use to place people into racial groups. However, someone of African descent may be the same skin shade as someone of Asian descent. Someone of Asian descent may be the same shade as someone of European descent. Where does one race end and another begin?"

So the point here is not political correctness. Although some experts cling to the concept of race… the American Anthropological

Association (AAA) may have had the last word in an official Statement on "Race" first published on May 17, 1998.

These racial experts concluded that "human populations are not unambiguous, clearly demarcated, biologically distinct groups. Evidence from the analysis of genetics (e.g., DNA) indicates that most physical variation, about 94%, lies within so-called racial groups. Conventional geographic "racial" groupings differ from one another only in about 6% of their genes. This means that there is greater variation within "racial" groups than between them."

So why has race been such an important concept historically? According to the AAA, historical research has shown that the idea of "race" has always carried more meanings than mere physical differences; indeed, physical variations in the human species have no meaning except the social ones that humans put on them.

Today scholars in many fields argue that race, as it has been understood in the United States of America, was a social mechanism invented during the 18th century to refer to populations brought together in colonial America.

The notion of "race" was a way for English and other European settlers to dominate conquered Indian peoples and African slaves.

Pretty nasty stuff, isn't it, Power-Packed Reader? Yet it's pretty difficult to move out all the conditioning and prejudice that all of us have received around race.

What we *can* do is to upgrade our views of so-called "racial characteristics." My hope as a physiognomist is to improve how people relate to people, one distinctive human to another.

In that brave, truth-finding spirit, let's go forward to interpret Nose Padding and how it ennobles all individuals.

Interpreting Nose Padding

Nose Padding refers to your preferred number of people for sharing a project at work. What is your comfort zone?

If you prefer to start a project alone, continue it alone, even finish it alone, you probably have **Small Nose Padding.**

This personal style emphasizes a specialized form of independence related to work. Understanding it can help you to take best advantage of a major talent.

Just one catch though. How do you like it when a boss looks over your shoulder and starts in on you:

"Did you finish the job yet? When is this job going to be done? Are you doing it my way?"

Ugh! Small Padding nose-wearers are allergic to bossy bosses. As a workaround, you might say this to anyone who tries to micromanage you:

"Once I commit to a project, I'm one of the most self-motivated people you have ever met. I push myself harder than you ever could. Leave me alone and I'll do my best work for you."

In addition, you might casually mention that bossing you around is no more effective than flogging a dead horse, except that in your case, it's more like flogging a *racing* horse.

At the opposite extreme comes **Large Nose Padding**. To describe your version of "Job Hell," only two words are needed: Solitary confinement.

However, on a good day at work, you do have contact with other human beings. How come you need this? People give you energy. Then you give energy back. It's a dynamic interplay. Without other people, work would drain you.

Should ample Nose Padding extend all the way to the bridge of your nose, you are one of the rare beings who actually prefers to start a project in a committee. Like Valerie, for instance. She is soooooooo social! (Most folks loathe starting projects in a group. Take your own survey.)

As for **Triangular Nose Padding**, you prefer to begin work projects independently. As the project gathers momentum, however, you feel more comfortable about sharing it through teamwork and delegation.

Just how comfortable do you feel? Look at the relative width of nose right above the tip. More dramatic triangling represents comfort and skill with leading huge numbers of people.

Extra Special Face Data: Combination Nose Padding

What about Combination Nose Padding? That's where the central ridge of a nose stands out distinctly. Yet there's also a great deal of fleshiness on either side.

Power-Packed Reader, how can you interpret a nose that simultaneously has both VERY Small Nose Padding and Large Nose Padding?

Combination Nose Padding hints at complexity. If you have that abundant nose padding, your work style convinces other people that you love being a team player.

To some extent, you do enjoy managing or delegating. Mostly because you are so good at it!

However, in secret you prefer doing things your way. This can lead to a type of sneaky fun. When people are looking, you act like The Great Team Player. Privately you rig the system so that the group does things exactly your way.

Your potential challenge? Ouch, the guilt! Over the guile! When you are so darned good at playing this game, how can you stop?

One way out of this challenge is simpler than the contours of your wonderful nose. Lose the guilt.

Having a secret agenda doesn't necessarily hurt anyone. You are merely more complicated than others in having personal style around teamwork at your place of employment.

That doesn't make you Machiavellian. It doesn't give you Machiavelli's nose padding, either.

In case you are wondering, Mr. Me-Me-Machiavelli had VERY Small Nose Padding. This collaborated with a Down-Turned Nose Tip. (More on that face data soon.) Most important, Machiavelli's free will enforced a rather extreme set of inner choices that brought out the worst in his nose and the rest of him. Now, speaking of Nose Tip Angles....

Nose Tip Angle

Our first Nose Tip category is about angle. We'll check this out in profile, examining our final work-related nose news.

Afterwards, with a deft swivel to full frontal face, we will sniff out different Nose Tip and Nostril categories to find money news lodged in that self-same tip.

To check out your Nose Tip Angle, you will need two mirrors. The **tip** is where your nose comes to a point. The **base** of your nose lies between the nostrils. Researching your Nose Tip Angle, compare the height of the tip to the base.

- If the tip is higher, you have an **Up-Turned Nose Tip**. See Anthony. And a VERY version belongs to Madison.
- If the tip is lower, either you are upside down or you have a genuine **Down-Turned Nose Tip**. Annette illustrates this from a front view.
- What if you are scratching your head (or your nose), puzzling over the Nose Tip Angle? It's probably an **Even-Angled Nose Tip**. See Gary.

Interpreting Nose Tip Angle

Nose Tip Angle relates to your timing related to work, with an **Up-Turned Nose Tip Angle** related also to impetuous speech, impulsive career moves, and an all-around good time.

To clarify, here's a rather detailed hypothetical example. Suppose that you work for a big-city Department of Public Transportation. You are young, idealistic. Like all your co-workers, you consider cars to be loathsome engines of pollution. When nobody's looking, you spit on them.

However, one way you differ from others in your office relates to your VERY Up-Turned Nose Tip Angle. When it comes to curiosity, you are the champ. Co-workers have learned to put you at the top of the office gossip grapevine. (Talent, yeah!)

Therefore, you are among the first to learn that your own boss has stopped riding his bike to work in favor of a car. And not just any old car, mind you, but a model that's notorious for being a gas guzzler. Multiple choice quiz:

What would you do, based on Nose Tip Angle alone:

A. Go outside and spit on more cars, just to relieve your pent-up anguish?

B. Consider taking your car to work tomorrow, too, and parking it near the one belonging to your boss, all the better to buddy-buddy up to him

C. March straight into your boss's office right now, confront him, and quit.

Power-Packed Reader, if you chose B., your own nose tip probably angles downwards. Answer C. represents the potential challenge with an Up-Turned Nose Tip.

Down-Turned Nose Tips suggest a deliberate style in making career moves. Once you define your career plans, you will probably get there. Focused ambition in the workplace is a specialty of yours, whether or not this shows to others.

And the very best part of this talent is the lack of flaunting. You won't tweet to a soul, not directly, not when it comes to your personal career strategy. Smart!

Your potential challenge? Until you grow comfortable with your pace of success, there can be a coldness about your clear focus. Do you open up much to other people's feelings or is your pursuit of success pretty much about Number One?

By contrast, what about an **Even-Angled Nose Tip**? This characteristic corresponds to moderately deliberate focus on career. Decisions will seldom be made impetuously. Risks may be taken, but those would be calculated risks.

What a fine, steady way to steer through the seas of employment! That nicely balanced Nose Tip Angle gives you a fine rudder, as it were. Your potential challenge? It's merely a lack of tolerance for the rest of humanity.

Why on earth are some of your friends or co-workers so impetuous? That Madison, for instance. Foolish career move she made at the Public Transportation gig!

And what's with those chillingly calculated characters you know, those survivors who are so adept at kicking others off the island? As if you want to stick around to watch their selfish reality show!

Why can't all those nose tip wearers be wise and workplace friendly and wonderful, more like you?

Nose Tip Size

In this Age of Vanity, people have funny ideas about Nose Tip Size. Quick survey: Have any of your friends recently rushed off to the cosmetic surgeon because their nose tips seemed too darned small?

No, Large Nose Tips are more often the seeming problem. This physiognomist laments such a reaction as one more perfectly fine face attribute considered undesirably "ethnic" or just "unfashionable."

Funny thing is, no matter which "Race" box you check off on the census forms, people who check off that very same box can have any size of nose tip. Start looking!

Power-Packed Reader, let your point of reference be the rest of the person's face. How does the size of the nose tip compare to the rest of the nose, to the width of the mouth, to the length of the eyes?

- A **Large Nose Tip** is like a bargain at the supermarket, the large economy size. See Valerie, Lloyd, Kathryn. And a VERY version belongs to Fred.
- At the opposite extreme, you might find a different kind of bargain, an exquisite **Small Nose Tip**. See Oliver: And a VERY version belongs to Joyce.
- If the Nose Tip Size isn't immediately obvious, count it as an **Average Nose Tip**. See Jesse, Wayne: And a VERY version belongs to Shirley.

Courage, now, as you hoist up that mirror. Remember to look on the level.

Interpreting Nose Tip Size

Nose Tip Size relates to personal style with financial security. For a balanced interpretation, be sure to immediately round out this category by reading the two nostril categories that follow.

Unless you read the full trio, your findings may be distorted. And if there's one part of the face where distortion would be especially unwelcome, that's your nose, right?

People with **Average Nose Tips** don't stress about how they're doing financially. If there's a problem, they solve it. Otherwise they don't worry... unless they're dealing with that little problem I call "Lack of tolerance for the rest of humanity — especially the silly ways they deal with money."

By contrast, **Large Nose Tips** reveal that saving for the future is a major concern.

How much money is actually in the bank? Sorry, the nose tip alone won't divulge. Your secret is safe, even among physiognomists.

The desire for financial security doesn't necessarily match the size of a person's nest egg.

Who thinks about savings most often? People who live in poverty. Also people who are ambitious, greedy, philanthropic, art collectors....

Hey, the answer can't be limited to any one category. When you read the Secrets, you will find that savers come from every income bracket and ethnic heritage.

And if you have ever agonized, "Why, oh why, do I have this Huge Nose Tip?" I have one answer for you: Anchor! (Go back to the "Eye" chapter to refresh your memory, if needed.)

Small Nose Tips correspond to **Prosperity Consciousness.** This means having a spiritual understanding of money as a symbol.

Money isn't just a number of bills in the bank. Money symbolizes the flow of energy, skill, work, appreciation.

According to Prosperity Ponsciousness, money is a flow, rather than something to hoard. And it won't flow any faster due to worry.

If you have a Small Nose Tip, there are practical implications to having this prosperity consciousness. Isn't it a given for you that there will always be enough? And don't you find that, somehow, you are always provided for?

Then you are a natural at Prosperity Consciousness. The benefit is freedom in your own life plus the chance to teach other people by example, elevating their spiritual understanding about money.

Obviously your potential challenge involves paying enough attention to saving responsibly for retirement, etc. But feather your nest as best you can. Never be ashamed of yourself for not worrying.

Nostril Size

Take a deep breath. Add a gulp, if necessary. We're about to delve into nostrils.

I know, I know. Before you become a fully-fledged physiognomist, nostrils may seem like the ultimate in embarrassing face parts.

Meaning-wise, too, the subject is considered taboo. Even close friends may be reluctant to discuss what Nostril Size means. Money.

Personally, I can't wait to lead you into nostril research. Partly it's because no face reading data embarrasses me. Partly, anyone in sales has a critical need to know about nostrils... and so does anybody who isn't independently wealthy.

And partly, I get a kick out of nostril reading because that facial structure reminds me of my son's keen intelligence.

When Matt was a toddler, one of his major hobbies was, to put it bluntly, picking his nose. Parental corrections didn't seem to discourage him, either. During one conversation between Matt and my husband, Mitch, this nose jazz had been going on entirely too long. So Mitch said politely, "Your finger doesn't belong there, son. Please take it out right this minute."

Instantly Matt obeyed, taking that finger and sticking it directly into his Daddy's nose.

Our face reading pursuits won't be that wild. But in our more reserved fashion, let's delve boldly into nostrils.

How do you gauge Nostril Size? No worries. You won't need anything conspicuous, like a finger. Simply view each nostril from the front, at a level angle. Notice how much of the shape of that nostril shows.

When it comes to seeing your nostrils, many a nose gazer does a weird kind of upward tilt. Well, you are not preparing for a deep sea exploration here, folks. No need to help miniature observers leap directly into a swan dive and then a Fantastic Voyage inside your body.

Avoid that upward head tilt. Just pivot your head back to a reasonable angle, on the level. Also, maybe, calm down. Power-Packed Reader, you're just face reading your Nostril Size, that's all.

- When you can see the whole shape, count that as **Large Nostrils**. See Rowan. A VERY version is modeled for us by Joyce.
- Air holes you can barely see mean **Small Nostrils**. See Annette and Wayne. Plus a VERY version belongs to Kathryn.
- No air holes? Either you are looking at a Barbie doll or it's someone with **VERY Small Nostrils**.
- **Moderate Nostril Size** means that you can see some of the shape. See Lloyd, Shirley, and Cliff.

Look straight up Cliff's nostrils if you dare, he makes it so easy in his multi-face photograph in Chapter 7. Try to gauge Nostril Size from the angles provided and this may remind you anew... how face data can be distorted... unless the face you're reading is on the level.

Power-Packed Reader, when you look in the mirror for this face reading category, check two different angles. Keep the mirror's angle on the level, of course. And then check the tilt of your head. Happy nostril hunting!

Interpreting Nostril Size

Nostril Size can be compared to the withdrawal capacity of a bank. Remember piggy banks? They have a narrow slit for depositing coins. Most of us toss our loose change into a container with easier access, such as a pocket.

In physical terms, too, some of us have chosen a slot that makes the money easy to reach. Other souls have decided to make it harder to take the cash out.

And just when did this momentous decision take place? Personally, I believe that each soul sets up a **Life Contract** about major talents and challenges when planning the overall lifetime.

Once we live on earth, character is shaped further by the use of free will. Over time, consequences of our speech and actions out-picture in face data like Nostril Size.

Of course, if you prefer to think about this as some sort of cosmic gamble, you could always imagine that your nostrils came directly from a slot machine!

Whatever the ultimate explanation, for thousands of years physiognomists have found a fascinating correlation between Nostril Size and spending habits.

Large Nostrils correspond to large spending, like easy access pockets. If you have this style, you know spending is fun. As a consequence, you greatly enjoy the things your money can buy.

Your potential challenge? More spending means less money in savings. With all the wide variations among economic theories, surely, here is one point of agreement.

What if you possess **Small Nostrils**? You tend to be frugal. Not an easy sell, you are a clever sell instead: Willing to buy if it's a bargain, otherwise not so willing.

Your potential challenge? Unfortunately, it's called "Stingy."

With **Moderate Nostril Size**, what is your automatic inclinations about spending vs. not?

Nothing.

You have no automatic inclination. This frees you up to spend money, or not, in a situational manner. Depending on what's for sale, whether you need it, how much money is available... you decide based on factors like these.

Of course, your potential challenge is a lack of tolerance for the rest of humanity. However there's a twist.

Not a nostril twist, Silly. Nostrils don't generally do twirly yoga asanas.

Conflicted Over Your Nose Data?

Sure, nose tips are fraught with conflict. Between Nose Tip Size and Nostril Size, plus our next category, financial conflict is the lot of nearly every nostril owner.

Before adding that third relevant category, let's pause for a breath or two.

Perhaps you are wondering this about Nostril Size: How does this spending style stack up with the need for financial security? Do Large Nose Tips automatically go with Large Nostrils?

Any combination is possible. And I don't just mean comparing Joyce's matched Small Nose Tip and Large Nostril Size versus George with his hefty Nose Tip plus Small Nostrils.

Think about your own experience pre-physiognomy. Some folks can love to save and also love to spend. Logic concerning finances is not necessarily built into the human heart... or nose.

After you get the point in theory, take a moment to assess your own personal styles for spending versus saving.

Also did your Nostril Size survey turn up differences between right and left? It's fairly common to have differences, such as being cheap about spending at work or in public (such as how you feel about taxes) while, in your personal life, self-indulgence rules the day.

Matt from our Cast of Characters is a great example of this, incidentally. Note the Medium-Sized Right Nostril (work related) compared to his Smallish Left Nostril (corresponding to spending money on himself in his personal life).

So much Nostril Size variation! Such potential trickiness comparing the divergent impulses to spend and save!

You know how all this adds up, don't you? One way or another, there's great opportunity for growth here at The Learning Planet!

Nostril Shape

Four major patterns of Nostril Shape can be found — just not all on the same nose.

Identifying the face data, Power-Packed Reader, take it easy. Nostril Shape will look like a shadow or, perhaps, a fleshy contour around a shadow.

To put it bluntly, nostrils are holes. So look at the skin right above that breathing hole and, sure enough, it will have a shape. The question is, what kind of shape?

- **Round Nostrils** have a circular shape. (Only the top-most part is round. Nobody's nostril is going to look precisely like a Cheerio.) See Rowan's left nostril. And a VERY version belongs to both of Joyce's nostrils.
- **Flared Nostrils** may be the hardest of the four shapes to recognize at first. But you will have plenty of practice seeing them because this shape is also the most common. Look for a nostril that starts out straight, close to the center of that nose. Moving out toward the side of the face, that Nostril Shape curves, more or less. See Rowan's right nostril. Also both of Alexander's nostrils.
- **Rectangular Nostrils** are somewhat rare. Recognize them by a straight, longish shape, like part of a box lid. Thank you, Gary, for providing a fine example with your left nostril.

- **Triangular Nostrils** are the most unusual variety. Finding them is like roaming across the vast desert sands of Egypt and bumping into a pyramid. Some day, you will be amazed to behold a pair of nostrils like two miniature pyramids and you will know that you have found a matched set of Triangular Nostrils.
  You would be noticing just the point of a triangle, right? Nose holes are not large or nuanced enough to contain equilateral triangles, rhomboids, pentagons, or any of those other tricky shapes you may remember from Geometry Class.

In our Face Reading Class, we are lucky enough to have two folks with Triangular Nostrils. See Jesse's left nostril and both of Shirley's.

Power-Packed Reader, before you start looking at yourself, be aware that unmatched sets of two Nostril Shapes are quite common. Even if left and right nostrils have the same shape, one might be a VERY. For instance, at this time in my life, the right nostril is larger than the left and has a steeper angle of the flare — more of a VERY Flared Nostril.

So when you hold your own nose up to the mirror, inspect one nostril at a time. Maybe you have already noticed asymmetries regarding Nostril Size. Regardless, you may find two different shapes in your personal nostril collection.

Doesn't that prospect bring new adventurousness to noses? Just think. Some day you may become a sort of nasal travel agent!

Interpreting Nostril Shape

Although I have tried to make a case for adventure, you still may not be entirely convinced that nostril reading is a superb way to see the world. I, your teacher, can handle this. I know that once you learn the true meaning of Nostril Shape, you are going to go gaga over this category.

Here's the deal. Nostril Shape informs you about spending style. Not the likelihood of spending, which you already have learned to read with the Nostril Size category. No, this is more about personal style with spending in general.

Salespeople, you may want to be extra nice to customers with **Round Nostrils**. If the Lord loves a cheerful giver, these folks must have front-row pews reserved in heaven. Their money style is resourceful, and they specialize in finding creative ways to manage their cash flow.

To put it bluntly, people with VERY Large, Round Nostrils are the biggest spenders on earth.

When a woman with this combination took one of my workshops, I told her so. Then I informed Gladys that her Round Nostrils also went with resourcefulness at juggling her debts. She laughed so hard, she fell off her chair. When Gladys could talk again, she said:

"I have 22 credit cards, and they're all charged up to the limit."

Next time I gave this workshop, a woman with the identical nostrils sat in the very same chair. I made my same tactful assessment. She laughed hysterically too, but didn't fall off her chair.

"I also have 22 credit cards," she told the group. "But not every one of them is charged up to the limit."

So any of you Power-Packed Readers with **Large, Round Nostrils**, beware of that potential challenge called "Consequences of spending."

What's so special, by way of talent, is the sheer enthusiasm for buying things. Purchases bring you more pleasure, dollar for dollar, than joy felt by folks with other nostril shapes.

Flared Nostrils flaunt a flair for adventurous spending. Power-Packed Reader with Flared Nostrils, 'fess up. If you like it, you will buy it, even if the item in question isn't the practical sort of purchase that would appeal to others you know.

Whether your purchase is trendy or practical, regardless of whether family members value that service or product, who cares? Not you.

That style of spending independence can prevail regardless of how regularly you buy yourself things.

Your potential challenge is a lack of tolerance for the rest of humanity. How weird their spending choices may seem to you. "Why can't they enjoy spending, in moderation?"

Easy for you to say, unless you happen to also have a Large Nose Tip or Small Nostrils. Then forget about easy. You'll be battling financial conflicts of your own.

Rectangular Nostrils present an analytical style of spending. If you possess even one Rectangular Nostril, you are good at budgeting.

Of course, I'm not suggesting that you stash an accounting notebook into your nose, like a foldaway bed in an efficiency apartment.

Nor am I trying to prohibit the sale of accounting notebooks or software based on scanning the would-be customer's nostril shape. Budgets are good for any responsible adult.

My point here, Power-Packed Reader, is this. If your nostrils are rectangular, you have got talent for budgeting. Maybe you keep all those figures in your head. One way or another, you have a talent for knowing where your money is going. Restraint comes naturally.

Your potential challenge? Responsible choices can box you in, stifling the freedom and fun of spending.

And this challenge can be exacerbated if you have a Large Nose Tip or a Small Nose Tip, Nostril Size Large or Small.

If it helps, repeat after me, "Money challenges at The Learning Planet can be important for my spiritual evolution."

Triangular Nostrils reveal a highly developed awareness of just how much money can buy. The potential challenge is stinginess — from an outsider's point of view, anyway.

Quite apart from that potential challenge, guess what? Power-Packed Reader, Triangular Nostrils are this Face Reading Program's first example of something I really, really love finding in faces, a Major Compassion Awakener.

Extra Special Face Data: Major Compassion Awakeners

Power-Packed Reader, here comes one of the deepest secrets of reading faces. A very small number of facial characteristics do not only contain a potential challenge. They reveal that a major challenge has already been suffered... and overcome.

Ever hear someone say, "That horrible experience left its mark on me"? Physiognomists know that to be literally true. Faces can change significantly after trauma or prolonged anguish.

Actually, this happens quite often.

If you pick up this book again 10 years from now, you might be able to go through every chapter and find one significant change to your face *per facial feature.*

And then you could find soul-stirring meaning about the meaning of all your facial evolution, e.g., Going from Large Nostril Size to Small, or vice versa.

Whatever the change, it is sure to be personally meaningful. Every natural change to the physical face symbolizes a way that you have inwardly grown, like it or not.

In this basic introduction to physiognomy, we don't have the luxury of exploring in full detail this free willish aspect of faces. Although it is my favorite use of face reading!

At least I can introduce you to something that goes even beyond the everyday, every-year, shifting that documents personal evolution.

Major Compassion Awakeners are these special face changes. Each shows a one-way change that matters, a distinctive change whose cause is so extreme and poignant that learning about it can really open your heart of compassion.

Down-Angled Eyes, which you already learned to read, count as a Major Compassion Awakener. Another of these special face items is Triangular Nostrils.

Nobody is born with Triangular Nostrils. Instead, they are earned. To me, those pointy nostril contours are like gold medals for valor here at The Learning Planet. What causes a person to develop a Major Compassion Awakener?

Someone like Shirley undergoes a terrible financial insecurity or loss. Note that the terror has to be personally felt to leave a mark on the soul, or the face. And one more something has to happen. I'll get to that soon.

Think first about the idea of terror personally felt to such an extent it leaves a physical mark. What would it mean to have financial problems that frightened you so badly, you feared that you would never, ever recover?

Fear like this isn't necessarily about the amount of money, because millions of Americans face poverty now. Growing up poor, or living from paycheck to paycheck, can be a way of life. It doesn't necessary shake a person's trust of life.

Even short-term financial challenge doesn't necessarily frighten a person. For instance, I have worked as a teacher of personal development since 1970. From 1971-1972, I worked with my husband Donald to open up a meditation center in Miami, Florida.

We were really poor, had no savings, could barely pay rent. For two weeks, we lived on cornmeal and tomato paste.

That didn't frighten us, though. As graduates of a top university, we didn't expect to wind up as bums. We kept at our work because we believed so passionately in what we were doing. Poverty didn't even seem like a sacrifice, more like a temporary problem that went with the territory.

Here's a contrasting example. Remember President Herbert Hoover? When campaigning for president, the man had a Rectangular Nostril Shape. One year after his inauguration, the stock market crashed, sending America's economy into the Great Depression.

Hoover's nostrils turned triangular.

Yes, an entire generation lived through those harsh years. Most suffered, but some were affected so deeply that they never really emerged. Although years of prosperity followed, these survivors still kept a scarcity mentality. Either way, most of these depression survivors did not earn Triangular Nostrils.

That privilege was reserved for folks who looked their own terror straight in the nose, as it were, and found new strength. In some new way, through the pain, these courageous survivors lifted themselves up inwardly. It's a rare kind of spiritual triumph. That is the extra soul choice that wins a Major Compassion Awakener like Triangular Nostrils.

This was true even for President Hoover, not known as one of America's greatest leaders. But his face change suggests that he felt deep responsibility and showed courage the only way he knew.

In my work as a face reader, I have been able to test this Compassion Awakener context on many individuals with Triangular Nostrils. During the face reading, I would explain that the corresponding talent was knowing the value of every penny. Then I would ask my client, "I'm curious. If you don't mind my asking, have you gone through a period of time that was really terrifying to you, financially?"

Yes, yes, yes. One woman told me, "I just declared bankruptcy last week."

Without exception so far, my clients with Triangular Nostrils have gone through hardship that really scared them. Afterwards they found courage to go forward as winners, neither victims nor wallowers.

Finding strength from within, these courageous souls earned the special symbol of courage that shows in Triangular Nostrils. So when you see them on somebody's face, Power-Packed Reader, may it open up your own heart of compassion.

Let's Get Practical: Dating a Nostril

On to a cheerier topic: Which sort of nostrils are the best to date?

If you are single and desperately lonely on a Saturday night, it may seem that a date's ways with money would count as the least of your troubles. Still, I do recommend that you seriously examine the nostrils of a *serious* date. (Well, not so carefully that you lose the date by seeming like you have an obsession with nose hair.)

Gather your data quickly and then proceed with the flirting. Afterwards, in tranquility, recollect those nostrils. Contemplate how their corresponding style might impact your financial comfort.

Maybe a wild, free-spending courtship appeals to your sense of adventure... all the way up to your nostrils. Suppose that you date someone with **Large, Round Nostrils** (and hopefully other fascinating attributes as well). You will have a great time, especially if that big spender is paying for at least half of your evening's entertainment.

But would it be wise to marry the owner of those particular nostrils? Factors that influence your decision might include your own spending style and the presence (or absence) of an enormous personal trust fund.

Dates with an owner of **Rectangular Nostrils** will be different. Do not expect such a date to equate courtship with lavish spending. However, if your bank accounts get hitched, your mate's budgeting style could add greatly to your financial peace of mind.

Neither Nose Tip Size nor Nostril Shape nor Nostril Size can guarantee a certain amount of money in the bank. Spending style is a matter of proportion, given the money available. But that style does matter enormously, long term. Will your prospective partner uplift your financial standards or bring out the worst in you?

Willingness to *discuss* money can matter nearly as much as how your mate spends it. Self-awareness matters as well. Remember the two nostril tales I shared with you earlier? Both of the women with the huge credit card debt (and nostrils) were honest with themselves, a first step toward overcoming any challenge in life.

Well, how financially aware is that new love interest of yours?

Don't just read faces to find out. Supplement that by asking questions.

"How's the weather?" won't do the job. Boldly ask questions related to potential challenges linked to that person's nose tip and nostrils.

Listening to the answer, use your inner Truth O'Meter. To start you thinking like a Savvy Face Reader Who Dates, here are some questions you might pose after the first few dates:

- To someone like Joyce, with a Small Nose Tip or VERY Large Nostrils, "Have you started saving for retirement yet?"
- To someone like Fred with a Very Large Nose Tip, "Do you go on big vacations often? Where are your favorite places?"
- To someone like Gary with Rectangular Nostrils and/or a VERY Large Nose Tip: "Do you like shopping? Which stores are your favorites?"

Money management doesn't require a degree in finance. Unless you're a Certified Public Accountant dating another CPA, you might not want to discuss money much during a first date.

But later? It's smart to discuss your current money habits. How much do you tithe or give to charity? How much do you save?

Whatever your nose tip and nostrils, you can manage your money and not have money wind up managing you. Not a bad discussion topic with a serious date!

Let's Get Practical Some More: Your Best Sales Prospects

Now here's a tip for those of you who work in sales. A Nose-Tip-Type tip.

Does the term "Screening customers" have meaning for you? Then lavish time on potential customers with VERY Up-Angled Eyes, also those with VERY Large, Round Nostrils.

Find someone with both? Such prospects are any salesperson's dream. They tend to be huge financial risk takers, believing in every glorious possibility.

For all you Power-Packed Readers, secrets about work and money make noses a truly delightful part of the face. Whether choosing a date or a job, whether closing a big business deal or running routine errands (that otherwise could be mind-numbingly dull) now you can stop along your path to smell the noses.

They have so much to tell you.

Nose-related secrets can add significantly to your power of face reading.

17. Mouths

Socially it's common to stare at eyes. Mouths, not so much. Usually we'll avert our eyes unless a quick look reassures us with a warm smile.

Yet mouths reveal just as much as eyes, even without a welcoming expression. Power-Packed Reader, you can have great fun learning how much mouths blab... about their owner's personal style with different aspects of communication.

Lipfulness

Lipfulness means how full, even chubby, lips are. To read this category, or anything else about mouths, you'll need to resist the temptation to see lips as simply big or small. Physiognomy demands way more nuance.

To research Lipfulness accurately, concern yourself with that attribute alone. Usually the upper lip has a different fullness than the lower lip. In which case, average them more or less. Another strategy is to view Lipfulness in the context of that person's Nose Tip Size and overall size of eyes.

- **Full Lips** chat at one extreme of lipfulness. See Oliver and Gary. A VERY version belongs to Kathryn.
- **Small Lipfulness** blabs at the other extreme. See Lloyd and George. A VERY version belongs to Annette.
- **Moderate Lipfulness** utters nothing extreme in either direction, just a moderate proportion when compared with the rest of the face. Examples from our Cast of Characters include Anthony, and Alexander, plus the left side of Matt's mouth.

Dare to Go Counter-Culture

Before we start interpreting Lipfulness, I think it's pretty important to debunk a huge social myth. Power-Packed Reader, have you ever heard that the plumpness of lips is supposedly clear evidence of sexiness?

You can't go to the movies without seeing women with plumped-up lips. Even girls under 10 are injected with this fake form of appeal.

(Ugh, don't get me started on how vanity surgery has become the new makeup. If I'm lucky, by the time this book is published, the Age of Vanity will have given way to an Age of Enlightenment, or at least an Era of More Common Sense.)

As face readers, we can provide a welcome alternative to this ridiculous concept. For the sake of sexiness, in physiognomy at least, there is no requirement to pump up mouths like tires at a filling station..

Now hear this: Everyone is sexy. At least everyone who wishes to be sexy can be sexy.

Really I can think of only one sex-related advantage to having extra-full lips. What if the person trying to kiss you has really bad aim? An extra-large target could help.

Otherwise, really, ridiculous! Let's fling aside social stereotypes, fads in makeup and pressures to trade in body parts as though participating in a white elephant sale. Power-Packed Reader, you can relax about your natural degree of Lipfulness, whatever that is.

Lipfulness isn't about sexiness but something else. Something that, unlike your sexual performance, can be shared with every single person you meet.

That said, take a look in that dependable mirror of yours. Please avoid the temptation to smile in the mirror. I know you like you. (At least I hope so.) But smiling changes how your mouth looks. (At least, I hope so).

Interpreting Lipfulness

Lipfulness whispers secrets about self-disclosure. Do you enjoy talking about personal matters, like shameful emotional quirks, psychological traumas (both mini- and maxi-sized); my personal relationship with My Savior; my sexual preferences and how I discovered them; a complete life list of my ice cream experiences including detailed descriptions of mouth feel for each spoonful; plus why the socks I am wearing today don't match and what I believe everyone else can learn from this?

You get the idea. Potentially, everyone has loads to share about me-me-me. Lipfulness means self-disclosure on parade. What is your personal comfort limit for discussing all those juicy topics?

Full Lips are great for breaking a conversation wide open. A share won't feel authentic to you unless it includes loads of juicy details.

Even if your generous Lipfulness doesn't make you sexually superior to other mortals, you've still got something great corresponding to those wonderful lips. You specialize in fascinating conversations. For this, thank your willingness to share your truth, your whole truth.

Indirectly you may even help people who are more reserved. You model for them how sweet it can be, sharing confidences in a deep-dish manner.

Your potential challenge? Embarrassing others.

Incidentally, will those embarrassed folks directly reveal their discomfort? Not necessarily. It could still cost you, at work or in your personal life.

To overcome this challenge, read a stranger's lips, especially the Lipfulness. Unless that person has Full Lips, too, downplay the personal aspect.

Another way to overcome this challenge is to offer your chatting companions a choice, e.g., "Which would you rather talk about next, the weather or a detailed account of my natural childbirth experience?"

Now, what if you have relatively **Small Lipfulness**? Probably you don't have to worry about embarrassing total strangers with your personal revelations. No, your potential challenge is saying enough about yourself to embarrass anyone.

Kidding. Of course, you can talk. And each person you talk with has an inalienable right to feel offended, especially embarrassed, whatever you say.

Your potential challenge is finding it hard to divulge personal information when people ask you for it. Such as a lover who begs you, begs you, "Tell me what really turns you on."

Well, hello! Communication under such circumstances doesn't have to be verbal at all. Why do you think God gave you hands, etc.?

As for revelations of a non-sexual nature, such a great talent accompanies Small Lipfulness! You don't automatically feel compelled to share every minute detail of your personal life.

So how about giving yourself credit for that? You can be hugely effective as a communicator especially because you *don't* feel the need to make all your conversations especially intimate.

Consider how effectively you can talk with friends and do business. Most human endeavors do not require huge self-disclosure. Friends who talk to you might actually feel great relief, as if being on holiday from watching reality shows on TV. Imagine, you can get through an interpersonal transaction without turning it into a form of lay psychoanalysis.

With **Moderate Lipfulness**, you are totally flexible about self-disclosure. A little, a lot, just a twinkle — you decide for yourself in a carefree, spontaneous manner.

If it wasn't for the potential challenge, I would congratulate you on having no self-disclosure issues whatsoever.

Except, oops! What about that lack of tolerance for the rest of humanity?

Many a time you may scratch your head over friends who clam up like Wayne. Or you might puzzle over a buddy like Kathryn, who keeps breaking her record for divulging way too much information.

"Really," you wonder in exasperation. "Why can't they be more normal, more like me?"

Power-Packed Reader, I think you know the answer to that one.

Speaking of answers, when introduced to reading Lipfulness, you were told something important: Your top and bottom lips could have entirely different amounts of fullness.

To read the Lipfulness category, you made a general assessment of both lips averaged out. Were you wondering, though, about those Lipfulness differences between upper and lower lip? Smart wonder! Here come some answers.

Lip Proportions

To read the category of Lip Proportions, all you need do is compare the fullness of upper and lower lips.

- Usually the lower lip is somewhat fuller than the upper one, which I call a **Moderately Fuller Lower Lip**. For examples, see Valerie and Alexander.
- How about lips that differ from this norm? An **Extra-Full LOWER Lip** means the lower lip is two, three, or more times fuller than the upper one. (I have a more colorful name for this that I'll tell you about later.) See both sides of Kathryn's mouth, also the left side of Jesse's mouth. VERY versions belong to Gary and Madison.
- As for an **Extra-Full UPPER Lip**, that means an upper lip at least as full as the lower one. Way different from what you just saw with the Extra-Full Lower Lip. In order to count as extra full, the upper lip doesn't have to be two or three times fuller. Just equally full on top. See Oliver for an example.
- A slightly fuller upper lip, compared to the lower lip, counts as a **VERY Extra-Full Upper Lip**. Nobody from our Cast of Characters wins that contest, but walk down a city street long enough and you will find some examples.

Now, Power-Packed Reader, do check out your personal Lip Proportions. (Don't say, "Cheese." Maybe "Glue"?)

Interpreting Lip Proportions

Just as human mouths generally contain a set of two lips, human speech can fall into two categories:

Speech about **objective reality**, (factual and physical things; any material object that can be counted, for instance) is represented by the lower lip.

Speech about **subjective reality** (e.g., Memories, dreams, reflections, beliefs, emotions, and intuitive perception), all that huge inner world, is represented by the upper lip.

Lip Proportions disclose a person's preferred type of speech.

Holy modem! What about the degree of emotional honesty or, perhaps, the intelligence behind your words? Or the truthfulness? As toy manufacturers might say, "These batteries are sold separately."

So let's be clear. Speech from the lower lip specializes in factual emphasis, not necessarily precision. While speech from the upper lip relates to topics are that are personal, even secret, with a degree of insight that might be less than bed sheets on a clothesline, flapping in the wind.

Power-Packed Reader, *you* undoubtedly speak insightfully whatever your Lip Proportions. Nonetheless, you and all your significant others have specialties within this category, so here goes.

An Extra-Full Lower Lip is a big deal. It's such a big deal, the following information alone could be worth the full price of this book. (Although I'll leave it to those of you with Rectangular Nostrils to make the precise calculation.)

Huge persuasiveness corresponds to those lip proportions. Lailan Young, my favorite contemporary practitioner of *siang mien*, has coined the perfect nickname for it, **Blarney Lips**.

Have you ever heard of kissing the Blarney Stone? According to Irish folklore, this is definitely the rock to kiss. One smooch will download a lifelong gift of gab. After the instant your smackers make contact, whatever you say from then on... can charm your listener. Regardless of what you are talking about. Or how true it is.

Why is it so important to be able to detect Blarney Lips?

When dating, seeing this in your new companion could help you keep your wits about you. Also your clothing.

As a consumer, noticing this mouth characteristic in others can put you on appropriate High Alert. A Blarney-Lipped salesperson could cause you to develop an urgent need for designer ice. Even though you live in Minnesota and it's February!

Soon as you eyeball such lips, arm yourself with skepticism. Not that everyone with Blarney Lips is necessarily dishonest; folks with these lips are just such darned good convincers. When "Washingtonian Magazine" ran a list of the nation's 50 most influential journalists, I went through the head shots. A physiognomist's version of head hunting!

Sure enough, I spotted 46 out of 50 top journalists with Blarney Lips, most of them VERYs. With average folks you would find maybe one pair out of a group of 50, and a VERY pair for one in 500.

Power-Packed Reader, if you are the one with Blarney Lips, congratulations. Persuasiveness may come so easily that you haven't thought much about it. Well, consider this. More than any other item of face data, Blarney Lips bring success.

Just remember to combine your gift of gab with integrity. Otherwise your potential challenge could create heartache.

Heartache of a kind that is perfectly understandable: Being so good at convincing *anyone* you like to believe *anything* you like, how tempting it might be to explore the possibilities.

As for you Power-Packed Readers with an Extra-Full Upper Lip, here's a laugh. My nickname for your lippy talent is **Outspoken Perceptiveness.**

How does someone like you heap perceptiveness upon perceptiveness? Your distinctive gift for communication can work in this sequence:

1. You are irrepressibly curious about what makes people tick. Refusing to accept other people's theories, you perpetually seek insights of your own.
2. Whatever you learn, you are articulate. You can find words to capture the nuances that you discover. That's important because you are unlikely to learn the language from other people, like TV talk show hosts. Not, at least, the creative and accurate ways you find words to express your insights.
3. You want to tell.

Uh-oh. That third part is the glory of Outspoken Perceptiveness, but also the potential challenge.

What if the person you are telling doesn't want to listen? Overcoming this challenge involves learning when to hold back, even if what you have to say is important. Otherwise, you'll be casting pearls before swine.

Say, for instance, that Valerie is your friend from work. She is always complaining about her mother-in-law and expects you to play captive audience.

One day, you let her have it. Flinging perceptiveness at your friend, you ask in your gentlest tones, "Have you ever considered that your mother-in-law might not like when you insult her right to her face? Such as the example you just gave me."

Given your Outspoken Perceptiveness, had Valerie offered you that kind of spot-on insight, how would you respond? Probably with something like:

"Wow, you are right."

"Thank you."

"I'll have to think about that."

From Valerie, alas, you are more likely to hear:

"You are wrong."

"You are inappropriate."

"You must be crazy."

Consider yourself warned. Comments like these would be voiced in Valerie's ascending order of defensiveness. (None of her accusations necessarily being true, and definitely not the part about alleged craziness.)

Actually, if Valerie were more honest she might say, "The only acceptable answer to my problems is blaming others. If you won't cheerfully enable me, I never want you to speak to me again. If you insist on contradicting my world view, I must put you on my Enemies List."

However, the important point with Outspoken Perceptiveness is about you, not blaming otherwise sweet people like Valerie. Overcoming the challenge with your speech style can be easy.

Before blurting out insights (even if you have Lowbrows, with their wonderful associated spontaneity), simply brake first. Ask an intermediary question before delivering your truthsome goodies. For instance, you might ask your friend:

"Valerie, I have an idea about that. Are you interested in hearing it?"

What if you work in sales and you have those Outspoken Perceptiveness Lips? Would it be wise to get collagen injections to turn Lip Proportions into Blarneys?

Never, please! You can be successful with any personal style. That's the underlying message of my system of Face Reading Secrets, along my assurance that you can make whatever you have work for you.

You can always find a way to express your soul gloriously. (Not to mention, authenticity is way more fun than trying out something fake, supposedly to become more successful.)

Most people, possessing a Moderately Fuller Lower Lip, talk more about the facts than the nuances. This talent has no special nickname in my system of Face Reading Secrets. Unless you want to call it **Perfectly Normal Communication for Most of Humanity**.

Flexible you. On occasion, your speech will emphasize facts of objective reality. Other times, you will emphasize subjective aspects, flinging out words as appropriate given the situation.

Okay, you might have that potential challenge about lack of tolerance for the rest of humanity. Honestly, don't the facts-mostly folks like Kathryn annoy you on occasion? Maybe once, just once, you don't want to be sold.

Or how about the countless times you don't want to hear a peep more, not one single gushy word more, about the very complicated inner life of Oliver?

Why, oh why, can't these people be normal and civilized? You know, like you.

Mouth Length

Checking out Mouth Length is trickier than you might think. Whether looking at photos or seeing yourself in a mirror, you are duty bound to look past illusions... at least while reading faces.

In an earlier chapter on "Smiles," you were educated about fake smiles in general. Here I want you to consider the version of fake smile that distorts Mouth Length.

Many people have trained themselves to deliver a lips-together half-smile. This is supposed to look pleasant. Lloyd is doing it in his photo, for instance.

Honestly, has an expression like this ever fooled you into thinking "What a nice person"?

Lloyd might well be very nice. But making a fake face isn't the way to prove it, not in my opinion anyhow.

Power-Packed Reader, can't you tell the difference between a relaxed mouth in repose versus this mask-like nonchalance? Pay attention and you will get it right away.

Except that TV trains us to accept that kind of face as "smiling," just as we are trained not to notice when most women over the age of 30, appearing on network television, have had their faces "fixed."

So it's understandable if you, personally, have caught this accept-mugging shtick from TV, like a computer catching a virus.

If so, you might wish to debug. To the discerning eye, a mouth-lengthening fake smile whispers "Phony" more than "Pleasant."

We face readers aren't hunting for expression of course. Just that, on the level of seeing face data accurately, we need to be able to spot trickery.

What else will help you to read the Mouth Length category accurately? Remind yourself — as all face readers must, occasionally — to research only one category at a time.

It's so easy for mouth watchers to be distracted by lipfulness, lipstick, mustaches... especially if you find both lipstick and mustache on the same face.

How can you research Mouth Length, once you find lips that aren't half-smiling? Find yourself a reasonable point of reference, the width of one eye.

Make that an eye belonging to the same person whose Mouth Length you are reading!

- **Medium-Length Lips** are a bit longer than two of your eyes placed horizontally. Ugh, don't try too hard to picture this, but see our examples of Matt and Oliver, with a VERY version on Ava.
- **Short Lips** are closer to the length of two eyes. See Jesse and Alexander. And a VERY version belongs to Kathryn.
- Relatively rare are **Long Lips**. When the lips are neither smiling Duchenne style nor smirking, you could still fit three eyes alongside each other. See Annette.
- As usual, start reading this category with an appreciative look at yourself.

Interpreting Mouth Length

This category whispers secrets about a speaker's most comfortable audience size.

Glossophobia (fear of public speaking), is a common problem. This can especially be a challenge if you have **Short Lips**. But the corresponding talent with this face data is so lovely: Sincere, honest speech.

Your preferred conversational size is one-on-one. Power-Packed Reader with Short Lips, you'll make that lucky companion of yours feel really special.

As for overcoming that potential challenge, practice helps. So does looking at one friendly member of your audience as you speak.

Friendly as in *sympathetic,* not as in *wearing underwear.* Maybe you have heard the famous advice to overcome fear of public speaking, "Imagine that everyone in the audience is wearing underwear." For someone whose lips are both short and thin, even one faint attempt at doing this could result in a year's worth of nightmares.

My hunch? Folks with **Large Lipfulness** are the ones who do best with the Underwear Technique.

Nudists might also find it funny, as in "How sad to find people who would resort to wearing underwear in a group like this when they could be totally naked." Okay, back to face reading....

Long Lips broadcast talent for talking with anyone, people wearing anything. Talking with the largest group possible, why not?

Lucky you, if you have this verbal form of leadership. It's a gift that keeps on giving, sincere friendliness being contagious.

The potential challenge involves being a social chameleon, saying "Whatever" just to go along with the group.

For instance, suppose that happens to Annette while at a party. Being the life of that party, she feels compelled to speak in alignment with the majority. "My favorite color is definitely mauve," she agrees.

Back home, after the party, Annette realizes that she doesn't even know what color "mauve" is. There she is, stuck, trying to make sense of her life. Soon Annette might rationalize that, since she said it, mauve must really be the color she prefers.

How deeply confusing is that? Until overcome, this challenge could eat away at Annette's integrity. Few sights in human life are sadder than a company woman, or a party gal, left alone with her conscience.

With **Medium Mouth Length**, your range of communication is flexible. You feel equally comfortable talking one-on-one and addressing crowds (especially if you've had the chance to practice a dozen times or more).

Truthfulness is your strongest mode of self-expression but you are better at lying than short-mouthed folks, who tend to be terrible at it.

"Life of the party" is a role you can play well with Moderate Lip Length, depending on which particular party. Unlike someone with a Long Mouth, you might also steal away for an intimate chat with a close friend or two.

In general, an adaptable speech style makes life easier for you. Your only challenge with that Moderate Lip Length? Not that we need speak the name aloud. It's merely, ahem, some lack of tolerance for the rest of humanity.

Why can't folks like Jesse get over that childish form of shyness? As for your friend Annette, you know you can't trust a thing she says in public. Besides, she looks so silly in that mauve wig.

Let's Get Practical: Outsmart Celebrities

Sadly, if you watch TV in America these days, most of the female faces you see will be semi-fake. Between the vanity surgery procedures, the digitally enhanced images, the tricky camera angles, what's a face reader to trust?

Just do your best to read each face as it is. Valid insights will flow, due to the reciprocal relationship between the physical face and the soul. When a star's face has been radically altered and Botoxed and lifted, however, a plastic look does set in. Surely you have noticed.

Power-Packed Reader, I won't blame you a bit if you feel weird seeking insights about a celebrity's mask of a face. Consider supplementing face reading with other types of deeper perception. For instance, at my blog, "Deeper Perception Made Practical" (www.rose-rosetree.com/blog) I will sometimes profile celebrities, reading auras from celebrity photographs taken at different times.

This research suggests that, in general, there is a terrible price to pay for walking around with a face that could belong to your daughter or granddaughter.

But here's some good news for those of us who love to read faces. Currently Mouth Length is one of the few facial attributes that's unlikely to be surgically altered. (Another is your reference point, eye length. Ha ha!)

So enjoy reading this facial category in its authentic state. Un-retouched face data does tend to express the soul best. (Granted, cosmetic surgery will transform a person inwardly, so those altered faces still count as valid to read. Plus, celebrity or not, a person may have very good reasons to get optional facial procedures. And be very happy with the results!)

Still, I find this mouth category so refreshing to read. Cosmetic surgery may change a face from the outside in, and collagen shots may change several mouth characteristics, but Mouth Length tends to speak… like a virgin.

Mustaches

Mustaches aren't merely hair but clear symbols of masculinity.

Ladies, don't feel bad that society denies you a comparable opportunity to use your face as a sexual billboard. Ever hear of makeup?

Makeup lies outside the scope of physiognomy. Not so the noble mustache.

Of course, mustache grooming is informative even before you get around to the face reading part. When a man fusses over his facial hair, trims it immaculately, or develops mannerisms around curling it while he talks to you — perhaps twirling it, tweaking it, or stroking it — sexiness is very much on this man's mind.

Gary does all that, for instance. Does that mean he is very secure or very insecure? Each observer must decide for herself or himself, one twirl at a time.

I applaud every adorable manly mustache, however. It takes courage to let one spread over your face, like an irrepressible smile. Any mustache broadcasts something about your sexual confidence. It's a show-and-tell for all the world to see.

Nonverbally, what are you saying? Maybe that you can't help it if your virility is supersized!

Unfortunately, the impression made by facial hair does depend on how that hair is controlled. A man runs the risk of having the world overlook his virility message and assume instead that he's a slob. Which brings us to the main mustache category in physiognomy: **Upper Lip Display**.

As a physiognomist, you read this category by noticing whether or not the hair has been trimmed to cover the man's upper lip. If you have a mustache of your own, check out this category in the mirror. Otherwise, find examples from our Cast of Characters.

- A **Lip Framer Mustache** is trimmed to deliciously highlight a man's upper lip. The hair may deliciously flirt with the edge of your mouth, as if to say, "Shall I touch you or not? Perhaps not, just for today. Do ask me again tomorrow." See Jesse and Alexander. Fred wears a VERY version.
- By contrast, a **Lip-Hider Mustache** covers some of a man's upper lip. See George.
- The **VERY version of a Lip Hider** is an immense, slipcover-like creation. It upholsters you from overlip to beard, leaving any bare mouth to a minimum. (Examples are as near as Santa Claus.)
- Finally a **Semi-Hider Mustache** contains portions that cover the upper lip; other hairy bits frame the upper lip. Thank you, Lloyd, for not grooming yours too meticulously in advance of your photo shoot.

When your mustache is a Lip Framer, it symbolizes willingness to divulge feelings. Not incessantly, not compulsively, but as a talent. So let's be clear. This face reading data does not mean that you necessarily need to "Man up."

Symbolically how you trim your mustache reveals your personal notions of manliness. With your kind of mustache, wow, a real man can have feelings! Consequently you are willing to discuss them with a friend or lover, as appropriate.

Hey, you could even play the lead in "Romeo and Juliet" (provided that, besides having this cool type of mustache, you are also an actor).

To assess the full impact of your **Lip Framer Mustache**, try the following math calculation: Note your Lipfulness and interpret what that means about your spontaneous talent for self-disclosure. Add points for how full your mustache is in the first place. Next, multiply this by how VERY decisively that mustache clears your upper lip.

VERY emphatic framing times a VERY full mustache would signify the greatest talent for a masculine style of maximum self-disclosure about personal feelings.

Will you find that often? Nope.

Such computations aside, any upper-lip-revealing mustache will brand you as a "Sensitive Man," the sort who admits to taking growth seminars or (Gosh!) becoming a face reader.

All you Power-Packed Readers, use imagination to translate how this sensitive style of masculinity would impact a guy's bedroom behavior. Many lovers, with appropriate gender and sexual orientation, prefer your style of virility.

Your potential challenge? Nothing about masculinity is more controversial than a man's willingness to appear sensitive. Although some strangers will instantly like you for this, others most definitely will not. Prejudice can be harsh.

Soon as they can see the whites of your eyes, folks will be close enough to assess how much skin peeks out between your upper lip and that mustache. Whatever you do, certain people will dislike you for your facial hair. Unless you shave it off completely.

What happens when a guy doesn't have much of a visible upper lip yet he still wears this tell-all type of mustache? Is his potential challenge an exploding head?

No, a physiognomist's answer is far more nuanced. That VERY Small Lipfulness corresponds, of course, to extreme dislike for self-disclosure. However the guy has trimmed his mustache in a way that delivers the subconscious message that he *adores* sensitivity-based conversations. What's going on?

Check out Lloyd, for instance. He has this mouth-mustache combo.

- Either the man is making a heroically extreme effort to become more self-revealing.
- Or he takes pride in speaking his mind and expressing an extremely unsentimental approach, substituting a rational approach. (That's exactly what I think goes on with Lloyd. For more about this interpretation, skip over to my discussion of his management of facial hair in our "Chins" chapter.)
- Or perhaps he just trims his mustache way vigorously, caring more about neatness in the mustache than the inner consequences of his baring an upper lip along with VERY Small Lipfulness.

Realistically though, how often do you see this combo of lip-framer mustache and no upper lip? Men who don't self-disclose comfortably seldom portray themselves at the opposite extreme. They're far more likely to grow a **Lip-Hider Mustache**.

Maybe you've just seen one in the mirror. Then you're a guy who defines masculinity ruggedly, even outrageously. Your sort of tough guy discuss anybody's emotions. You kidding?

What, kidding? Don't expect laughter over such a joke, or any joke that might make you appear "weak."

George has this type of mustache, for instance. Don't expect him to gush any time soon.

Note: Displaying a crinkly smile (when he chooses) doesn't mean the guy likes gushing.

His Lip-Hider Mustache signifies talent for being a certain type of man, an old-fashioned Real Man, even a strong silent type.

That takes some doing, as you know if you also wear a Lip-Hider Mustache. Unless you do outrageous big smiling like George, people can take you really seriously. Only your closest friends will dare to ask personal questions. Even if consciously they're not face readers yet, subconsciously they get the message.

Your potential challenge with sending out the message of a Lip-Hider Mustache? It's the waste of a perfectly fine upper lip, especially a full one. Whatever the Lipfulness on that upper lip, might you be hiding your ability to have close relationships?

Finally we must consider the **Semi-Hider Mustache**, which inconsistently frames and hides your upper lip. Neither here nor there, this type of mustache may begin as a grooming omission yet the consequences remain. As you know, face reading is based on a very consistent reciprocal relationship between the physical face and the inner person.

For instance, consider Gary's Semi-Hider Mustache. To a hot new date like Valerie, he might seem like the guy of all possibilities. Maybe intimate as a communicator, yet also an old-fashioned manly man.

Over time, though, Valerie will get wise. Or if Valerie reads faces, she will know immediately about Gary's potential challenge. She won't trust Gary much around the topic of self-disclosure – unless Valerie happens to be similarly evasive, in which case her heart strings may quiver "Soul Mate."

Otherwise, Valerie might find it vexing, how inconsistently Gary can act. Unless the potential challenge is overcome, sometimes he will be available for tender talk; other times he will turn into a hard-to-get sort of guy. Adorable Gary might be predictable only in his unpredictability as a close communicator.

However, any Semi-Hider Mustache represents a talent, too. When a mustache semi-hides his upper lip, a man enjoys the benefits of ambivalence around self-disclosure.

Let's Get Practical: Commitment

Unwillingness to commit isn't limited to mustache wearers or, even, to men. The challenge shows in many different face reading characteristics. Here are three you might have, mustache wearer or not:

- **Deep-Set Eyes** present a potential challenge with hiding. Specifically, hiding your true feelings. Even significant others may not know the truth about you. How do you really feel about them?
- **Straight Lower Eyelid Curve** can signal your making people work really hard to earn your trust. And have to win that trust repeatedly.
- **Out-Angled Ears** hint at being a contrarian, committing to a relationship only when your partner doesn't.

By contrast, a **Semi-Hider Mustache** brings the potential challenge of withholding support for others, doing this on an intermittent and mysterious schedule.

All these potential challenges share a payoff. Maybe you even know somebody who has all four attributes. Consciously he may never think about power in his relationships. He is, however, used to expecting total control.

It's only human for a person to enjoy this. Overcoming such challenges would be such a man's human potential. Even ennobling.

However, let's continue being practical, Power-Packed Reader. When you notice even one of these four characteristics on somebody else's face, consider yourself warned. The power of face reading helps you to discern other people's character, not necessarily improve it.

Overlips and Philtrums

Successful actors don't look like you and me. Or, at least, me. Philtrums are definitely a relevant issue.

Most performers show something interesting above their mouths, in their overlip sculpting. We will get to that. First, though, what is an overlip anyway?

Overlip is NOT your upper lip. Instead it lies above your upper lip, forming the area between nose tip and mouth.

Overlips contain many categories in physiognomy, such as Length, Width, and Thrust. Most important for a new face reader is an overlip's two ridges of flesh, sculpted into a face with a sort of valley nestled between the ridges.

Call this your "**Philtrum**," Power-Packed Reader. Unless, like my friend Joe, you prefer calling it "The vital link." (This term comforts Joe when he nicks it while shaving.)

Razor optional, take a quick look in the mirror. Do you see two raised ridges, more or less parallel, forming a groove in between? Or don't you see much contouring of anything?

Put down that mirror. Calm down, too, if necessary. This face reading system is based on the premise, "God don't make no junk." Remember?

Whatever you noticed in that preliminary glance, your life will work out perfectly fine.

Now, more nuance for reading this relatively mysterious part of your face.

Your degree of philtrum sculpting has a name, of course, Power-Packed Reader. Because how can you empower yourself as a physiognomist by calling things on your overlip "Whatsies"?

So meet the face reading category of **Philtrum Definition**. Explore just how ridged a philtrum might be.

To refine your research, I recommend the **Philtrum Definition Index**. Ranging from 1 to 10, the Index's #10 means the strongest quality of chiseling, with a #1 corresponding to neither visible ridges nor much of a valley-like hollow between those sorta-ridges.

Right before you hoist up that mirror, stop. Arrange your expression to avoid smiling. You know, smiles are done with lips, not overlips. But any smile will distort Philtrum Definition, plus all the other philtrum categories not discussed here. (If you are a philtrum fancier, you can find additional categories in a companion how-to, "Read People Deeper.")

Most of our Cast of Characters did smile somewhat for their close-ups, unfortunately. So I'm reading this category as best I can. You know, Power-Packed Reader, a pragmatic approach keeps a physiognomist sane — a trade secret I'm happy to share with you.

At least, when inspecting your own overlip area, you have the advantage of controlling whether or not the face in question is smiling.

- A **Well-Defined Philtrum** shows two chiseled ridges very distinct from each other. In the mirror, you might see the high definition range from 8-10, with 9 or 10 counting as the VERY version.

Bad boy Alexander scores a 10.

- If you can't find much by way of ridges (chiseled or not), name what you Have "**Low-Profile Philtrum Definition**." This means a score of 1-3 on the Philtrum Definition Index, with 1 or 2 being considered the VERY version. Ava scores a 3, Annette a 1.
- Otherwise, you have been blessed with **Moderate Philtrum Definition**. This means you score somewhere between 4-7 on Philtrum Definition Index. I would score Kathryn a 5, Oliver a 4.

Interpreting Philtrum Definition

Philtrum Definition can whisper the most fascinating secrets about sex appeal. Do you make heads swivel, even if you haven't just come from the hairdresser's? With a **Well-Defined Philtrum**, the answer is probably "Now that you mention it, yes!"

Out on the town, you could be grumpy, unsociable, sweaty, exhausted. Who cares, far as sex appeal is concerned? You could be fatter than you'd prefer, or thinner. You could be old enough to be the mother or father of the person who beholds you now with undisguised lust.

Probably, though, you and your Well-Defined Philtrum have dressed in a way that does emphasize your sexiness. After all, strangers have been responding to your vibe ever since those hot, hormonal teenage years. You're used to a certain sexual self-consciousness.

What explains this link between an obscure facial characteristic and being a hottie? Where is the justice?

One of my students has astutely referred to a woman's well defined philtrum as "Upper cleavage." Regardless of whether or not you happen to be in the mood, some people near you will think about sex.

Consolation alert, if you have Low-Profile Philtrum Definition. Some of the implications may have already occurred to you. Well, stop sobbing. Think. Would you really want to live, day after day, with that degree of magnetism?

That's right, would you truly enjoy being like the mega-sexy actor Hugh Grant, fated to have otherwise normal people stammer and drool in your presence? Once I read his aura for the "Chicago Sun-Times" newspaper. To quote reporter Paige Weiser, quoting me:

"To really capture how far his sex appeal sticks out, I'd have to jump through the wall in my office and go out about a mile.'"

Later Paige quoted my researching the price I thought mega-sexy Hugh Grant paid for being so fabulously fit:

"Grant's heart chakra is well protected. He has five walls around it, Rosetree says, and each is very thick. 'This is a way he's learned to handle being that sexy and getting that kind of reaction from people,' Rosetree says."

Even if your Philtrum Definition does not ascend all the way to a screaming VERY, perhaps being merely an 8 on the Philtrum Definition Index, your challenge with any degree of Well-Defined Philtrum is… handling all the attention.

Few people, deep down, yearn to be treated (by everyone) primarily as sex objects. So the question becomes: Once you get all that attention, what will you do with it?

"Become a movie star!" Sure, that is one answer. Did you know that VERY defined philtrums are practically a job requirement if you want to play the love interest roles?

However, facial characteristics do not mean automatic movie star placement through some Cosmic Employment Office. With a Well-Defined Philtrum, you don't really have to compete with millions already in show biz. Even without auditioning for a Philtrum Reality Show, you can make exceedingly good use of your talent. Sexual energy is, simply, energy.

Talent corresponding to a well-defined philtrum allows you to turn up the energy wherever you go. After that interest awakens, direct it however you like. Sales or politics, not just performing arts, may appeal to you professionally. Success in these fields is definitely enhanced by sexual charisma. Like your lucky Cousin Alexander, for instance!

As for **Low-Profile Philtrum Definition**, a relative lack of animal magnetism is your potential challenge. Don't be discouraged, though.

Sex appeal means nothing, absolutely nothing about real-life sexiness. Anyone can be sexy in an authentic way, with a suitable real-life partner.

Your Aunt Annette, for example, may have confided to you about some of those wild adventures from her past. Who would guess, just from looking at her philtrum…and searching for it without seeing much of anything. Ha ha!

Real-life sexiness depends on your free will. How you think, how you dress, how you speak: When you emphasize sex in everyday life, real-life sexiness will increase. Your target demographic will respond accordingly.

Besides, when you don't automatically turn up the energy with people, does that doom you to a life of great personal blandness, perhaps zero friending on Facebook? Not at all.

Witness the gift that does accompany your physical face data. With Low-Profile Philtrum Definition, you are wired to impress people first with other aspects of who you are. Perhaps your intellect, your kindness, your athletic prowess, your being a power-packed face reader.

When that adorable new date subconsciously reads your face, guess what? The sex appeal part of you may not reach out and grab attention — except for special times, like when you are in love. Instead your relationship can start growing because of your other gifts and interests.

Actually there's something to be said for having Hugh Grant, or whoever, fall in love with you first for those gifts, then discover your sexiness as a delicious afterthought.

For some souls, it could even be preferable to draw interest not based on your sex appeal. I'm living proof. This spiritual teacher and healer is quite relieved to have people relate to me as a spiritual teacher and healer, rather than a sex worker. As for my husband of decades, he isn't deterred by my score of 1 on the Philtrum Definition Index.

Regarding **Moderate Philtrum Definition**, that's the third delicious option out of three for this face reading category. If you're like Kathryn, your sex appeal can be flaunted or understated. You get to choose what's projected, one day at a time, one date at a time.

Your potential challenge? Aw, shucks, it's just the usual lack of tolerance for the rest of humanity.

Not that people usually have strong opinions and judgments about how other people flirt, or dress, or attempt other aspects of sexual display in public. Oh no. That would be like admitting to sarcasm.

Special Gifts from the Lip Fairy

And you only believed in the Tooth Fairy! There's a Lip Fairy, too. She has bestowed special gifts for communication on special people with certain extreme lip combinations. Might you have one of these?

- **VERY Long Lips + VERY Small Lipfulness**. See Annette.
- **VERY Long Lips + VERY Large Lipfulness**. Joyce from our Cast of Characters comes closest, with moderately large lipfulness and moderate mouth length. (That combo of VERY long lips with VERY large lipfulness is quite rare, Julia Roberts being a famous example.)
- **VERY Short Lips + VERY Small Lipfulness**. Rowan might be an example. It's hard to tell for sure unless you catch her not smiling.
- **VERY Short Lips + VERY Large Lipfulness**. See Jesse and Kathryn.

Just for fun, behold your mouth one more time. Not smiling, of course. It's possible that you have one of these unusual combos.

Anyway, Power-Packed Reader, it's very possible that you will encounter some. I want you to have the inside information just in case.

Each of these four special mouth gifts has a nickname that I use for convenience.

My nickname for VERY Long + Thin Lips is **Millionaire Mouth**. This combo of attributes is great for business, politics, or wry humor. It means you can comfortably talk to anyone about anything (so long as you are not asked to divulge personal information).

The words need not be, strictly speaking, true. But they will reach out to everyone in the group, no matter how large the gathering.

By not embarrassing potential clients with self-disclosure, Millionaire Mouths can discretely amass their fortunes.

The most exuberant way with words goes with VERY Long + Full Lips, which I call the **Born Talker Mouth**. It's hard to find someone with this face data who doesn't come across as a major extravert.

Actually, if you are familiar with the distinction between **extravert** and **introvert**, you will love how much extra nuance you find by reading faces.

Communication as an extravert is completely independent from timing for speech (Eyebrow Height), timing for making decisions (Ear Position), leadership style (Cheek Proportions and Cheek Prominence), or some chin categories you have yet to meet.

Back at the Born Talker Mouths, check out your favorite reality TV show or talk show. You'll find an unusually high proportion of talking heads with Long, Full Lips.

Although performers' Mouth Lengths come in every variety, speakers with Long, Full Lips is prepared to talk to anyone about anything. Personal topics are not off limits. Shockingly, not even while self-disclosing on television!

VERY Short + Thin Lips have their special excellence, too. I call them **Privacy Lips**. Yes, their owners may hold in feelings, replay old insults, and frustrate friends by playing way too much hide and seek.

When words do emerge, however, they can carry an uncanny soul-stirring power.

Let's not leave out another extremely interesting kind of mouth. I like to call VERY Short + Full Lips by the epithet "**Best Friend Lips**." This face combo suggests a willingness to tell the truth, the whole truth, without restriction. Just one catch, though — the juicy stuff will mostly be shared one-on-one.

Major Compassion Awakener: Mouth Puckers

Mouth Puckers look like miniature dimples on either side of the lips.

What are these puckers supposed to look like? Imagine what would happen to the corners of your mouth if you were to play the oboe. Except after you put the instrument down, you were to keep the puckers.

If so, they count as face data. For an example, see Lloyd. (In this photograph, he posed without an oboe.)

To see if you have Mouth Puckers, you will not require an oboe either. Nor will you need to smile in front of your mirror. Resume the unadorned version of mouth holding that you used when examining Lip Length. Most folks don't have Mouth Puckers. See if you do.

Interpreting, be prepared for one of those Major Compassion Awakeners.

People with Mouth Puckers excel at self-censorship. In particular, they have learned to avoid asking for what they need most. Show me a baby with Mouth Puckers. Just try!

Personal history is revealed in those puckers. We'll take your history for an example, if you should happen to possess this face data.

Before the Mouth Puckers appeared on your face, I suspect that you suffered major pain of a particular kind. A significant other consistently belittled your feelings, whether the scoffer was a parent, sibling, partner or teacher.

In short, Mouth Puckers appeared when you learned self-censorship. At the time, it was your best way to cope.

Now that can change. You can stop carrying that challenge forward. Practice asking appropriate people for what you need.

Start by asking someone you trust for something really small. For instance, suppose you have learned that your new yoga teacher, Helene, is gracious and kind. So kind that sometimes she will bring yoga students special pillows before the final relaxation exercise. Boldly, you might ask, "Helene, would you please bring me one of those fancy pillows?"

With practice you will learn to speak on your own behalf. Imagine, asking for favors as appropriate, and not just about pillows.

When the pain is fully healed, you may even lose those physical Mouth Puckers. Even then, your soul will remember what you learned earlier. This hard-won talent for verbal discretion can be highly useful.

As for you as a face reader, from now on, seeing Mouth Puckers can open up your heart of compassion. Wider and sweeter than ever!

With Lloyd, for instance, despite his cantankerous ways.... Yes, you might remember that he wasn't born with those Mouth Puckers. He has had a harder time in life than you might have supposed.

Let your heart of compassion open even more. Interacting with a tough guy like Lloyd, you might have to stand up for yourself extra assertively. Can you do that along with deep-down compassion?

Absolutely! The combination of pursuing appropriate self-interest plus caring and insight concerning others — absolutely, that can help you to live with the power of face reading.

18. Jaws

Granted, jaws and chins may not seem as soulful as your eyes, nor as kissable as your so-perfect mouth. Yet those nether portions are your face's bottom line, revealing vital secrets about principles, ethics, choices, and handling conflict.

Power-Packed Reader, you aren't really surprised that jaws could be meaningful, right? Not by now.

By now, you are so used to face parts taking on a life of their own that you could meet Mr. Potato Head walking down the street and not bat an eyelash — except perhaps to think he was on the short side for a grownup human.

And if he flung you an extra ear or nose, you'd probably pocket it cheerfully, thinking how it might come in handy some day. Such is the wisdom of a face reader.

You know there is no such thing as a throwaway, or insignificant, face part. All of it counts. That includes jaws, even though they're not generally loved or respected nearly enough.

Jaw Width

To explore jaw width as a face reading category, start comparing what you have with other people's lower face hinges.

- Exactly how wide are **Wide Jaws**, anyway? Let's put it this way. You can stash away several wads of chewing gum without their showing. See Matt. And a VERY version belongs to Jesse, on the right side of his face.
- **Narrow Jaws** don't catch your eye the way Wide Jaws do. You are more apt to overlook the width category and skip over to something else, like zooming over to your gorgeous eyes. Except you are reading faces now, so don't. See Lloyd on the left side of his face.
- **Moderate Jaw Width** is what most people have, neither especially wide nor narrow. See Ava, Valerie, Oliver, George, and Kathryn.

Interpreting Jaw Width

Jaw width reveals talent with commitment, as if you were clamping down your teeth like a dog, stubbornly holding on. As always with face data, everybody has something good in this category... just not the same kind of good.

Do you have **Wide Jaws**? Then congratulate yourself for exceptional loyalty. Folks at work or in your social life are unlikely to congratulate you for this loyalty, however. During the course of the relationship, you inadvertently train them to expect steadfastness from you, as though it were their inalienable right.

Hey, you have heard how rats leave a sinking ship. Who stays? People like you, with the Wide Jaws. You are an amazing gift to a company, a church, a cause, a spouse.

If I were getting a Ph.D. in Physiognomy Studies, I might do my thesis on jaws like yours. Specifically, I would research the correlation between divorce and Jaw Width. Inversely proportional, I suspect.

Meanwhile, do your own research. Start with the happiness and richness and depth to your important relationships, thanks to your strength of commitment. All your significant others can benefit from this toughness.

Think of the great British leader Winston Churchill. If it weren't for this tough leader, everyone in the world today might be living in some little Nazi suburb. Find a photo of Churchill's face and you will see an almost unbelievably wide set of jaws. He's famous for this motto: "Never, never, never, never, never give up."

The potential challenge with your particular wars? I mean jaws. ;-) It's knowing when to let a commitment go.

Sure that affiliation worked for you once upon a time. But what has it done for you lately? (This life lesson is especially important if you also have **Down-Angled Eyebrows**, which accompany talent for valuing wisdom from the past. But the potential challenge is not letting go of outgrown friendships and interests.)

Another potential challenge with Wide Jaws is making a commitment in the first place. My, how you might agonize!

Why? Deep down you know what you are in for. If you do decide to commit, you may stay in that relationship, or job, until death do you part. (Unless you have overcome the previously mentioned challenge, anyway.)

Finally, Wide Jaws relate to physical stamina. This face data is often found in professional athletes (unless the sport is golf, where instead you will likely find at least one Close-Set Eye). The more exhausting the sport — Think football! — the more likely you are to find players whose jaws bulge.

Of course, Wide Jaws on your own face don't mean, "Take physical stamina for granted." How well you care for your body today will show physically 10 years from now, same as for anyone else. What you have now, with those splendid Wide Jaws, simply means that you have an advantage right now.

Narrow Jaws go with a talent I call an "Early Detection Warning System for Conflict." Similar, perhaps, to those home security systems you may see advertised on television.

When was the last time you or Lloyd preened in front of a mirror, admiring your jaws and whispering to yourself, "Gorgeous Cuddles, you are just so refined"?

Well you could. (Just avoid making a YouTube.) You can feel justifiably proud of your Jaw-Width related talent. Only it's subtle. Here's how it works.

Say that you are friends with Valerie. Conflict starts creeping into your relationship. Which of you will notice first? You, of course. You with the Early Detection Warning System for Conflict.

This talent alerts you: *Something here is wrong.*

After a little thought, you will consciously figure out what bothers you.

Such knowledge is meant to be used. Not to be worried about, used. Used as the basis for a problem-solving conversation.

Your conversation might begin, "Valerie, could we talk a little bit about our relationship? You know how important our friendship is to me. But you keep on texting other people while we're together. It hurts my feelings. Would you please hold off on texting until our visit is over?"

How will Valerie react? Will she just text you, "Goodbye. Our friendship is so over"? I mean, "GB. Frendshp over. i wil nvr CYAL8R"?

In my opinion, you can't lose, no matter how Valerie reacts. (Easy for me to say, I know.) But here's why.

With the Early Detection Warning System for Conflict, one potential challenge for you is initiating conversations like these. When you manage to have any such conversation at all, in a close friendship, you are officially overcoming a significant life challenge.

Think about it logically. If your jaws are narrower than those of others involved, who is going to notice the problem first? Lucky you! Of course you run the risk of being told, "There is no problem, except in your fevered imagination."

To fully overcome that potential challenge, take my word for this: You are right.

You just are. You're the one with the Early Detection Warning System for Conflict, not those silly other people.

By having the best conversation you can, you will win. Regardless of a Valerie's reaction. Because that conversation is guaranteed to be informative. Either Valerie will agree to help solve the problem or she won't.

- If the conversation goes well, you will have cleaned up your relationship, maybe even deepened it.
- While a negative, defensive reaction from Valerie would be informative, too. Your imagination isn't fevered, and you definitely weren't wrong about her attitude. If this is a disposable relationship, go ahead and dispose.

Keeping relationships free of rancor matters for someone with Jaw Width like yours because, otherwise, guess which person in your relationship will suffer more? Other things being equal, it's the one with Narrower Jaws who will suffer more emotionally. (And perhaps be more likely to develop health problems from the unresolved conflict.)

You, the proud owner of Narrow Jaws, were given this gift for a reason. Your mind-body-spirit system is spiritually evolved in a manner that causes you to need harmony in relationships. Consider for a moment how spiritually beautiful that is.

Beauty of a different sort shows in our remaining option within this category. Commitment is easiest if you present **Moderate Jaw Width** to the world. Maybe you already guessed. By now you know the story of mid-range face data.

With Moderate Jaw Width, you don't agonize over commitments. A little conflict won't bother you, either.

Your potential challenge? Questioning the strange behaviors around you.

Why does Lloyd perpetually complain that his wife disrespects him. This has happened for years, yet Lloyd never tells her so much as "Excuse me."

And why won't Jesse admit that his job at Sweatshop Inc. is exploiting him? Jesse took a job there 20 years ago. Just a job. Did he think he was taking a vow?

Why not work there for a reasonable amount of time, then move on?

Unfortunately, defining "reasonable" isn't easy to do on behalf of others, any more than recognizing one's own tricky problem, a lack of tolerance for the rest of humanity.

Jaw Definition

Power-Packed Reader, it's good that you have practiced reading one face category at a time. That's excellent preparation for jaws, as many of us are used to face-judging instantly, "Is this a strong jaw or not?"

Fortunately you know by now that God doesn't make junk, not at the bottom end of a face, nor anywhere else. Face data expresses truth in a sacred alphabet that reveals the soul.

So relax, knowing that you are not going to be reading anything remotely like "Good vs. pathetic."

Hoist up your mirror on the level. Please keep your face muscles on the level, too, or at least relaxed in your normal resting position. No smiling or tobacco chewing right now. Avoid clenching your teeth together as if flexing biceps to impress me. I'm already impressed with you!

- **Jaws with Sharp Definition** appear angular, especially as they bend around the hinge on each side of the face. See Fred. And a VERY version belongs to Alexander.
- Jaws with **Soft Definition** look curvy more than bony. See George. And a VERY version belongs to Matt.
- Jaws with **Moderate Definition** make a face reader's eyes glaze over. Kidding! Those moderately sculpted jaws are like a moderately toned body, neither aggressively buff nor cushiony. Perfectly wonderful, and meaningful, too. See Joyce and Rowan.

Interpreting Jaw Definition

Self-discipline and determination are talents conveyed by **Sharp Jaw Definition**. You can push yourself if need be. And the "stronger"(i.e, more severely defined) your jaws, the more likely that you will push yourself very hard.

Resolve is lovely. It helps you achieve. But how much success is enough already? Unreasonable effort is your potential challenge. Likewise being hard on yourself.

Just because nobody else knows how harsh you can be, treating yourself in a punitive manner doesn't make it right. Or helpful to you in the long run.

So if you have been secretly cruel to yourself, do reconsider. Even if you believe that the end justifies the means, karma accrued along the way will unfold. Negative consequences, once set in motion, cannot be avoided simply because you don't believe in them.

Learning to be satisfied with yourself and your current level of success — that's not going to turn you into a couch potato, not really. Trust me.

In case you are wondering, Power-Packed Reader, **Soft Jaw Definition** does not brand you as a couch potato either. The gift here is being reasonable with yourself.

Yes, you can set goals and pursue them while maintaining full self-respect.

Yes, you can be kind to yourself in life, rather than whipping yourself along.

Yes, you may have learned to be patient with yourself. Somehow. Against all odds, imagine!

Think of statues you have seen of The Buddha. He takes time to laugh. Doesn't he also have pretty Soft Jaw Definition?

Your potential challenge? Blaming yourself is a possible danger. As in comparing yourself to others and then calling yourself lazy (or worse).

Of course, it's important to keep yourself motivated. This is best done one day at a time, and with kindness.

How about comparing yourself to your very own self, the version from younger years? Decades ago, you may have had Sharp Jaw Definition. Maybe you like that look better. Well, remember how you *felt* inside. Because that would be included in a real tradeoff.

Would you really like to swap places with the wisdom and self-acceptance you have now?

I know that American society currently values youth above all else. This form of cultural tyranny doesn't prevent you from opting out. Dare to be counter-culture and value the life you have now.

With **Moderate Jaw Definition**, you have got it made. Sometimes you can muster real push; other times you can cut yourself some slack.

Your potential challenge? Lack of tolerance for the rest of humanity around self-discipline.

What, George doesn't push himself the way you do? (Ah, but have you ever tried jogging in George's moccasins?)

As for Alexander, what's with that semi-secret self-cruelty? Sure, it's obvious to you how counter-productive that is.

"Ironic," you may think. "All that work to make himself look attractive, yet he has turned so hard. And who will ever be attracted by that?"

All Alexander may need is one lover who prefers that. (Actually, knowing Alexander, make that five or six lovers.)

Funny thing is, everyone on earth is evolving spiritually. Sometimes we evolve by making mistakes. Sometimes we know, deep inside, "This is definitely a mistake. And yet so fascinating."

Who has the right to change someone else's sacred experiment here at The Learning Planet? Whether or not a lifetime seems perfect by the final death breath, you can trust that soul will have learned a great deal. Maybe you and that other person you used to find so troubling... will giggle together in heaven.

Major Compassion Awakener: Pointy, Angular Jaws

Sure you have seen them. But did you consciously notice them?

Flip on your TV and you can find loads of women with Pointy, Angular Jaws.

Anorexia has become a job requirement for aspiring female celebrities. Extreme care to be sufficiently thin may not produce the desired jiggle-free limbs. But it sure can result in jaw hinges that are pointy or bulging or extremely muscle-padded or angular. Not always, but often.

Nor does this happen only to performers. Among the wealthy, the single, the impressionable, many women today feel social pressure. Supposedly they had better look thin enough or else....

Similarly today's men can feel terrible pressure to develop a six-pack, then keep on pushing until they develop Pointy Jaws.

Even to be a certified "Bad Boy" these days, you might achieve the desired reputation most dramatically by semi-starving yourself. (And I hope that I don't hurt Alexander's feelings when I mention him in this group. Take a good look at the pointy side of each jaw.)

Now, some folks are metabolically wired to be naturally slender. Or their bodies respond to reasonable fitness programs or an interest in sports. These thin people do not generally develop Pointy Jaws.

And, of course, Pointy Jaws do not always, inevitably, mean self-starvation. But take your own survey, Power-Packed Reader.

In my personal survey, it seems that plenty of ambitious folks are starving themselves like crazy or working out to the point of cruelty. And why? So that they can attain a look wittily described by novelist Tom Wolfe as "Starved to near-perfection."

Once you start noticing these jaws among celebrities, you may find it fascinating how many have adopted hairstyles that hide the jawline evidence.

Or maybe you will just take another look in the mirror and admit to yourself that this Pointy-Jawed description applies to you.

Regarding compassion, if you are one of these secret seekers of physical perfection, you have learned a truly valuable lesson at The Learning Planet.

For the rest of your life, you will be able to spot those in similar pain, including bulimics who weren't able to quite achieve anorexia (which may cause them to compound the inner torment, considering themselves weak-willed).

Given your history with Pointy Jaws, you'll naturally feel compassion for those men who have literally sacrificed so much for so little. Or to look so little.

Some of the Pointy-Jawed folk don't think they ever have had issues around body image or food. Why? They don't pay attention to any "issue" that doesn't show visibly to others.

Power-Packed Reader, you may notice such well concealed suffering in others from now on. Easier to notice when a life challenge isn't potential but past! In your history, if there has been physical pushing the body too hard, you can definitely move into greater kindness in how you treat yourself.

Let's Get Practical: Angry Jaws

Personally, I think it's fascinating that non-face-readers are so interested in so-called "**Strong Jaws**" when something far more informative can be read right at the surface of life. Stored-up anger in jaws can show clearly with expression reading.

Although not face reading per se, checking out jaw tension can make a fine extra hobby. Such a revealing display of muscle movement on **Angry Jaws**! "Angry Birds" (in the popular game), cannot match that expressiveness.

Quite apart from the face reading category of Jaw Definition, expression reveals a range of emotions from serenity through moderate tension all the way to "Start, just start. I dare you. Watch this dynamite blow."

Normally I don't advocate reading expression when physiognomy brings much more interesting insights. But researching rage in jaws is way too much fun to miss, and so many expression watchers do miss it.

A New Sense of Proportion

Having completed jaws, Power-Packed Reader, let's pause to consider the overall proportions of your face.

For 5,000 years, physiognomists have compared three different lengths on a face, often calling them "Life Priority Areas." Or "**Priority Areas**" for short.

Let's see how they stack up on your particular face. Don't raise your eyebrows, of course, when checking out this face reading category. And keep that fine mouth of yours closed. Otherwise, you'll distort the data.

- **Priority Area I** reaches from your hairline to the highest part of your eyebrows. Power-Packed Reader, note that the highest part could be at the start, middle, or end of your eyebrows. Also, that highest part could belong to either eyebrow.

  Basically, Priority Area I means your forehead. If your hairline has receded, use a reasonable approximation.
- **Priority Area II** stretches from that highest point of your eyebrows to the lowest part of your nose (either between the base of your nostrils or the bottom of your nose tip).

  Basically, this Priority Area is about eyes + nose.
- **Priority Area III** stretches from that lowest part of your nose down to the bottom of the chin. (Hey, that's the first chin.)

  Basically, that means everything from the mouth down.

How can you measure these Priority Areas? I recommend the **Handy Ruler Method**.

To make this Handy Ruler, you will need your thumb and forefinger. Use your other hand to hold your hand mirror on the level.

Back at your Handy Ruler, span the distance from hairline to eyebrow with those two parts of your hand. That's Priority Area I, remember? Keeping that hand-based ruler in place, freeze the positions of thumb and forefinger for now. There's your measuring tool!

Now move your Handy Ruler down to Priority Area II. Is that part of your face bigger or smaller? How about Priority Area III? If either is bigger than Area I, expand the distance between thumb and forefinger to set a new standard for the size of your Handy Ruler. What you are seeking now is your largest area.

Proportions between the Priority Areas vary more than you might suppose. Pick 20 people at random, in person. Doing this at a party might work better than trying to accost random strangers on the bus.

Checking them out with your Handy Ruler, you will find great variety. You will be ready to rock and roll (or race out of the bus). And definitely you will be prepared to read two different categories related to Priority Areas. First...

Largest Priority Areas

Every Priority Area can be the biggest or smallest. Since these differences are highly meaningful, let's start by exploring which Priority Area is the largest. Hoist up that mirror with the hand you will not need to form your Handy Ruler.

- With **Priority Area I Largest**, both of the other Priority Areas will be smaller according to your Handy Ruler. Nobody in our Cast of Characters, pictured with the full face showing, has this face data. But you certainly can find folks with this attribute. Search the world!
- With **Priority Area II Largest**, both of the other Priority Areas will be smaller according to your Handy Ruler. See Madison and Gary. Wow, are they VERYs! But Kathryn and Annette also count as having Priority Area II Largest.
- With **Priority Area III Largest**, both of the other Priority Areas will be smaller according to your Handy Ruler. See Anthony.
- Could T**wo Priority Areas Tie** for first place? Yes yes! Gleefully leap ahead to "When Two Priority Areas Tie" — our next heading. Reading here, Jesse and Ava would get to make this kind of leap.
- With **All Three Priority Areas Equal**, your Handy Ruler doesn't need to adjust for any of the three chunks. See Rowan and

Wayne. And then leap forward, two headings ahead, to "Equal Priority Areas."

If you are reading a photo, be selective. Avoid reading this category on someone with a big smile where lips part wide, like Joyce's. A very open mouth will distort Priority Area proportions.

Otherwise, with a photograph, make sure it is positioned on the level, plus it is large enough for you to see clearly. Then use your Handy Ruler in the usual way.

A picture so small that your fingers are touching together means a picture that is too small for reading this face category accurately. You are no longer reading faces. You are practicing how to squint.

Interpreting the Largest Priority Area

Human life requires that we specialize. Your current specialty shows in whichever of your Priority Areas is largest.

Power-Packed Reader, by now you know that quality physiognomy reveals far more than your surface personality. But if you were forced, say at gunpoint, to generalize about personality, this category would be your best bet.

Hey, who am I kidding? If somebody asks you, at gunpoint, for a face reading, guess what? You have my official permission to lie. For instance, you might invent dozens of flattering ways that the gunslinger's face is oozing with mercy.

Back in the realm of the serious and non-hypothetical, we were safely considering the meaning of Largest Priority Area. Whichever area is largest, that suggests a two-fold gift.

You are especially good at that area of life. Plus you naturally have credibility with other people who match you, regarding that same Largest Priority Area.

Now for more juicy details!

Priority Area I relates to thinking. If this area is largest for you, don't you positively revel in understanding, learning, abstract ideas, imagination, theories, and such?

Sadly, this face data does not prove you are smarter than others. Instead, your personal style displays patience for book learning. You crave intellectual challenge and prefer that your friends be smart, too.

Intelligence is not a universal requirement for being an interesting person. Except it is for you.

Romantically, you'll find ideas sexy. So you may value conversation as a kind of foreplay.

What could be a potential challenge with having Priority Area I Largest? Other people may be repulsed by understanding, learning, abstract ideas, imagination, theories, and such. Oops.

To overcome this challenge, downplay your intellectual proclivities to match your audience. It won't hurt to date someone who also has Priority Area I Largest, and you definitely want to avoid marrying someone with Priority Area I Smallest.

Priority Area II represents ambition. With this area largest, you are an unabashed go-getter, caring passionately about money, status, prestige, and owning the best.

Might you be as smart as someone with Priority Area I Largest? Definitely, maybe even smarter (same as with Priority Area III Largest). Your emphasis differs, that's all. Once you understand something new, you start thinking, "How can this make me some money?"

Impressive at work, you can also wow dates during courtship with how much you accomplish.

Your potential challenge? Early in the relationship, a lover will be impressed. Later, that same lover might be ignored, then turn resentful.

Regarding your love life, it's probably a bad idea for you to become involved with another person who has Priority Area II Largest. Competition may never end… even after a divorce decree.

What's the simplest way to overcome your potential challenge with such a focused personality? Purposely schedule plenty of play time.

Playing? Sensuality? Enjoying creature comforts? Hey, that's where you excel if you have **Priority Area III Largest**.

Remember the idea that folks with Priority Area II Largest enjoy owning the best? By contrast, you simply enjoy what you possess. For its own sake! Status doesn't matter nearly as much as enjoying your life.

Enjoying what you own, now you're great at that. And you just might shop for the best... because *owning* the best, to you, means *enjoying* the best.

Sexiness is probably on your mind often, if you have Priority Area III Largest, so let's include that aspect upfront when surveying personality characteristics. With Area III Largest, you may feel relatively secure about your sexiness.

What else is probably easy for you? How many times have you been told you are "The salt of the earth"? How many times have you been told you have a "Salty sense of humor"? Best of all, there's your built-in B.S. Detector.

This earthiness can bring you popularity and instant respect from other practical people. When you say something can work, it will.

Why? You have already checked to make sure that it will. Otherwise you wouldn't say so. People respect that practical bent, even folks with a different Priority Area Largest.

By this point in our survey, Power-Packed Reader, all of us without Priority Area III Largest may be drooling with envy. How can we hook up with someone like that?

Yes, given their street smarts and eagerness to dwell on physical matters, it seems obvious that a mate with Priority Area III Largest might serve as a human kind of Viagra. But wait.

Don't propose on your first date, lured by a gigantic Priority Area III. For a love relationship to last longer than a quick fling, consider your own Priority Area proportions. Make sure that you don't have Priority Area III Smallest. Like Jesse, for instance.

Otherwise your relationship could fail due to Area III Largest's potential challenge, lack of respect for people with a different life priority (especially Priority Area III Smallest).

When Two Priority Areas Tie

Whatever are you to do, on discovering two Priority Areas tied? Don't panic.

Let's spell out the personality talents that go with each possible combo. Then let's spice up the examples with implications for your love life.

With **Priority Areas I and II Both Largest**, you may first fall in love with how your crush thinks, then add a creative, practical spin to shared activities.

In relationships, you combine deep understanding with effective action. How wonderful!

Your potential challenge? There can be quite a gap between your ideals and reality. If you haven't overcome that challenge yet, here's a suggestion. Learn to make peace with what is. Then you'll have a much better chance at improving your circumstances.

To be effective, the biggest idealists need the strongest grasp on objective reality.

With **Priority Areas I and III Both Largest**, congratulations on having a down-to-earth personality that is strong on imagination (and I'll leave the sexual translation of that to your imagination).

Your potential challenge? Maybe you don't insert a whole lot of personal ego into your actions. Mostly that's wonderful, spiritually magnificent. Yet some fields of endeavor depend on personal pushiness if you aim to gain serious recognition; some friendships do too.

Avoid the temptation to fake your way into a pushier personality. Probably you can't win ego contests when folks have Priority Area II Largest, nor do you really need to compete.

For every person who admires pushiness, you can find plenty who are just as turned off by it... as you are.

With **Priority Areas II and III Both Largest**, your personality comes across as ambitious yet sensual. Although a go-getter, you care as much about physical pleasures as life's more monetary forms of success.

Regarding relationships in general, you can enjoy huge popularity. So many people crave one or both of these specialties. Folks with either Priority Area II or Area III Largest (only) may find your particular combo especially fascinating, even educational.

In your love life, the combination of street smarts, drive, and sensuality can make you irresistible. Your potential challenge? It's lack of tolerance for the rest of humanity… especially folks with Priority Area I Largest.

Equal Priority Areas

Having **Equal Priority Areas** is quite rare. With such a gift, you tend to keep your life balanced — at least relatively balanced, compared to most folks living in this frenzied age.

You are likely to manage time well, at least regarding all three major compartments of life. Somehow you manage to spend time on learning, additional time on doing, and still find time to simply enjoy life's sensuous pleasures.

Aside from personal balance, your Equal Priority Areas signal another spectacular advantage related to personality. Intuitively you understand people of every priority dominance, able to make friends with them all. With Equal Priority Areas, you might simultaneously date an exercise freak, an ambitious workaholic, and the most ivory-towerish of intellectuals.

Other factors being equal, your love life could include "happily ever after" with any of these partners, too.

Just not many such partners at once. Because nobody's face is that big.

Wait, trigamy isn't your potential challenge. Instead that would be a lack of tolerance for the rest of humanity… especially everyone but those fortunate ones like yourself, those who possess Equal Priority Areas.

Smallest Priority Areas

Power-Packed Reader, pull out your Handy Ruler. Then hold your nose. Joking! Why would it need to be an icky experience, locating one Priority Area that is more diminutive than the others?

Logically, something has to be physically smallest. In words and deeds, you can still be great.

For physically big everywhere, identically-built life forms, you will have to seek elsewhere than homo sapiens.

Of course, human life on Earth School is reputed to be one of the greatest opportunities in all the universe, if what you are seeking is spiritual evolution. Also rumor has it, we have the best food of any planet in the universe.

So boldly go forth, Power-Packed Reader. Investigate where you have a Smallest Priority Area.

Quick reminder: Look with your face in repose, neither eyebrows lifted nor breaking out your adorable smile.

From a level front angle, use your Handy Ruler to compare your three Priority Areas.

Reminder: Priority Area I reaches from hairline to the highest part of either eyebrow. Priority Area II stretches from that highest point of your eyebrows to the lowest part of your nose. While Priority Area III extends from the lowest part of your nose to the bottom of your chin.

- **Priority Area I Smallest** is one possibility. See Joyce.
- **Priority Area II Smallest** is a second possibility. Although nobody in our Cast of Characters models this set of facial proportions, you can definitely find it. Maybe even in the mirror.
- **Priority Area III Smallest** is a third possibility. Equally good, as in "Last but not least." Except this time the last is the least big, so maybe that saying could be confusing. See Kathryn as an example.
- Could two Priority Areas tie for smallest? Sure.
- You might even have all three Priority Areas tie for smallest. But, for goodness' sake, don't go there, because in that case you could also brag about having Equal Priority Areas, recently discussed.

What if you can't find an obvious winner. Skip the smallest Priority Area category entirely. Power-Packed Reader, you know why, right?

VERY = VERY is a vital time management principle for physiognomists. Muddling over sorta-smallest *anything* on a face will not be a good use of your time. If necessary, read the following just for insight about other folks.

Interpreting Smallest Priority Areas

In a way, I'm still recovering from my introduction to face reading courtesy of Timothy Mar in 1975.

Earlier I told you part of the story, how I met this world-renowned physiognomist at a Mensa meeting. There Mr. Mar delivered a rather unfortunate sales pitch but nonetheless changed my life.

In all fairness, I must add that Mensa folk tend to be an unusually tough audience. After becoming a face reading author myself, I would go on to give face reading talks at two different Mensa meetings.

A highly skeptical, cerebral culture at Mensa confronts anyone speaking about mind-body-spirit. Or it did, back in the day.

Also, consider Mar's point of view. He was a consummate professional who had spoken for free to a surprisingly squirmy, disrespectful group of New York intellectuals.

Before walking to the back of that room, with his little stack of books awaiting purchase, Mr. Mar probably felt the Universal Author's Book -Signing Sense of Doom, fearing he might not sell one single book.

Which would have proved true. I don't remember a single one of us purchasing a copy of his new book, "*Face Reading*." Yet Timothy still indulged us, providing free readings to everyone who asked. His generosity was lovely.

Back at my side of the story, however, I couldn't distinguish the shortcomings of *siang mien* itself from the kindness of Timothy Mar. And here is what I mean by shortcomings....

I raced over to the back of the room and got there just in time to hear Timothy Mar do his first, actual, face reading of the evening. Which made it my "Like a Virgin" experience as a physiognomist, only lacking Madonna singing in the background.

"You have a very small forehead," Timothy Mar told Gladys. "That means you had a very unhappy childhood."

Gladys had what we would call Priority Area I Smallest.

"Noooooo," I remember thinking, "That would be helpful how, exactly? Wouldn't Gladys already know about her own miserable childhood?"

I stayed around, however, curiosity aroused. Timothy Mar kept reading.

Soon he was talking about someone else's smallest Priority Area. For this guy, Joe, that was Priority Area II.

Mar sighed loudly. Then I remember him telling Joe, "You keep trying to be more in life than you are destined to achieve. You may as well save yourself the frustration. Become more humble."

Undoubtedly Joe would have been more horrified than me, but I was a runner up. What, face reading used for that dismal sort of fortunetelling?

Fast forward to now. In teaching you about the power of face reading, memories like these influenced me to save discussion of Priority Areas until close to last. In *siang mien*, traditional Chinese face reading, Priority Areas are often read first.

Now, as then, I feel disgust when folks interpret faces to imply inferiority. How dare an intuitive art be used to put people "in their place," whether in the future or the past?

In that first moment of disgust, back 37 years ago, a seed was sown within my heart: "There has to be a better way than this to read faces."

The system I later developed, Face Reading Secrets®, hasn't stood the test of time yet, compared to the 5,000-year-old art of *siang mien*. However, people do find interpretations like those that follow to be accurate, plausible, empowering, etc.

You can always seek, and find, fortunetelling systems of physiognomy.

Personally, I believe really strongly that the best way to have a good future is to fully be yourself in the present.

So, if you recognize yourself in the interpretations below, maybe that will matter more to you than being told about your alleged future limitations or past misery.

Folks with a **Small Priority Area I** do have a personality talent: Soon as you understand something, you want to use it.

Okay, maybe you won't be criticized for excessive subtlety. But how likely is it that folks will 'fess up in words like these?

"I'm jealous you got there first and made all that money."

Your potential challenge? It's a lack of patience for pure theory, idle speculation, endless debates about how many angels can dance on the head of a pin.

How about **Priority Area II Smallest**? Your personality talent is hard work, with motivation that transcends personal ambition.

For instance, hard work at your office might be motivated by the desire to make the company look good, rather than caring about making yourself look good.

Promotions and great marriages and life's other goodies can really be yours, sure as there really are such things as good karma for work well done, reputation for excellent service, etc.

Years ago, I reviewed mind-body-spirit books for Pathways Magazine. With practice, I could tell by the end of the first page quite a lot about the author's motivation.

Some authors wrote all about me-me-me, a flavor that grew only stronger with subsequent chapters... in books that I refused to review.

Instead of giving print time to shameless self-promoters, I used that precious review space to help authors succeed with books strongly positioned to help readers.

With Priority Area II Smallest, recognition may take you a while. But sooner or later, you will find people who appreciate what you do, humility and all.

Your potential challenge with this Priority Area smallest? Self-esteem may suffer until you properly appreciate your service orientation. Even members of your family may not understand it.

When you have fully overcome your challenge, their comments around the Thanksgiving table will make you laugh inwardly, not cringe. Because you, and you alone, are in charge of evaluating your life.

With **Priority Area III Smallest**, your personality talent leads you to hold a counter-culture view of the finer things in life. To you, they are not designer merchandise or other status objects.

Less *obvious* equals more *interesting*, far as you are concerned. This natural inclination helps you to seek greatness in your own way.

For example, you may care greatly about originality, ideals, hidden truths.

Sound familiar? Then shape your life accordingly, and don't worry about pleasing folks with different priorities.

Your Priority Area proportions can act like a motor, propelling you strongly forward in the direction of your purpose in life.

The potential challenge? Lack of interest in physicality can cause you to give awful driving directions, appear spaced out, act clueless about the prevailing culture, or dress more like a visiting anthropologist from Mars than a member of your current society.

Let's Get Practical: Why Priority Areas Can Change

Proportions within your face can change just as much as particular facial features. If you haven't felt thrilled while reading about your Priority Areas, know that time is on your side. So, too, the power of your free will.

Power-Packed Reader, so much about your face depends on your use of free will. Depending on how you spend your time and money and emotions, you will change inwardly. Guaranteed.

Change enough and the corresponding physical changes will develop, due to that fact of physiognomy you know so well:

There is a reciprocal relationship between the inner person and the physical face. Change one significantly and, over time, you will change the other.

Despite the emphasis in current society on cosmetic surgery, most face changes still work their way naturally... from the inside out.

Take Elvis Presley for an example. I have done detailed comparison face readings, and you can too. Base them on photographs in a book. Or go online and search at Google Images or elsewhere for two good clear comparison photographs, taken from a straight angle.

The young Elvis had **Priority Area II Largest**. He was a deeply ambitious performer.

Branding himself as a sex symbol, Elvis changed enormously over the years. By the time of his comeback tour, he had **Priority Area III Largest**.

Here are some other ways that Presley's face changed during his career.

- From Passion Power Style to Leader-Like Power Style.
- From Straight Eyebrow Shape to Curved Eyebrows.
- From Up-Angled Left Eye to Down-Angled Left Eye.
- From Wariness Index 10 on his right eye to Wariness Index 1.
- From Large Nose Tip to Small Nose Tip.
- From Small Nostrils to Large, Round Nostrils.
- From Philtrum Definition 10 to Philtrum Definition 2.

Depending on your own values and choices, your face will change too. All the more reason to pursue what is truly meaningful to you!

Chapter 19. Chins

In this chapter, it will be my special pleasure to restore the good name of what is commonly, if insultingly, known as a "**Weak Chin**."

Weak at what, exactly?

Maybe you will be surprised, right from our first category about your chinny-chin-chin.

Chin Bottom Shape

Imagine being able to predict how somebody else makes decisions. Might that ever help you? If your answer is yes, pay special attention to learning about the Chin Bottom Shape category.

Although you still won't be able read that person's mind, you can discern what motivates decisions. Make your argument based on that, and what an advantage you'll have! Bring on the power of face reading.

Of course, Power-Packed Reader, you will first need to develop your eye for facial butt watching.

That's *facial* butt watching, right? Many an invitation has come my way to read people's tushies, feet, hands, etc. I decline, of course. The only butt this physiognomist wants to examine in public is the face part between the jaws.

Admittedly, this is usually called something different from "Butt." It's called "Chin."

Start with your very own chin, looking on the level. What shape does it make at the lower edge?

- **Curved Chin Bottoms** are the most common. Your degree of curve may vary but here's the point: You are seeing a shape like a segment taken from a circle. See all the variety of curvy chins on Joyce, Wayne, and Rowan.
- Another possibility is that the mirror will show you a **Straight Chin Bottom**. See Kathryn and George. A VERY version belongs to Annette.
- Hardest of all to find (and to physically recognize), are **Angled Chin Bottoms**. These tend to be narrow in width. When you look carefully you will notice a tapering of the entire chin,

like the top of a pyramid, only turned upside-down. Also note: That chin would be made out of flesh and not pyramid construction materials. And all flesh has a bit of a softness or curve. Fred graciously provides an example of an Angled Chin Bottom.

Once again, make sure you are reading the face in repose. Duchenne smiles can distort the shape of your chin bottom.

Interpreting Chin Bottoms

A **Curved Chin Bottom** displays your compassion when making choices. You take people into consideration. How will your choice make them feel?

When your decision is practical or political, you won't emphasize ideology but how people's lives will be affected by your choice.

Your Curved Chin Bottom also represents something very practical: Hospitality.

Power-Packed Readers, if ever you are going to crash a party, go to one hosted by somebody with a VERY Curved Chin. Food-wise, you will be so glad you came.

With a **Straight Chin Bottom**, you are more likely to show your mettle by hosting parties with a strong concept, perhaps a theme like "Celebrate birthday."

You might plan some party activities designed to make the occasion memorable, since your choices tend to emphasize ideals. Or ideas. Or ideology.

Any of which can turn something as simple as a little party into a big, symbolic deal for you.

Think for a moment and you can find reasons why you have made major life decisions like marriage, voting, even consumer choices for big purchases. For you, the motivation wasn't simply "It felt right," was it?

Choices based mostly on feelings are more the style of someone with a Curved Chin Bottom.

Every chin bottom comes complete with a potential challenge. Curved Chinners can be hopeless mushballs at making decisions, preferring sentimentality over thinking "straight" about long-term consequences.

While Straight Chinners may struggle with an equally tricky challenge, thinking only in terms of black and white. Upholding "The principle of the thing," we may carry on about "Good" and "Bad," with no interest in finding other alternatives.

At its worst, every Straight-Chin choice is between "My way versus all the stupid ways."

Can you guess? I am one of those Straight Chin folk. For years, I have worked to overcome this challenge. Hence an unfortunate incident when my son, Matt, was five.

Driving him to preschool, I had missed breakfast, which I was determined to remedy. After strapping Matt into the car seat next to me, I asked him to hold a plastic container filled with my breakfast of dry cereal.

Since this container was shallow and wide, I anticipated what a mess there could be if Matt didn't firmly hold down the lid. One sudden stop could scatter crunchy little O's of goodness all over the car.

So I instructed my child to hold that lid down carefully unless I was reaching in to grab a handful of cereal. To motivate him, I supplied this little pep talk:

"Think of it like a fairy tale," I said. "The hero is given a difficult task. If he succeeds, he will get to marry the King's daughter. If he fails, they will chop off his head. It's like that, Matty, with the cereal. If you don't hold on tight, I'm afraid it's going to be a big problem."

"But Mom" protested my kid. "Aren't there any shades of gray about this?"

In retrospect, it affords me some consolation to think of the things that must slip out of the mouths of parents who have **Angled Chin Bottoms** because of their need to stay in control. Control is their blessing and curse all rolled up into one chin-sized package.

You know, if you have that rare kind of chin bottom. Pity the poor fool who tries to push you around. Wish I could eavesdrop in your car!

That commanding sense of self will prevail. You make decisions on your own, whether politely or not.

You'll make those decisions regardless of your personal style in other aspects of life — self-disclosure in communication (your Lipfulness), intimacy (Eyelid Fullness plus Eyelid Structure), typical pattern for reacting to social rules (Ear Angles).

Does your Chin Bottom Shape serve as an anchor because you are, otherwise, so sweetly pliant? (If you don't remember the significance of a physiognomy anchor, go back to our discussion of this in Chapter 11.)

Or perhaps your Angled Chin Bottom punctuates a long facial sentence about always doing exactly what you choose, everywhere, every time.

You could have loads of face reading data related to staying in control, such as Angled Eyebrow Shape, Out-Angled Ears, Triangular Nostrils, Angular Jaws.

So many contexts could be possible. They won't change your highly emphatic way of making decisions. Whatever choices you make, look out, world! Each important choice will be yours alone, regardless of whether you keep it a secret from others.

In any event, face data can't be kept secret from the rest of us Power-Packed Readers, ha ha!

Let's Get Practical: Scary Little Chins

Power-Packed Readers, consider yourselves advised. Angled Chin Bottoms are worth noticing.

On Fred, for instance. Your new next-door neighbor (from our Cast of Characters) may seem meek and mild, even sensitive and kind. Much of his face reading data supports this. But watch out for that Angled Chin Bottom.

In contrast to Fred's everyday personality, he will make his own choices. Don't get in the way.

No point in complaining about his fence or how he deals with his dog or the times he chooses to play loud music. Confrontation will not make this guy change his mind. The harder you push, the harder you'll see him push back.

For Fred, I suspect, that Angled Chin Bottom does serve as an anchor. He really is a sweet guy. Just stubborn in very particular ways.

Especially beware a **VERY Angled, Short Chin**, the sneakiest face bottoms of all.

I call them "**Scary Little Chins**." Their owners are nearly always women. Despite the chin owner's other characteristics related to sensitivity, such a chin conceals a will of iron.

Hey, you, owning such a chin. Stop giggling. Consider yourself both praised and warned. Your potential challenge is making what could be called, "Flaunting Choices." That's when you pointedly, and chinly, show others, "Nobody's going to tell me what to do."

A Flaunting Choice might be wise for you, under the circumstances. Or slightly weird. Or terribly, terribly awful. (Choose any one of a thousand theoretical shades of gray, something that I personally have learned to do, and not just when dealing with cereal management.)

With a Scary Little Chin, you will do exactly what you want, for better or worse. My advice to those who are dealing with you: "Surrender quickly. You might as well."

Beard Bottoms

Now that you can read Chin Bottoms, what about Beard Bottoms? Maybe you are wondering, Power-Packed Reader. How will you ever find the real Chin Bottom beneath a beard?

Good news here. You don't have to play archeologist, unearthing one layer of chin under another. The topmost civilization wins. Beard Bottom trumps Chin Bottom.

What if a man disguises his real chin shape with his beard? Goatees are probably a heck of a lot more common than Angled Chin Bottoms, for instance.

Doesn't matter. When you change your face on the outside, you also change your personal style on the inside. To rephrase a popular saying, "Be careful what you wish for… by way of disguising your face data. You will surely get it."

To develop your eye for Beard Bottoms, don't bother to look in the mirror unless you already have grown yourself a fine beard. Because drawn-on beards don't count for face reading.

When you can locate a real-live beard, head straight to the south end and look at the shape. With the examples provided from our Cast of Characters, all beards are quite short. This physiognomist freely admits that some prodigiously long beards might seem to be a matter of chest reading, rather than face reading. But they're not. Chest hair is different from facial hair!

- A **Curved Beard Bottom** has a shape similar to a Curved Chin Bottom. It's part of a circle, whether large or small. See Lloyd's somewhat Curved Beard Bottom. When a beard like this is way larger, I call it a "Santa Claus Beard."
- A **Straight Beard Bottom** is relatively straightish. You show me a man with a perfectly ruler-straight beard and he's a guy who could use an extra hobby. Jesse, glad to say, wears an unfussy, natural-looking, Straight Beard Bottom.
- An **Angled Beard Bottom** is usually called a "**Goatee**." Even a small one makes a powerful statement. What would happen to Alexander's look, for instance, without that triangular beard of his, petite yet stately?
- How about **Designer Stubble**? Do those barely-there hair looks still count? Sure they do. The shape is about the shape, not how much hair lies within the outline. For instance, Fred's manly Designer Stubble counts as an Angled Beard Bottom.

When you read a man's beard, it won't do to ask, "How long has it been since you shaved?" Like any item of face reading data, simply read it in the here and now.

For our purposes, it doesn't matter if Fred's beard look could have sprung up over the weekend while Alexander's chin fuzz has been a long-time, carefully-tended, bonsai project.

Interpreting Beard Bottoms

Count all Beard Bottoms as a VERY version of Chin Shape Bottom. Yes, even Fred's. However, you might want to note the grooming factor in your interpretations. (I'll explain soon.)

A **Curved Beard Bottom** reveals choices based on people's feelings. How sweet of you!

If you have such a beard, and it's the lush, curvy Santa Claus Beard variety, that symbolizes a spontaneous, big-hearted generosity.

While an accidental-looking barely-there version is more about unintentional generosity. Still, far as I'm concerned, whatever giving you do still counts as sweet.

As for a Lloyd-style meticulously groomed Curved Beard Bottom, it makes me think of the saying, "The Lord giveth and the Lord taketh away." Substitute Lloyd's name here and you'll just about have it:

"When feeling benevolent, Lloyd will bestow generosity upon thee. Otherwise watch your step, Buddy."

A **Straight Beard Bottom** points to your making cerebral choices… related to a certain intellectual independence.

Despite the huge curve to his Wariness Index, that Jesse is nobody's fool. He'll make choices based on his principles and standards.

Then what about an **Angled Beard Bottom**? A goatee means trouble. Not for you, the beard wearer. Just for everyone else.

Many folks instinctively cringe at the sight of a goatee.

Power-Packed Reader, if you are daunted by a Scary Little Chin, be on your guard even more around any goatee. It's the VERY version of Angled Beard Bottom which, in turn, is the VERY version of an Angled Chin Bottom.

A goatee owner takes extra huge pride in making all choices based on what he wants, no compromising.

He may revel in behavior that controls other people. And, to him, that may not seem like a potential challenge but, rather, a chance to have fun.

Power-Packed Reader with that statement of a beard, when you just read this didn't you laugh a bit? Someone has to play that strong directorial role in life, right?

Let's Get Practical: More About Facial Hair

What else can you easily tell from a man's facial hair, be it beards or mustaches or eyebrows?

First, consider **Care in Grooming**. How messy or neat is that man's facial hair?

Then, consider **Consistency in Grooming**. Lloyd presents a superb example of inconsistent grooming of facial hair.

- Lloyd sports a VERY carefully trimmed mustache. This degree of grooming suggests that Lloyd stays in strict control of self-disclosure.
- Beard trimming is less careful. Lloyd has chosen a Curved Beard Bottom, which conveys a talent for making choices with kindness.

Note the lack of consistency to the shape; perhaps Lloyd could have trimmed that curve more evenly but didn't bother.
(This physiognomist wonders if he might have some with-holds about the kindness. Of course, it is also possible that Lloyd just didn't have had the perfect tools available on the day of his photo shoot. Maybe only hedge clippers were handy?)

- Along with the moderately messy Beard Bottom, notice the meticulously groomed area beneath Lloyd's lower lip. Here the beard has also been razor sculpted to do something unusual. Notice the Upward-Thrust Beard Knob, where you might expect a straight shape. Such a one-of-a-kinder!

In our "Chin" Chapter you will learn about the fascinating characteristic I call a "Macho Knob." Lloyd's **Upward-Thrust Beard Knob** is a bit like a Macho Knob, only the meaning relates to verbal intensity.

And the potential challenge with the beard characteristic? It is vigorous displays of temper.

By contrast, a Macho Knob lies under the chin rather than above it. The chin data relates to expressing pride through actions, not only speech.

- Most quirky of all, Lloyd's **VERY Wild Eyebrow Hairs** reveal a certain pride in his superior and untamed intellect. As if he were Tiny Tim, telling his own random thoughts, "God bless you, every one."

As a face reader, I would expect Lloyd to have unconventional ideas, lots of them. Plus considerable dislike for anything that seems too simple.

Isn't it fascinating, his extremes of Care in Grooming of Facial Hair? From the sublimely wild to the meticulous, partly free but otherwise controlled.... All this adds up to Lloyd's distinctive, outrageous charm.

By contrast, how consistent is Alexander's facial hair management?

- Although that beard is small, Alexander has trimmed the edges beautifully.
- Eyebrows are neat as well. They may have been carefully brushed upwards, to make the most of them.
- Also, Alexander has chosen to carefully trim his mustache so the philtrum shows through clearly, not necessarily an easy thing to do. Scoring 10 with his Philtrum Definition, why wouldn't Alexander want it to show that off? Still, a **Semi-Transparent Mustache** like this one is a rare sight.

This physiognomist concludes that Alexander shows impressive predictability with his grooming of facial hair. Thinking Patterns, Decision Making, and Sexual Self-Presentation (Eyebrows, Beard Bottom, and

Mustache characteristics, respectively) are well balanced. None of these three aspects takes over his life.

All this Care and Consistency adds up to Alexander's distinctive, bad-boy charm.

Power-Packed Reader, you get the idea. Whether you are managing your own facial hair or reading somebody else's, you can learn a lot by face reading Care and Consistency with Grooming Facial Hair.

Where a man takes care, he broadcasts to the world that he is very, very interested in the aspect of life represented by that facial hair. Where he chooses to go wild and free, that can inform you too... about the aspect of life corresponding to that particular item of face data.

Chin Thrust

How much a chin sticks out from the rest of the face — that face reading category is Chin Thrust.

With practice, you can see Chin Thrust from the usual straight angle. Pay attention to your 3-D vision.

Does the chin pop out? That's Out-Angled Chin Thrust.

Tilt neck-ward? That's In-Angled Chin Thrust.

Not do much? Probably you are seeing moderate versions of Out-Angled or In-Angled Chin Thrust. So you might want to take another look. True Even-Angled Chin Thrust is quite rare.

In short, this category can be tricky to see from the front. So it's better to start with profile views.

Doing this, don't view only the chin. Context matters.

Your context for this face category is the overall sweep of face, punctuated by the angle of chin. So let me prepare you more thoroughly than usual before you hoist up your mirrors.

1. Create an imaginary line for viewing the angle of Chin Thrust. Start that straight line at the forehead directly above the eyes.
2. Skip over the nose. Continue drawing that imaginary line at the overlip.
3. Skip over the mouth. Resume drawing that imaginary line all the way down to the bottom of the chin. (Often that part of your imaginary line will lie inside that person's physical chin, because most chins have Out-Angled Chin Thrust.)
4. A Once you have created that imaginary line, compare the outermost edge of the physical chin to that straight line. That gives you the angle of Chin Thrust.

Thus, Power-Packed Reader, you have perspective now. You can appreciate that the context for reading this chin category does not start at the chin but, rather, places Chin Thrust in the context of a whole face.

- When the line of thrust goes outward at the chin, that is **Out-Angled Chin Thrust**. This chin thrust is by far the most common. See Helene and Madison in profile, Wayne from a front view.
- When the line of thrust goes inward at the chin, that counts as **In-Angled Chin Thrust**. We have no profile example, but Kathryn and Jesse provide examples from a front view.
- **Even Chin Thrust** is rarest of all. See Anthony.

What about your own Chin Thrust, Power-Packed Reader? You control the angle, so move yourself into true profile position.

Using both mirrors to see that side view, pivot your head on your neck. Slowly move up and down and then ease into an even angle. Subtly you may feel your jaws relax, your head feel more open, your breathing deepen. Aligned, yum, that feels good!

Plus you are prepared to assess your Chin Thrust. What is it, Out-Angled, In-Angled, or Even?

Interpreting Chin Thrust

Competition is one of those bottom-line survival needs. At least, if you have **Out-Angled Chin Thrust**, you most likely feel a strong need to win at competitions.

The more intensely out-angled, the more likely you are to relish a "Good fight." Not necessarily win with words but your actions. Competition can bring out the best in you.

What if that chin of yours is attached to a rather athletic body? Then you may enjoy proving your worth through sports.

Your potential challenge? Beware unnecessary aggression. No need to shoot an ant with a cannon!

Guess which people cringe at competition? It's the crew with **In-Angled Chin Thrust**. Cringe, at least, until the potential challenge has been overcome.

Either way, what a mistake it would be to call these "**Weak Chins**." The terminology is revealing, however. It demonstrates how people can undervalue a deeply spiritual gift.

Sometimes an In-Angled chin is called a "**Receding Chin**." I'm not fond of that metaphor because it implies that the chin is moving out from shore, much like a "Receding" hairline. Are hapless pieces of hair floating in disarray like so much seaweed, caught in the outgoing surf?

Surely chins and hairlines are not beaches with their inevitable tides. No seaweed covers these face parts. Hair loss has meaning beyond the scope of this book, but Chin Thrust? Let's get to it!

Chin Thrust has so much meaning, in fact, that it belongs to the group of facial characteristics that seldom change, what I call **Soul Signature Traits**.

About 10% of your face data will not change over the years, however much you evolve, whatever the direction of your personal changes.

Chin Thrust is one of your Soul Signature Traits. Which makes it all the more annoying how people speak of these angles at the face bottom. Sometimes In-Angled Chin Thrust is called "Weak" as well as "Receding" And sometimes small chin size is called "Weak" too. Neither chin characteristic deserves contempt. On the contrary.

Kathryn, for instance, she's no wimp. **In-Angled Chin Thrust** accompanies a deep-down preference for conflicts to be resolved in such a way that everyone prospers, a.k.a. "win-win."

If you, too, have In-Angled Chin Thrust, you know what I mean here. What is the fun of winning if others must automatically lose?

And the talent you have motivates you to find an alternative: Rather than fight or push, you prefer to compromise and learn.

To keep relationships harmonious, you may volunteer to do more than your share of the work. Volunteer work for which you won't even attempt to take credit....

That brings good news and bad news. First the good: Even if you don't know the meaning of the word "Karma," you may sense that any good that you do in this world will come back to you, sooner or later. So true!

But the bad news? Your potential challenge with In-Angled Chin Thrust is obtaining respect. Most folks have the opposite Chin Thrust. They undervalue community and overvalue aggression. Don't buy into that belief system. It's optional.

As for **Even-Angled Chin Thrust**, sure you might have this. "Rare" doesn't mean "Never."

Anthony has Even-Angled Chin Thrust and so might you. In which case, congratulations on demonstrating instinctive balance regarding compromise and aggression. With this Chin Thrust of equanimity, you handle one situation at a time, neither taking advantage of others nor allowing them to take advantage of you.

I remember telling a man about his Even-Angled Chin Thrust during a presidential inauguration event. Reading faces there for hours, my favorite interaction took me by surprise. I found myself at a table of extreme VIPs where Even-Angled Chin Man listened to his face reading with an unusual degree of interest.

Gravely he concluded, "I'm glad you noticed that about me. I work at the Pentagon."

Both of us shared a long moment, feeling relief.

Power-Packed Reader, maybe your line of work doesn't include activating drones or dropping bombs. Whatever your career, if you have this line of chin, it can help you succeed.

Your potential challenge? Perhaps you don't get to work in an exalted position for your nation's Department of Defense.

Kidding, of course. There's that little matter of lack of tolerance for the rest of humanity.

Knowing Wayne as you do, you wish he would drop the pushiness? Even pretend occasionally, just for the sake of variety.

When Jesse tells you his latest saga of life being unfair, it is so much like other stories you have heard from him. You might be tempted to shriek, "Would you please man up?"

However, being a "Real Man" doesn't mean that Wayne must behave like somebody with Out-Angled Chin Thrust.

Nor does femininity require the personal style suited to In-Angled Chin Thrust. It's so much more informative (not to mention interesting) to take life one person at a time, one situation at a time, one gender at a time, one chin at a time.

Let's Get Practical: Fake Profile Pix

What is a true profile view of your face or anyone else's? The torso and head line up, facing forward. The head is level, chin neither tucked down nor thrust forward.

Obvious? Hardly. Let's revisit three of our profile pix.

- **Madison**: If you look closely, you will find something tricky about Madison's pose for this photograph.

  See how far her head is tilted back? Perhaps this is meant to accentuate the drama of Madison's haircut.
- **Helene**: Her chin isn't aligned naturally either. See that?

  Overall head tilt isn't as extreme as Madison's pose. But you, the viewer, are still being played.

  Helene is supposed to be showing her profile, right? Actually, Helene is gently sticking out her chin. Ha!
- **Anthony**: Is this really supposed to be a profile shot? Take a closer look at the clever camera angle and cool coordination that conspire to make his photo look so captivating.

  Anthony's torso is posed to face mostly towards the front, not the side. Perhaps years of yoga classes helped him to then twist his neck way to the side. Then he has tucked his chin slightly down. This makes him appear to be in profile, although he's not.

For comparison, check out shoulder placement on Madison and Helene.

Back at coordinated Anthony, not only does he hold this twisty asana without a grimace. But his mouth is artfully bent into a great big photogenic smile — although fake, visually compelling.

Power-Packed Reader, think that is easy? Try copying both the photo angle and expression in front of some mirrors:

Face front. Twist neck. Downcast eyes. Big secret smile.

Feels pretty different from how it looks, doesn't it?

Anthony sure is coordinated, appearing so natural in this position. I wouldn't be surprised if he could hold the same expression while doing Downward Facing Dog.

Power-Packed Face Reader, sometimes you may want to practice seeing photographs in a more sophisticated way. You don't have to become an expert on lighting, photography or makeup. Good old physical mimicry can help you dispel illusions.

Just take time to notice how a face is physically positioned.

Practice doing the pose yourself, so you can viscerally feel how different it is from the illusion being conveyed. Your quick 'n casual look at a photo does not mean the model has had an equally quick 'n casual approach.

About reading photographs as a physiognomist: Until you have practiced quite a bit with professional pix, you may find it easiest to discern Chin Thrust from a front view, especially if the person is not smiling.

When you read faces in person, however, check that first impression with a true profile angle.

Looking at our Cast of Characters who are pictured from a front view, can you find anyone with Out-Angled Chin Thrust?

- I notice Wayne has a VERY Out-Angled Chin Thrust.
- While Lloyd, Matt, Joyce, and Annette have more moderate versions.

Chin Length

Your simplest way to read Chin Length is to regard a chin from your usual straight angle.

Look when the person's mouth is closed, as an open mouth can distort chin characteristics.

Make a quick, even carefree, decision about length, relative to the rest of that person's face.

- In proportion, do you find a **Long Chin**? See Annette. Or Valerie's chin, especially the right side. A VERY version belongs to Wayne.
- Or might you be having a close encounter with a **Short Chin**? See Fred. And a VERY version belongs to Kathryn.
- Perhaps you are locating **Moderate Chin Length**. See George. And a VERY moderate version belongs to Ava.
- All good!

Interpreting Chin Length

Chin Length relates to ethical and physical courage. Whatever the face data, everyone wins something. (Of course, nobody wins *everything*, either.)

A **Long Chin** marks you as having the kind of courage known as "Resiliency." When misfortunes arise, you can "Take it on the chin" and recover relatively quickly. (Literally, there's plenty of chin to take "It" on.)

With this Chin Length, you may also be splendid as a physical risk taker. Notice how you drive a car, for instance.

If athletic, you might win friends and influence owners of faces based on your physical prowess. Because you are likely to be bold, even daring, on those ski slopes (or the equivalent).

Your potential challenge? Unfortunately, you may also be bold about taking ethical risks. Avoid getting carried away by the fun, or adventure, of doing anything that you know is wrong.

How about a **Short Chin**? Does it deserve to be called "Weak"?

Sure, if you mainly value taking physical risks. But Short Chins accompany talent for taking emotional risks. One of the greatest things about a Short Chin is the internal courage, whether you apply it to spiritual practices, psychological growth, or simply taking responsibility for your actions in life.

With a Short Chin, for instance, you might courageously ask a friend about "The elephant in the room."

Your potential challenge is not with ethical courage but the physical kind. Count how often you go bungee jumping, for instance. Hey, notice how *you* drive!

Ethical strength is another plus if you have a Short Chin. Most likely, you walk your talk. To you, Sunday ethics aren't only for church. In fact, you may give yourself an awfully hard time over those personal ethics.

Let's say you are at the bank, opening a new checking account. Using a pen to fill out a form, you pocket the cheap pen absent-mindedly. After returning home, say that you discover the pen and realize you appropriated it. How do you respond?

- With a Long Chin, you might think, "Too bad. But the thing couldn't have cost more than a quarter. Anyway, those bankers can afford to give me a cheap pen. They have pens galore."
- By contrast, with the relentless conscience of a Short Chin, you are more apt to worry, "Abraham Lincoln would have walked 15 miles to return that pen."

Honesty is admirable. Honesty, however, doesn't require that you torque your life out of shape due to guilt. Which is the main potential challenge with a Short Chin.

To overcome that challenge, consider my Guilt-Busting Technique.

1. Ask yourself, "Which do I think matters more to God, that I made this mistake or that I care so much to never repeat it?"
2. Make reasonable amends, if you can.
3. Learn from the experience, if you can.
4. Then move on already.

With a **VERY Short Chin**, your talent is a truly exquisite conscience. However, you may be wired for guilt to an alarming degree. Not only sins of omission, like accidental pen thievery, can set off the alarm. So can criticism from other people.

Consider yourself forewarned. Just because you possess that degree of ethical refinement doesn't mean you must use it incessantly. In the words of Sigmund Freud, who supplemented his own Chin Length by adding a considerable chunk of beard, "Sometimes a cigar is just a cigar."

With **Moderate Chin Length** — whether enhanced by a beard or not — you naturally take a situational approach to risks of any kind. Physical adventurousness? Emotional and spiritual adventurousness? You'll deftly make one choice at a time. Superb!

Your potential challenge? How annoying, that pesky lack of tolerance for the rest of humanity.... Now there's a truly risky sport!

Chin Width

Having learned to see Chin Length as a separate category, let's go horizontal and appreciate Chin Width.

- Some chins are small from the sideways direction, however long they may be. Call them "**Narrow Chins**." See Kathryn. And a VERY version belongs to Alexander.
- **Wide Chins** are built firmly into the jaw. Sometimes they're short and broad. Other examples are longer. But either way, what counts is the horizontal distance. See Lloyd and Cliff. VERY versions belong to Annette and Rowan.
- **Moderate Chin Width** fits somewhere in-between. See Ava and Oliver.

Interpreting Chin Width

Mini Quiz: Let's see if you can figure out the meaning of Chin Width. Here come some hints.

Width on a *nose*, the Nose Padding, is about the number of people you feel comfortable having on your team at work.

Width on *lips*, Mouth Length, is about the number of people in your ideal audience for communication.

So might the Chin Width category also involve a person's most comfortable number of people for some aspect of life?

Yes indeed! Chin Width concerns personal style when handling adversity, recovering from difficulties, disappointments, and delays. Such problems come to us all. Power-Packed Reader, when they come to you, do you recharge better from contact with other people… or from solitude?

A **Narrow Chin** suggests that, when faced with adversity, your instinct is to go it alone. When ready, you will reach out first to a very significant other. Then, gradually, you will reach out to other friends or family members.

What a lovely talent for depth healing! Your potential challenge? Let's not call it being unsociable. Not exactly. Your need to go it alone when upset can be a magnificent strength. However, isolating yourself can cause social repercussions.

Disappearing without explanation isn't the potential challenge. No, that would be neglecting to inform your closest friends in advance about your personal style.

Each of us needs to find strength the best we can. So it need not count as an act of betrayal if you disappear socially when upset. To overcome the Narrow Chin challenge, just give just a little clue to new friends, once you get to a stage of true closeness. For example:

"Since our friendship is growing, there's something I need to tell you. When I go through hard times, I gather my strength by being alone. This isn't personal. So if, in the future, it happens some time that you don't hear from me for a few days, please know this is how I need to do things. I'll get back to you soon as I'm feeling better.

"Are you like that too? Because I know that many people are just the opposite."

Sure you could probably read this information from your good friend's Chin Width. But conversations out loud are important for maintaining a friendship.

With a **Wide Chin**, companionship gets you through the tough times. Support groups, 12-step programs, and peer counseling were all developed for people like you. Help from others can speed your way to personal balance.

Your potential challenge? Other folks may disappoint you by not giving enough. The more VERY your Wide Chin, the more likely you are to expect others to support you in the style to which you have become accustomed.

Sure, you would give that much support to others without thinking twice. It is normal to you.

Only everybody is not like you, as proclaimed by Chin Width. Although you, the proud owner of that Wide Chin, would leap to comfort a friend, folks with different Chin Width may not leap at all. Considerately they give you plenty of space.

This happens to be what they would prefer to receive under similar circumstances.

Oh, how hard it can be, giving people what they need rather than what you expect them to need! Except there is one group of people who don't have that problem. And I suspect you know who is in that group, Power-Packed Reader. Only everybody with **Moderate Chin Width**.

Are you in that fellowship? Then you know plenty about appropriate support. Sometimes solitude might help you best; other times you might reach out to others. Perhaps you will choose one sociability style for a few days, then experiment in the opposite direction.

You know what you need. Lucky you, there is also an ability to easily discern the comfort style belonging to others. (Even without reading faces! Although there remain plenty of good reasons for you to read faces.) When it comes to social smarts around helping others to handle adversity, you are a natural.

Your potential challenge? Expecting others to be just like you... oh, that lack of tolerance for the rest of humanity can appear in so many guises. Unreasonable people, Chin Width and all, can surprise you with the horrible mess they make of their lives. Really, why can't they be "Normal, just like me"?

Extra Special Face Data: Macho Knobs

Some chins include a raised, circular wad of flesh that looks like a doorknob. I call this a Macho Knob. Power-Packed Reader, do NOT ignore it, especially the VERY version, which is punctuated by a dimple.

- See George and Wayne for that combo of Macho Knob + Chin Dimple. While Alexander sports an un-dimpled Macho Knob.
- Women can have Macho Knobs, too. Except none can be found on the women in our Cast of Characters.

Male or female, can you find one in the mirror yourself? Take a look.

Macho Knobs relate to pride, but nuance varies according to your gender, sexual identity, and cultural background. Below I am going to address differences in terms of being "Male" and "Female." Adapt the context for meaning, as appropriate.

If you're male, the pride symbolized by a Macho Knob involves an old-fashioned standard for manliness. You may insist on using your power, getting your way, expecting others to defer to your wishes. (Although savvy partners may be able to coax out your inner Benevolent Despot).

What about the potential challenge? This probably doesn't worry you but, more, could be a problem for your significant others.

Power-Packed Readers, do not mess with a man who has a Macho Knob. Actually, some of you will be too intimidated to want to cuddle with him, either... unless you sport a Macho Knob of your own.

Hey, there's one compatibility advantage, the union of two Macho Knobbers. Beneath that Knob may lie a tender heart!

If you are a guy with a Macho Knob, your extra share of manly pride can help you greatly with career. Family status and other personal relationships can benefit, too, since many other folks under-use their power, so you gain a competitive advantage.

Your potential challenge? Over-using your power, a.k.a. Bullying.

If you are the female owner of a Macho Knob, you have your own ways to intimidate foes. Possibly subtler ways, no less effective for being concealed.

Because of your pride, when someone treats you disrespectfully you may react with an intensity of rage that surprises everyone concerned.

Anyone can get mad. However, other factors being equal, folks with Macho Knobs tend to get madder. Take a survey among your friends and acquaintances.

What is the trick to making a Macho Knob work in your life in a positive way? Use the pride without going overboard on the pushiness. There's no harm in aggressively making your dreams come true. Just don't act like the stuff that nightmares are made of.

Does the meaning of the Macho Knob change for people who are gay or lesbian?

The characteristic under discussion may be a knob but it isn't a peg. No chin characteristic (or data anywhere else on the face) means you automatically must have any particular sexual orientation. Each of us responds to certain qualities as masculine or feminine. Macho Knobs relate to strongly asserting your masculine energy, and every human has a mix of masculine and feminine energy.

What if you are a guy without the Macho Knob? Can't you still be very masculine?

Absolutely. You may be equally manly. even devastatingly sexy. Only you won't be so concerned with defending your manhood. You may be so confident that you dare to eat quiche, or let your sensitivity show in public, or experiment with the sexual message broadcast by a Lip Framer Mustache.

As for how strongly you broadcast anything about your personality, let's introduce one of the most fascinating mysteries about sex, personality, face data, and so much else in social life....

Extraverts or Introverts

Power-Packed Reader, it's not necessarily easy to categorize **extraverts** versus **introverts**. For physiognomy adds deeper understanding.

Shirley, for instance, has the teamwork style of Large Nose Padding. While at work, she loves to socialize; the more interactions the merrier. As a communicator, Shirley is friendly as could be. With her VERY intense Permanent Dimples, Shirley charms folks, too.

In personal life, as well as work life (corresponding to left and right cheeks, respectively), Shirley charms people so much, you might consider her the ultimate extravert.

Only then, check out Shirley's Eyelid Fullness. Those double eyelids of hers have No Eyelid Fullness at all. So a date might be shocked to discover how independent this gal really is. She needs her own room, her own things. That's an anchor for Shirley, built right into her face.

Hey, these qualities could rightfully be considered the signature of an introvert.

As for Chin Width, allowing for the distortion of her smile (which I consider myself skilled enough to do, after decades as a physiognomist), Shirley has a Narrow Chin. Interpreting how she reacts to adversity, you can expect her to seem like a huge introvert in that respect as well.

Friends might hear sad news about Shirley, say the death of her beloved ferret, Adonis. Soon as they find out, friends are calling, texting, and tweeting like an Impromptu Ferret Loss Support Group. They're so used to sharing with Shirley, Ms. Congeniality.

Only now Shirley won't respond. Suppose that so far, she hasn't overcome her potential challenge with that Narrow Chin. Neither is she comfortable talking to others right now (which is fine) nor has she learned to communicate in advance this need of hers (which is where the personal style challenge could have been overcome).

Overcoming that, perhaps all Shirley needs to do is post on Facebook, "I'm taking some time alone to get my head together. I'm okay. When I'm ready, I'll be in touch again. Promise."

That's all her friends need to know. It could make such a difference to them. Despite appearances, Shirley isn't such a huge extravert after all.

As for what you need to know as a physiognomist, Power-Packed Reader, you get the point, right? People are interesting. People are funny. People are not necessarily simple.

Reading faces, you can delve into the mysteries of human contradiction, gaining wisdom and spiritual discernment. In pop culture, chins are often judged harshly and inaccurately as "Weak." Now you know better.

Personally, I find it amazing how much chins express about ethics, risk taking, and style of handling conflict. I hope this chapter has inspired you to greet the lowest part of your face with a healthy respect, maybe even a new-found delight.

20. Sex

Does any single item of face reading data provide a quick summary about who is sexy? Of course not. Even if, say, one part of the face corresponded to the size of a new lover's sexual organs, how much would that mean about sexiness? Wouldn't it matter how the lover actually used all that fine equipment?

Besides, ask any sex therapist. A good love life depends on more complex factors than "I'll show you mine if you'll show me yours, and then we'll both take out our rulers."

By now I have logged nearly 1,000 media interviews. One that I don't count began with a surprise phone call from Cosmopolitan Magazine. Within minutes the Cosmo Reporter asked, "Is it true that the size of a man's nose corresponds to the size of his penis?"

Not in my experience! However, my personal survey wouldn't be impressive enough to rate for any magazine article, so I simply denied the relevance of that cliché and asked the reporter for her next question.

Gamely, the Cosmo Reporter interviewed me for another half hour. Punctual as a cuckoo clock, every five minutes she would repeat her first question. If this was supposed to trick me into saying "Yes," it failed.

For some reason, Cosmo never published a word of that interview. Guess I didn't know enough about face reading to suit the editors.

Power-Packed Reader, it's obvious that you have way more patience than my Cosmo Reporter. You already know about philtrums and sex appeal. If you think about it, you have learned loads of information relevant to sex, both learning about yourself and learning to read all love partners.

Good Reason to Review All You Have Learned

Face reading categories with relevance to your love life include:

1. Eyebrow Thickness
2. Eyebrow Startup Hairs
3. Eyebrow Shape
4. Eyebrow Height
5. Eyebrow Range

6. Wariness Index
7. Eye Width of Set
8. Ear Length
9. Ear Position
10. Ear Angles
11. Earlobe Size
12. Ear Circles Proportions
13. Cheek Emphasis
14. Cheek Proportions
15. Dimples
16. Nose in Profile
17. Nose Tip Angle
18. Nose Tip Size
19. Nostril Size
20. Nostril Shape
21. Lipfulness
22. Lip Proportions
23. Mouth Length
24. Mouth Puckers
25. Mustache
26. Jaw Width
27. Jaw Definition
28. Chin Length
29. Chin Bottom or Beard Bottom
30. Chin Width
31. Facial Priority Areas
32. Philtrum Definition

When you are looking for love, go back and read every one of those categories. Read them with sex on your mind and you will find many interesting sexual implications.

Except what if you are impatient and have a one-track mind, like Cosmo Reporter? Then you might want to skip face reading altogether. Because we physiognomists do stop short at the chin, the first chin. And the goodies you seek are probably located lower down on the body.

In Conclusion

Power-Packed Reader, you never really have to conclude your study of physiognomy. This book needs to end somewhere, though, and that somewhere is almost here.

I'd like to leave you with a thought to consider. Each of us has a unique contribution to make in service to humanity. Work that involves face reading may be part of your mission. Or perhaps discoveries about yourself through face reading will help you to *find* your mission.

Aha!s about even one part of your face may inspire you to use your talents more fully. Don't underestimate how important that is. Whatever your work, you help people most when you use your talents — and they will shine brightest only when you consciously acknowledge them.

As you do this, aligning speech and action with your true strengths, the power of self-knowledge will show in your presence. Your example can spark the light of deeper self-knowledge in others.

So may you go forth as boldly as a Jedi knight. Power-Packed Reader, go light up our world. And may the face be with you!

Acknowledgments

For the field of physiognomy, back in 1975, brilliant Timothy Mar was my awakener. Lailan Young, a British face reader and delightful writer, also inspired me greatly. (I recommend her "*Secrets of the Face*" to anyone curious about the venerable tradition of *siang mien.*)

Face reading is the first system I developed in what would, over time, become a body of work about energetic literacy.

This whole group of techniques can be used one skill set at a time: Face reading, aura reading, empath empowerment techniques for doing skilled empath merge.

I am so grateful to all who helped me present workshops on these methods, including leaders at First Class, Inc. in Washington, D.C.; Adult Education for Fairfax County Public Schools, Virginia; the Learning Light Foundation in Anaheim, California; Unity Churches in Virginia, Maryland, Cincinnati, and Seattle; both the College of Psychic Studies and the Inner Potential Centre in England; VOICE in Japan.

And, of course, I am grateful to colleges and businesses who hired me as well, including Georgetown University, George Washington University, Long & Foster, USA Today, The Event Group, The Food Marketing Institute.

Face reading students and clients have inspired me, also, especially graduates of my Correspondence Course in Face Reading.

Using Energy Spirituality skills with clients, in 2012 I began to discover that some of my long-term clients were moving into a state of self-actualization, a quantum leap of personal growth that has historically been called "Enlightenment."

That, plus shifts to my own personal experience this year, have made it possible for me to add one more skill set to the assortment, Enlightenment Coaching.

Timothy Mar set all this in motion, giving an insecure stranger the gift of a free face reading. I am so grateful to him, and to all those who have provided me with a sacred and continuing education about what it means to be human.

Face Reader's Guide

Beards 32-33, 226-230
Angled Beard Bottom 227
Curved Beard Bottom 227
Designer Stubble 227
Goatee 227
Straight Beard Bottom 227

Cheeks 49, 135-150
Big Cheek Padding 140-141, 147
Cheek Emphasis 141-146
Cheek Padding 139-141
Cheek Prominence 136-139
Cheek Proportions 124, 129, 146-150
Cheeks Widest/ Leader-Like Power Style 146, 147-148, 150
Close-Set Cheeks 141, 144, 146
Even Cheek Proportions/Polite Power Style 147, 150
Far-Set Cheeks 141, 143-144, 145, 146
Forehead Widest/Passion Power Style 147, 149
High Cheek Emphasis 141-142
High Cheekbones 141, 142, 145-146
Low Cheek Emphasis 142, 143
Moderate Cheek Padding 140-141
Modest Cheek Prominence 136-139
No Cheek Emphasis 142, 144-145
Prominent Cheeks 136, 141, 143, 147
Small Cheek Padding 140-141, 143
Under-Cheeks Widest/Pacifist Power Style 146, 148-149

Chins 49, 223-240
Angled Chin Bottoms 223-224, 225, 227
Chin Bottoms 223-225
Chin Length 234-238
Chin Thrust 230-234
Chin Width 236-238
Curved Chin Bottoms 66, 223, 224
Even Chin Thrust 231
In-Angled Chin Thrust 231
Long Chin 234-235
Macho Knob 229, 238-239
Moderate Chin Length 234, 236
Moderate Chin Width 236, 238
Narrow Chins 223, 236
Out-Angled Chin Thrust 231
Receding Chins 231-232
Scary Little Chins 226
Short Chins 234-236
Straight Chin Bottoms 223, 224-225
Weak Chins 32-33, 223, 231-232, 240
Wide Chins 236

Dimples 129, 133-136
Chin Dimple 238
No Dimples 134, 136
Peekaboo Dimples 134-136
Permanent Dimples 134-136, 240
Powerline Dimples 134, 136

Ears 49, 107-126
Attached Earlobes 118-119
Balanced Ear Circles 121-124
Ear Angles 15, 33, 114-116, 124, 129, 225
Ear Borders 124-125
Ear Circle Proportions 119-126
Ear Length 107-109
Ear Position 110-114
Earlobe Attachment 118-119
Earlobe Size 116-118, 157
High Ear Position 12, 111-114
In-Angled Ears 114-115, 198
Large Earlobes 116-118
Larger Inner Ear Circles 66, 121-124

Larger Outer Ear Circles 121-124, 138
Long Ears 107-108
Low Ear Position 111-114
Medium Ear Length 107-109
Medium Earlobe Size 117-118
Middle Ear Position 111-114
Moderate Ear Angles 114, 116
Out-Angled Ears 114-115, 225
Short Ears 107, 109
Small Earlobes 116-117
Unattached Earlobes 118-119

Eyebrows 49, 51-54, 63-78
Angled Eyebrows 66-67, 225
Arched Eyebrows 66
Big Eyebrow Range 71-73
Curved Eyebrows 66-67, 156--157
Distribution of Hair 51-54
Down-Angled Eyebrows 206
Ender Eyebrows 51-53
Even Eyebrow Distribution of Hair 51-53
Eyebrow Hairiness 63-65, 154-116
Eyebrow Height 69-71, 129
Eyebrow Range 71-73
Eyebrow Shape 33, 66-68, 124, 129
Highbrows 69-70
Large Eyebrow Hairiness 63-65, 66
Lowbrows 69-71
Middlebrows 69-70
Moderate Eyebrow Hairiness 63-65
Moderate Eyebrow Range 71-73
Small Eyebrow Hairiness 63-65
Small Eyebrow Range 71-73
Starter Eyebrows 51-53
Startup Hairs in Eyebrows 68-69
Straight Eyebrows 66-67
Unibrow 74
Wild Eyebrow Hairs 229

Eyes 49, 79-106
Average Eye Set 85-88
Beady Eyes 32-33
Close-Set Eyes 33, 60-61, 85-88, 206
Curved Lower Eyelids 66, 83-84
Deep-Set Eyes 33, 89-90, 198
Double Eyelid Fold 91, 93-95, 96-97
Double Whammy Eyelid Fold 98-99
Down-Angled Eyes 100-103, 181
Even-Angled Eyes 100, 104
Eye Angles 99-104, 124, 129, 153-154, 158
Eyelid Fold 90-92
Eyelid Fullness 93-96, 129
Far-Set Eyes 85-88
Horizontal Eye Set 85-88
Large Eyelid Fullness 93-94, 94-96, 97-98
Lower Eyelid Curve 79-85, 124
Moderate Eyelid Fullness 93, 95
Moderately Curved 83-85
No Eyelid Fullness 93-95, 240
Shifty Eyes 32-33
Single Eyelid Fold 91-95
Slanted Eyes (*Also see* Eye Angles) 20, 92-93
Small Eyelid Fullness 96-97, 98
Straight 83-85, 198
Up-Angled Eyes 100-101
Wariness Index 82-84, 104, 129

Jaws 49, 205-222
Angry Jaws 212
Jaw Definition 208-210
Jaw Width 129, 205-208
Jaws with Moderate Definition 209
Jaws with Sharp Definition 209
Jaws with Soft Definition 209
Moderate Jaw Width 205, 208
Narrow Jaws 205, 207-208
Pointy, Angular Jaws 201-212, 225
Strong Jaws 208, 212

Wide Jaws 205-207

Mouths 49, 185-204
Best Friend Lips 203
Blarney Lips 188-190
Born Talker Mouth 203
Extra Full Upper Lip 188, 190-191
Extra-Full Lower Lip 188-190
Full Lips 185, 186-187, 193, 202-203
Lip Proportions 72, 163, 188-191
Lipfulness 32-33, 72, 185-188
Long Lips 192, 193, 202
Medium-Length Lips 192, 193,
Millionaire Mouth 202-203
Moderate Lipfulness 185, 187-188
Moderately Fuller Lower Lip 188, 191
Mouth Length 191-195, 236
Mouth Puckers 203-204
Outspoken Perceptiveness 188, 190-191
Privacy Lips 203
Short Lips 192, 193, 202-203,
Small Lipfulness 185, 187, 196, 202-203

Mustache 228-230
Lip-Framer Mustache 195, 196-197, 239
Lip-Hider Mustache 195, 197
Semi-Hider Mustache 195, 197-198

Noses 49, 159-184,
Arched Nose 163, 164-167
Average-Sized Nose Tip 174
Bumpy Nose 166-167
Combination Nose Padding 171-172
Down-Turned Nose Tip 172, 173
Even-Angled Nose Tip 172, 173
Flared Nostrils 178, 179, 180
Hanging Columella 21-22
Large Nose Padding 168, 240
Large Nose Tip 174-175
Large Nostrils 176-177, 180, 183
Long Noses 160, 161-162
Moderate Nose Length 160, 162
Moderate Nose Padding 169
Moderate Nostril Size 176-177
Nose Bonus 21-22
Nose in Profile 162-168
Nose Length 160-162
Nose Padding 129, 168-172, 236
Nose Tip 129, 172-175
Nostrils 176-158
Rectangular Nostrils 178, 180, 181, 183
Round Nostrils 178-180, 183
Scooped Nose 163, 164
Short Noses 160-161
Small Nose Padding 168,
Small Nose Tip 175
Small Nostrils 176-177
Straight Nose 163-164
Triangular Nose Padding 169
Triangular Nostrils 179, 181-183, 225
Up-Angled Nose Tip 172-173

Overall Face Proportions
(See Priority Areas)

Overlips (*See* Philtrums)

Philtrums 198-202
Low-Profile Philtrum Definition 200-202
Moderate Philtrum Definition 200, 202
Philtrum Definition Index 199
Well-Defined Philtrum 199-201

Priority Areas 124, 212-222
Priority Area I 212, 213, 214-215, 216, 218-220,

Priority Area II 212, 213, 215, 216, 218-221
Priority Area III 212, 213, 215-216, 217-218, 220-221,
Priority Areas Equal 213-214, 217

Wrinkles 34, 60-61

Index

Accidents 76
Accuracy 5-6, 109-110, 152
Age 7-8, 24, 25, 210
Aggression 231-232
Ambition 215, 216 (*Also see* Determination)
Anchors 96-97, 225
Asymmetry 37, 57-62, 86, 89, 146
Aura reading 17, 87, 104, 110, 130, 148, 157
Beauty 24 -25, 210
Career 49, 57, 67, 84, 115, 116, 138, 150, 159-172
Cast of Characters 41-42
Choice (*See* Determination, Free Will)
Clairvoyance 87
Coloring 26-27, 34, 52, 92
Commitment 143, 198, 206-207, 208
Communication 49, 54, 185-204, 68, 72, 98, 113-114, 185-204, 207-208
Conflict 49, 142, 231-233, 237-240
Conformity 14-15, 114-116, 225, 229
Confrontation 67, 207-208, 226
Cosmetic Surgery 25, 75-78, 99, 142
Creativity 52, 123, 163-167
Cruelty 209, 210-212
Curiosity 36, 67
Dating 24, 30, 97, 183, 214-222
Deception 29-30, 39, 84, 90, 104-106, 129, 136, 184, 188
Decision Making 112-113, 224-228
Destiny (*See* Fate)
Determination 209-212
Discrimination 83-84, 87
Drama 72-73
Emotions 66-67, 71-17, 122, 223-224, 278
Energetic Literacy 17, 31-32, 104
Energy Spirituality 26
Enlightenment 117-119
Ethics 6-7, 9, 49, 126, 142-143, 205-222, 235-236, 240
Expression 29-34, 44, 67-68, 79, 127-134, 186, 192, 212, 233-234
Extra-Special Face Data 68, 96, 98-99
Extravert 203, 239-240
Eyebrow Plucking and Waxing 63, 65-66
Face Reading Program 35, 38, 47, 51
Face Reading Secrets 12-13, 19-22, 23-27, 39, 124, 126, 129, 158
Facebook 21, 64, 137
Facelifts (*See* Cosmetic Surgery)
Fame 138
Fate 4, 15, 219-220
Fears 193
Femininity 137-138, 233
Free Will 14, 18, 145, 181, 201, 226
Friendliness 83-85, 237-238, 239-240
Genetics 17 (*Also see* Heredity)
Gifts 17
Go Flippo 62
Goodness 32
Gossip 172-173
Grooming 195, 198, 227, 278-230
Guilt 171-172, 235-236
Health 26, 144, 206-207 (*Also see* Macrobiotic Face Reading)
Heredity 18, 145
Highly Sensitive Persons 67
Intellect (*See* Thinking Patterns)
Intention 40
Intimacy 83-85, 90, 93-99, 225
Introvert 239-240
Jealousy 64

Leadership 137-139, 140, 147-150, 170-171, 225, 278
Left and Right Sides of a Face 55-62
Life Contract 177
Loyalty 206
Lying (*See* Deception)
Macrobiotic Face Reading 13
Major Compassion Awakener 102, 181, 203-204, 210-212
Makeup 37, 44, 99, 155, 195, 234
Masculinity 137-138, 233, 239
Mind-Body-Spirit 18, 157
Mirror Skills 44-47, 54-62, 111-112
Money 49, 138, 174-184
Multi-Racial People 21
Multi-Tasking 47, 64-65
Objective Reality 122-125, 138, 188, 216
Online Dating (*See* Dating and Photograph Reading)
Overwhelm 108-109
Personal Style 14-15, 115, 137, 138, 142
Personality 214-222, (Also see Personal Style)
Personology 13,
Photograph Reading 55-62, 214, 233-234.
Phrenology 32-34
Physiognomy (See Power of Face Reading)
Power 1, 49, 135-150
Power of Face Reading 2-3, 13-14, 47, 75, 150, 151-158
Power-Packed Reader 2-3, 39, 139, 234
Predictions 13
Prejudice (See Race)
Problem Solving 69, 101-102
Proxemics 115
Psychic development 17, 35
Quiz 32-33, 128-129, 153-154, 158, 173, 236-237
Race 19-22, 24, 32-33, 145, 169-170
Reframing 16-17
Relationships, Personal (*Also see* Career.) 57, 66-67, 138, 202-203, 237
Respect 55, 56
Sales (Also see Decision Making) 184, 185-204
Self-Disclosure 186-188, 197-198, 202-204, 225
Sense of Identity 5, 95, 99, 243
Sensitivity 66-67, 96-97, 123, 207-208, 226
Sex 24, 33, 123, 185-186, 195, 198-202, 215, 216, 239, 241-242
Shyness 54
Skin (Also see Coloring) 25
Smile (See Expression)
Social Attention Deficit Disorder 150
Social Connection 49
Social Status 17, 25
Soul 18, 31, 66, 73, 77, 145, 204
Soul Signature Traits 231-232
Spontaneity 70
STUFF 109-110
Subconscious Patterns 107-126
Subjective Reality 122-125, 138, 188
Success 17, 215
Tattoos 63
Thinking Patterns 49, 51-54, 63-78, 112, 214-215
Thoroughness 52-53
Tricky Facial Characteristics 74
Trust 137
VERY (in physiognomy) 38, 151-158
Voting 125-126, 224
Weight 139, 211-212

Rose Rosetree

Rose Rosetree teaches energetic literacy. She uses it as a basis for healing with the separate skill sets of Energy Spirituality. Or sometimes she just reads faces for fun.

Previous face reading books by Rosetree have sold over 100,000 copies worldwide. (By 2012, her other books on perception and self-healing have amounted to an additional 200,000 copies in print.)

Widely acknowledged among professional face readers, Rosetree has been called "The Mother of American Physiognomy."

Based in Sterling, Virginia, Rose offers consulting services, workshops and trainings, personal sessions of face reading, event entertainment, and a Correspondence Course in Professional Face Reading.

JAICO PUBLISHING HOUSE

Elevate Your Life. Transform Your World.

ESTABLISHED IN 1946, Jaico Publishing House is home to world-transforming authors such as Sri Sri Paramahansa Yogananda, Osho, the Dalai Lama, Sri Sri Ravi Shankar, Sadhguru, Robin Sharma, Deepak Chopra, Jack Canfield, Eknath Easwaran, Devdutt Pattanaik, Khushwant Singh, John Maxwell, Brian Tracy, and Stephen Hawking.

Our late founder Mr. Jaman Shah first established Jaico as a book distribution company. Sensing that independence was around the corner, he aptly named his company Jaico ('Jai' means victory in Hindi). In order to service the significant demand for affordable books in a developing nation, Mr. Shah initiated Jaico's own publications. Jaico was India's first publisher of paperback books in the English language.

While self-help, religion and philosophy, mind/body/spirit, and business titles form the cornerstone of our non-fiction list, we publish an exciting range of travel, current affairs, biography, and popular science books as well. Our renewed focus on popular fiction is evident in our new titles by a host of fresh young talent from India and abroad. Jaico's recently established translations division translates selected English content into nine regional languages.

Jaico distributes its own titles. With its headquarters in Mumbai, Jaico has branches in Ahmedabad, Bangalore, Chennai, Delhi, Hyderabad, and Kolkata.

SINCE 1946